THRICE A STRANGER

THRICE A STRANGER

New Chapters of Autobiography

by

VERA BRITTAIN

LONDON
VICTOR GOLLANCZ LTD
1938

PRINTED IN GREAT BRITAIN BY PURNELL AND SONS, LTD. (T.U.)
PAULTON (SOMERSET) AND LONDON

"*The desire of the moth for the star,*
Of the night for the morrow,
The devotion to something afar
From the sphere of our sorrow."

PERCY BYSSHE SHELLEY

"*Man shall spread his wings and fly*
away like a mighty swan."

LEONARDO DA VINCI

To

G. P. B.

AND

H. S. L.

who made for me a new America

AUTHOR'S ACKNOWLEDGMENTS

Among the friends who have so kindly helped me with material for this book, I would like especially to thank Mr. Oswald Garrison Villard, Mr. Norman Thomas, Miss Izetta Winter Robb, the President and Vice-President of the Macmillan Company of New York, and the President of the Macmillan Company of Canada. My sincere gratitude is also due to my husband, whose ten years of residence in the United States gives expert value to his advice.

I am indebted to the following authors, publishers and editors for generously permitting the quotation of copyright material:

Mrs. Franklin D. Roosevelt, and Messrs. Harper & Brothers (THIS IS MY STORY); Miss Edna St Vincent Millay, and Messrs. Harper & Brothers (WINE FROM THESE GRAPES), published by Harper & Brothers, Copyright 1934, by Edna St. Vincent Millay); Miss Dorothy Thompson, and the Editor of the *New York Herald Tribune* (extracts from "On the Record"); Mr. Paul Engle, Messrs. Doubleday, Doran and Company, Inc., New York, and Messrs. Jonathan Cape, London (AMERICAN SONG); Mr. Stephen Vincent Benét, and Messrs. Farrar & Rinehart, Inc. ("1936" from BURNING CITY); Sir Philip Gibbs, Mr. Leslie Baily, and Mr. Charles Brewer (SCRAPBOOK FOR 1918); Miss Elise McDougald, and Messrs. Albert and Charles Boni, Inc. (THE NEW NEGRO); Mr. E. Leslie Spaulding, and the Editor of the *Chicago Tribune* (INVULNERABLE); the Editor of *The New York Times* (extracts from Christmas editorial, 1937); the Editor of the *Christian Science Monitor* (extract from an article by the late Right Hon. Arthur Henderson); Mr. John Gunther, and the Editor of *The Saturday Evening Post* (extract from "This Peace Is a Cheat"); and the Editor of

AUTHOR'S ACKNOWLEDGMENTS

Time, The Weekly Newsmagazine. My thanks are also due to the Editor of the *Atlantic Monthly* for kind permission to incorporate in the text material from my article, "Listeners English and American", which appeared in his magazine; to Mr. George V. Denny, Jr., President of the Town Hall, Inc., New York, for kindly allowing me to use a portion of his speech delivered at Harvard University on June 26th, 1937; to the New York Economic Council, Inc., for permission to reprint their appeal on behalf of Private Enterprise; and to the editors of British and United States newspapers for the use of brief paragraphs from their columns.

V. B.

CONTENTS

FOREWORD

A STRANGER LOOKS BACK

So MANY BOOKS have been written by British authors against an American background, that nowadays it seems necessary to justify a new one.

Having spent, altogether, about two years in America, and having visited thirty out of the forty-eight States, I repeatedly told my American publishers that I would never attempt to describe their country in a book. Over a period of thirteen years it has played an intimate part in my personal life, and I felt that I knew it too well to emulate those courageous visitors who produce a volume of American impressions after spending a fortnight in New York.

But as it happens I have known the United States at three widely different periods, separated from one another by long intervals—such intervals as those which enable an occasional family visitor to notice changes in a growing child which are imperceptible to its parents. I first lived in the country between 1925 and 1927, when the era of golden swaggering prosperity seemed destined to endure for ever. I returned in 1934 to find the long shadows of the great depression still lying over the land. More recently, in 1937, I went back to discover a national temperature which, in spite of the "business recession", seemed closer to sane normality than the boastful affluence of the first period or the retrospective apprehension of the second.

One day in the late October of last year, as I wandered round the vivid sun-drenched Campus of a Junior College in Dallas, Texas, reflecting upon these contrasts, the summer warmth of the South-West stirred my northern blood to excitement, and I almost shouted to the sulphur-hued butterflies flitting lightly above the scarlet cannas, "There's a book in all this!"

And despite my previous severe resolutions, before I realised what I was doing I had begun to write it.

The title that I have chosen is not intended to suggest any lack of welcoming generosity on the part of the American people, for no nation could be more benevolently anxious to make a foreigner feel at home. The only time when their reception of me fails to command my envious admiration is the few moments during which I am herded with the "aliens" for passport inspection as the steamer moves slowly up the Hudson towards the docks. The word "alien" seems always to carry with it the adjective "undesirable", and I cannot acknowledge without inward resentment that description of myself when I am coming to a country which shares a thousand years and more of the same history, speaks a language approximately if not exactly the same, and follows some—though now not many—of the same habits and customs.

But I am willing to accept the description "stranger". I cannot, indeed, escape it, for if I were to visit the United States a hundred times, I should not come to the end of the topics, manners and practices about which the Americans and I have different points of view. They cannot, for instance, understand why I prefer a train to an aeroplane, and a steady lumbering Pullman to one of the new streamlined "Hiawathas" and "Zephyrs" of which they are so proud. They are uninfluenced, to an extent which seems to me astonishing, by the fact that I on my ponderous Pullman can get through satisfactory hours of the very correspondence or literary composition that they, on their rapid rocketing trains which make letter-writing impossible and eating a matter of manual and facial gymnastics, are hurrying to Boston or Chicago to begin. To them, too, my desire to walk everywhere when it is so much quicker to ride seems quite incomprehensible, while I am equally puzzled by their habitual description of an hour's drive in a car with all the windows closed and the heater turned on, as "getting a little fresh air".

Again, I have repeatedly been a stranger in the United States because, on each of my visits, the indefatigable architects of that unresting country have deliberately altered so many of the features peculiar to its civilisation. Even after a year or two, the very silhouette of its most famous horizons has changed. There are new buildings, new bridges, new highways, a new Northern shore to Lake Michigan in Chicago, so that one has perpetually to re-learn one's landmarks and re-adapt one's impressions. Somebody once said that New York would be a magnificent city if they could only finish it—but they never do. The New York that I have known has constantly revised its appearance, like a woman who is always altering the style of her make-up. In its passion for doing, constructing, improving, it is never satisfied that tomorrow's experiment may not be better than today's.

In the seven years between 1927 and 1934 during which I did not visit America, the Empire State Building and "Radio City" went up, dwarfing the down-town skyscrapers which I had innocently supposed to represent the loftiest limits of man's architectural skill. Between 1934 and 1937 the George Washington Bridge was constructed and a number of new highways, such as the Henry Hudson, have changed and simplified the exits from the city into its commuter's hinterlands.

The restaurants too are different. Between the resounding epoch of Prosperity and Prohibition, and the less sensational drama of American living today, the "speak-easies" of 1925 have disappeared, and various cheap eating-places, such as the Horn and Hardart Automats, have sprung up like convenient mushrooms for the sustenance of a less extravagant and more law-abiding people. Even the methods of cheap transport have altered. In New York and other cities tram-rails have been torn up, and cross-town buses have supplanted the clattering street-cars. Many taxi-cabs are now equipped with radio sets, and others have developed "sunshine roofs" of clear glass through which the brilliant daylight can penetrate, though no one seems as yet to have discovered a method of introducing light, air and order into that underground inferno, the New York subway.

But the true significance of a country, as of a person, lies not in its face but in its spirit. For me the essential temper of America, which I have audaciously tried to interpret through the medium of a personal story, has altered beyond recognition in the last decade. And to the extent that, instead of criticising, I have tried more humbly to understand it as the years have passed, I have become, not more of a stranger, but infinitely less.

June, 1938.

I

(1925-1926)

" . . . this destiny moved outward to the farthest
    Of the man-living lands. But the American
Soul, that should have soared, flapped in the driving wind
That blew with the stench of sweat and oil and the fetid
Fat breath that cried for gold. The rational
Imagination brooding on the stuff of earth,
Lucid science like a living spirit
Shaping the crude ways of light, was held only
As the convenient author of our ease.
Eyes that watched their ships circle the ultimate
Oceans of earth could not see beyond
The diamonds flashing their hands."

                              Paul Engle, *America Remembers*.

I

Let me confess from the outset that on my first visit to America in 1925, I made two major mistakes.

The worst of these was one common to most Europeans, though I had experienced enough of the dire consequences of national antagonisms to know much better. I carried my English prejudices with me across the Atlantic; I judged American civilisation by European standards, found it congenial where it conformed to them and displeasing where it did not.

This is the last error into which an English traveller should allow himself to fall. Before he leaves Southampton he must give up expecting that the United States will be a copy of England or even responsive to English ideas. Its very resemblances, which yearly become more superficial, are a snare in themselves. When we visit France or Norway or Hungary, we do not hope to discover English values or Anglo-Saxon customs; the chief attraction of these countries lies in their strangeness, in their differences from our own. Yet in America, merely because of a decreasing similarity of language, we look for the familiar acceptance of antique traditions or time-honoured habits, and feel exasperated when we do not find it.

In retrospect I realise that I should have saved myself much resentful heart-burning if I had paid more attention to a warning given me shortly before I sailed by an English Professor attached to an American University, who had spent two years in learning to follow his own advice: "To understand America, wash out England and Oxford and all classical culture from your mind, and go out as a little child."

My second mistake was to enter the United States by way of Canada, creeping as it were through a back door into the uninviting shack-dotted emptiness of up-state New York, instead of sailing majestically up the Hudson straight into that fantastic vision of audacious splendour which is America's proudest gesture to the staid Old World. Journalistically the famous sky-line of New York has become a hackneyed story, staled by admiring repetition, but for a foreign traveller nothing can replace that first crashing impact of fearless magnificence upon his astounded senses. No nation has ever come so close, in the quality of its experimental achievements, to the scientific imagination of Leonardo da Vinci and his symbolic prophecy: "Man shall spread his wings and fly away like a mighty swan."

Ten weeks before that voyage to Canada, G. and I had been married. I had known for some time that my first exploration of the New World would coincide with the psychological explorations of our first year together, for he was then an Assistant Professor in a large New York State University, which followed a tradition of appointing English scholars to its Faculty. Although our hopes and ambitions made ultimate residence in London desirable for us both, I had promised him, not without many misgivings, that I would try the experiment of living for twelve months in a small American University town.

Our economical choice of a small Montreal-bound cabin boat was made because G. wanted me to see the sombre majesty of the Canadian coast and the maple-scarlet banks of the St. Lawrence in September. It was also due to our limited means, for we began our married life in a state very far from affluence. Our combined incomes made only a modest total, upon which we had also an elderly relative to support, and I could not count upon supplementing it by fees from articles and lectures—which I had begun so satisfactorily to gather in London—in a new country where I was quite unknown.

As we watched Liverpool dwindle into the distance until nothing was left but the humped mistiness of the spireless Cathedral and the twin pagodas of the Cunard Offices, the misgivings with which I had so often wrestled crowded upon

me like a dark battalion of marauding birds. Already, though
I could not have described my malady in words, I was
suffering from a twofold antagonism towards the country to
which we were travelling. Possessed by an overmastering
passion to write which the War and its comfortless aftermath
had already frustrated again and again, I was obliged to
leave England just when my stories and articles were
becoming known, for a new struggle with obscurity. And I
had little assurance that the people of an unfamiliar
continent would be interested in anything that I had to say.

I knew, for G. had told me, that apart from their soldiers
who had gone overseas, they had little knowledge of the
War and no experience of post-war suffering. Their thoughts,
I anticipated, would be exclusively possessed by the golden
progress of their abounding prosperity, while mine could
never quite break loose from the stricken poverty and
humiliating griefs of Europe after war. Twice during the
past twelve months I had visited the sorrowful territories of
the conquered nations, travelling through Germany and its
occupied areas into Austria and Hungary during the
autumn of 1924, and again staying in Vienna and Budapest
for two weeks of our recent honeymoon. Could I hope to
make any American understand the significance of a story
told me during my last term at Oxford four years earlier by
one of our tutors who came from Central Europe?

In October, 1914, a few weeks after the outbreak of war,
my tutor had walked with an Austrian officer through one
of the parks of Vienna. Pointing to the fallen leaves which
in autumn cover the wide paths with a rich drift of gold,
the officer sighed and exclaimed: "We are living on the
shadow of a shadow. On what shall we live afterwards?"
And the don replied: "You won't live at all."

Meditating upon the heavy truth of that prophecy, I
walked up and down the deck of the small unsteady liner,
now plunging past the grim silhouette of the dark Welsh
hills. Beneath transparent orange banners from the stormy
sun, the Great Orme and the rocky coast of Anglesey stood
out black and menacing against a sky of red and inky

purple, like the copybook of a peevish Titan. Unreasonably I began to be seized with a vague frightening dread, to understand what the Greeks meant by "the envy of the gods" and its constant threat to human happiness. When blue-grey darkness descended upon the sea and the eyes of the stars winked slyly between the hurrying clouds, I went down to join G. in our tiny cabin, still unconsciously clasping my passport with its immigration visa which I had obtained at the cost of much time and exasperation from the American Consulate in Cavendish Square.

I had gone to the Consulate during the last week of August in the happy expectation that I should return an hour or two later equipped with my visa. During the past year I had succeeded, without any difficulty at all, in entering France, Germany, Italy, Austria, Hungary, Czechoslovakia and Jugoslavia, and it had not occurred to me that admission into the United States was a proposition of quite another order. G., from the happy security of his American job, blithely assured me that I should have "no trouble whatever", and I started optimistically forth in my best clothes, which I naïvely supposed—having then no knowledge of the laconic democracy characteristic of American officialdom—would ensure me immediate attention.

The morning was serene and lovely, and the birds in Hyde Park, disregarding the subtle march of autumn, were singing as though the spring had just begun. To go in search of a new continent seemed, at that moment, a grand and appropriate adventure, and I wondered pityingly why people made such a fuss about passports and visas, and all the necessary little preliminaries of travel. The Americans, after all, were a free and noble people; they had every right to be particular about the type of person they admitted. Now I, I felt agreeably certain, was exactly the type of socially valuable immigrant that a discriminating nation would welcome with open arms.

For an hour I waited inside the doorway of the Consulate, happily confident of success in spite of having to admit that, no, I was afraid I had not an appointment. At length I was ordered to "go home" and provide myself, for reasons not vouchsafed to me, with two copies of my birth and marriage certificates, and two photographs of myself. I was also required to produce a statement, in duplicate, from "someone in authority", to the effect that I had never been in prison. The tone of the command suggested that if I had not, I certainly ought to have been. Thoroughly crestfallen, I returned meekly to our flat.

By the end of the month I had conscientiously collected all the necessary documents, and was able to return apprehensively with them to the Consulate. This time G., suddenly alarmed lest the United States might refuse to admit me after all, came with me in order to convince the Consulate that I was genuinely his wife, and not some perfidious little spinster creature sneaking into America to encourage polygamy, atheism, Mormonism, divorce, or any other of the immoral occupations in which a protectionist continent—whatever the liberties permitted to its own citizens—refuses to allow its resident aliens to indulge. Being no longer alone I was evidently considered less dangerous, so we were shown through a long passage resembling an Underground tunnel, which terminated in a bench crowded with would-be travellers like the solitary seat on a Metropolitan Railway station.

For an hour we waited, while the other applicants for visas played General Post between the Metropolitan bench and the portentous series of offices behind the closed door. At last, by the time that I had been reduced to the mentality of a school-child waiting on the mat outside the Principal's study, the door opened again, and a disapproving official appeared like a genie before us.

"Have you an appointment?" he enquired sternly.

"Yes, I have," I replied hopefully, having remembered this time to take that precaution. Since it was now almost eleven, I thought it unwise to mention that the appointment had been for nine-thirty.

"Come this way, then," he said, in a pessimistic tone,

calculated to dismay any optimist who imagined that
entering the United States was an easy matter, and we
followed him humbly into the inner sanctuary.

I was destined, it appeared, to be a marked woman from
the beginning; all the occupants of that office seemed to
take an immense dislike to me as soon as they examined my
passport, and discovered that it was still made out in the
name of Vera Brittain. Undesirable aliens, from America's
point of view, were evidently not only the unwashed, but
the unconventional. The Consulate was already preparing
to classify me, to its own satisfaction, as a 'D (wife)', and
its departmental soul was outraged by the notion that I
proposed to enter God's own country wearing the wrong
label.

"I don't know what the Foreign Office meant by making
out your passport in your maiden name!" my interrogator
commented indignantly.

"They only did it because I asked them to," I replied in
a conciliatory tone.

He capitulated with a gesture of resignation.

"Oh, well, put her down as she wishes; copy the name on
her passport," he said to his girl clerk, but he murmured
in lugubrious tones to G. "You may have *trouble* about this
at the other end, you know!"

So the clerk entered my name as Vera Brittain, adding
that I was the wife of my husband. Then, with her fingers
poised expectantly above the typewriter, she began to fill in
the rest of my particulars.

"When were you married?" she asked.

I pushed forward my marriage certificate, which stated
that I was married in London at St. James's Church,
Spanish Place, on a June Saturday two months previously.
Mechanically she entered the details, and turned to me
again.

"Any children?" she enquired energetically.

"No," I answered severely.

She then began to fill in some of the other columns, only
to discover, long before she reached the end, that the date

at which my offending passport expired had been filled in wrong, or filled in twice, or not filled in at all. At any rate, whatever it was, there was something the matter with it, and I must go at once to the Foreign Office and have it put right.

This, as anyone would expect, took the rest of the afternoon. As for the American Consulate, it shut at 3 p.m. or thereabouts, and was quite determined to have nothing more to do with me that day.

The next morning I rose even earlier, and managed to arrive at the Consulate by nine o'clock. When I reached the end of the Underground tunnel, I immediately encountered the official who had so deeply disapproved of me the day before. As the office was empty and he had just come on duty, he was doing nothing in particular, but as soon as I approached he switched on a bureaucratic expression of extreme preoccupation.

"What do you want?" he asked. "Have you an appointment?"

Then my appearance struck him as familiar and at once he recalled my unorthodox passport and the perturbations which it had involved.

"Oh, yes, I remember you. You're *married*!" he exclaimed crushingly.

I agreed with him meekly that, in spite of all indications to the contrary, I *was* married; it appeared to be the only fact in my circumstances which interested the Consulate at all. Alas, I reflected, that a simple ceremony, lasting for twenty minutes, should so easily transform an individual with qualities into a type having a status! So long as a woman remains unmarried, she continues to be known as Mary Jones, lecturer, or Jane Brown, barrister, or Vera Brittain, author; but once let her agree to live with some man as his lawful spouse, and everyone conspires to rob her of that unbecoming individualism. Henceforth, for social, journalistic and legislative purposes, she is anonymously included in the category of "wives-and-mothers"—except when there is a war or a revolution or a shipwreck, when she becomes "women-and-children" for a change. Even the steamship companies no longer permit her to book her cabin reservation by name; she is merely listed as "and wife".

"The next thing you have to do," said the official, after looking round to see if there was any possible reason why I could be told to wait for an hour, and deciding that—the office at the moment being completely free of adventurers —there really was not; "the next thing you have to do is to go over to No. 18 and have your medical examination."

I had foreseen this instruction. I had, in fact, anticipated it by again putting on my best clothes in order to satisfy the medical officer that I had no secret intention of carrying contagious diseases into hygienic America. This time, at last, my confidence was almost justified. After walking through several mysteriously empty rooms, I had only waited in the ante-chamber for quite a few minutes when the doctor put his head round the door, wearing the stern expression of one who expected to see a Chinaman from Limehouse or a naturalised Lithuanian from Bethnal Green. When he observed my fawn coat-frock and scarlet Bangkok hat, his face lighted up and he announced flatteringly: "Oh, *you* can come in!"

I went in, and he said that he supposed I had been vaccinated. He then wrote down that I was not verminous, added a few more equally picturesque details, and handed me my certificate without examining me further. I felt quite stunned by this celerity—which, however, proved unavailing. When I returned to the other building to have my papers, which now seemed to be complete, initialled by Mr. X., I discovered that Mr. X. was no fonder of arriving in Cavendish Square at nine o'clock than I was. He did not, in fact, appear till nearly eleven, so I spent the interval examining the blue paper with the red seal and green ribbon which represented my non-quota immigration visa.

This document asserted, with substantial truth, that I was neither an imbecile, an epileptic, a person with chronic alcoholism, nor an individual afflicted with a loathsome or dangerous disease; that I was not a polygamist, an anarchist, a prostitute, an illiterate, or an unaccompanied child. It informed the American immigration officials that my "calling" was that of a writer, my height five feet three inches, my eyes hazel and my hair dark brown; also that I was able to speak English and even to write it—a long-standing ambition which I was delighted to know that I had at last fulfilled.

But Mr. X., when I was finally ushered into his presence, appeared quite unimpressed by this literary achievement. After we had looked at each other with mutual suspicion for a few moments, he summoned me to his desk with the air of a police officer who warns the arrested criminal that anything he says in his defence may be used against him, and with impressive deliberation initialled my papers.

By this time the cashier had departed, probably to have a cup of tea and a biscuit. I envied her. I waited. When she returned ten minutes later, I paid her £2 1s. 8d. for the privilege of enjoying the hospitality of the American Consulate for three instructive mornings.

"Well," enquired G. anxiously, "did you get it this time?"

Triumphantly I indicated the clauses which certified me as a solvent traveller, a sound monandrist, and a 'D (wife)'. At last, I assured him, I was entitled to leave my own country for another, potentially still mightier and far more particular about its immigrant aliens.

The country that I was leaving, though secure and tranquil compared with Central Europe, was facing a period neither happy nor comfortable for any political party. Throughout England appeared ominous portents of that industrial unrest which was to lead a few months later to the General Strike. In September, 1925, one of its manifestations took the form of a firemen's strike, which caused our boat to sail for Canada with inexperienced firemen, including a number of unemployed shepherds from Wales.

It was an autumn of blustering winds and heavy seas; a month afterwards the *President Harding* stood by for forty-eight hours to rescue an Italian freighter sinking in mid-Atlantic. When, half-way through our voyage, a malicious storm (described by the Captain as "a nice swell" and by the ship's log as "Moderate gale, high head sea") turned our cockle-shell of a liner into a little hell of banging doors and creaking timbers, the reactions of the pastoral "firemen" to their job were anything but helpful to crew or passengers. Incapacitated by sea-sickness they refused to work, and a steward told us that for two or three days the engineers themselves were obliged to stoke the ship. Not only was our arrival at Montreal delayed, but we were haunted through the voyage by the fear of fire.

Owing to my inconvenient memory of war-time terrors when we sailed through the submarine-infested Mediterranean in the hospital ships *Britannic* and *Galeka*, I was an unhappy ocean-goer in the quietest weather, and this miserable journey did nothing to lessen my fear of the sea. It took several voyages to America and back in later years to cure me of the idea that an Atlantic crossing was an excessively perilous experience.

When the storm was at its worst I lay abjectly on deck, trying to eat cold scraps of food from a tray brought me by a sympathetic steward. Too sick to go down into the dining-room, I felt also too terrified to retire to my cabin and stop looking at the sea, for I was obsessed by the ridiculous notion that if once I took my eyes off the riotous waves, they would become gigantic and overwhelm the ship. Around me a group of women on deck were lugubriously discussing all the gales that they had ever known—gales in the Channel, the Atlantic, the Bay of Biscay, invalids, corpses, how they carried them out. Close to these female jeremiahs, a taciturn American Professor and an irrepressible Irish student from Dublin University, who disagreed fundamentally on every topic but appeared to have a morbid fascination for each other which kept them perpetually together, had now reached quarrelling point, their nerves jarred by the wind.

"Young man!" the American exclaimed in loud exasperation. "Have you never heard the words of Abraham

Lincoln: 'My friend, the Lord loves ordinary men; that is why He made so many of them'?"

"Indade!" responded the Irishman, staggering jauntily away with his hands in his pockets. "And if that's so, why was it the Lord took care not to be an ordinary man Himself?"

As he disappeared at the end of the swaying deck, scraps of conversation floated to me from those infuriating travellers who never notice the weather but toughly persist in tramping their daily mile.

"Didn't see Oxford? Gee, it was some spot! There's a wall there that's been exta-ant since ten hundred!"

Behind my chair the steward, with the nonchalance characteristic of ocean stewards, was discussing the storm with G.

"We expected better weather last night, sir."

"Oh? but it didn't come off?"

"No, sir. It failed to materialise."

Few sights in the world have ever brought me greater relief than the red and green lights of the pilot-boat at Father Point, creeping out of the darkness like a star growing into an enormous firefly. But the weary, long-drawn voyage had left me too dizzy and exhausted to appreciate the grandeur of earth and water which I had been brought to admire. I could only think what a long, long distance the New World seemed from the Old, where I had so unenterprisingly desired to remain, and resent the journey up the St. Lawrence as a prolongation of experiences already intolerable.

Though I was no longer a girl even then, several years were to pass before I realised that the quality of one's fatigue is dictated by the measure of one's courage, and that seasickness, tiredness, minor ailments and a craving for sleep can be rendered negligible by the pedestrian expedient of getting on with one's job.

Never, I thought, had I seen anything in the world so cold as the Gaspé Peninsula, an endless stretch of austerity clouded by fog. I contemplated it distastefully across a flat stretch of leaden-coloured sea beneath a sky of steel-grey clouds with oases of dull yellow and periwinkle blue, like beds of northern flowers cultivated in an inhospitable soil. Even the frozen Base in war-time France during the bitter winter of 1917 had seemed less forbidding than this. Though cruel winds had lashed our faces and icy mud soaked our feet, humanity, suffering, sentient, warm, had mitigated its rigours with rueful humour and gay insouciant endurance.

On the previous day, when we passed through the Straits of Belle Isle, my jaded spirits had been temporarily lifted by the sight of land after the long tedium of hostile ocean and stormy sky. Not the challenging pagan towers of New York, but the low olive-green coast of Newfoundland shelving palely to the shore, gave me my first glimpse of North America. I knew no other territory which looked so empty and undiscovered, yet the grass appeared exhausted, as though generations of men had trodden out its vitality. I soon learned that the grass of these regions seldom grows emerald like that of the British Isles; the winter snows lie upon it until its colour is lost and its young sap withered.

That night from the deck we watched the Aurora Borealis —a cold, ghostly incandescence which was yet bright enough to drive indoors the ship-board lovers, who had now passed the publicity stage. Balls of phosphorus tumbled like lighted cigarette-ends in the frothy wake of the boat. Even at night the huge estuary of the St. Lawrence has a peculiar lightness and rarity of atmosphere; it is cold and dry and brilliant, like iced champagne. There seems to be so much of it that individuals can take possession of islands as large as Cornwall—like Senator Meunier, the "Chocolate King" of France, who used the Island of Anticosti as his private game-preserve.

When you travel in the Old World, I reflected as we swung from the Gulf into the river, you are continually pressed and crowded by its overwhelming history, but when you first reach the New you find nothing but geography—

geography which suggests the soullessness and infinitude
of higher mathematics. The Gaspè Peninsula, arctic-blue
and covered with spruce, looked lonely, reticent and autonomous. If human beings became equally autonomous, there
could surely be no future generations; the race of man with
its awareness and its chronicles would die out, and the
whole world became an illimitable vista of unself-conscious
geography.

"So much the better!" commented G., who in his more
academic moments pretended to view with an unapprecia-
tive eye the tempestuous drama of humanity. "History is
nothing but a morass of little tufty facts in which many
people seem to lose their wits!"

At that moment we were passing one of the settlements
of white, crouching villages, with red-roofed churches out of
all proportion to the size of the community, which spring
from the shores of the St. Lawrence at intervals of fifty
miles. From the ship we could see no sign of life, no smoke,
no people, no activity. Only in front of every village, a line
of little black boats, like dots and dashes, made a primitive
telegraphic code along the shore.

"Well," I retorted, pointing to the solitary settlement,
"your New World is nothing but a mass of unwieldy
geographical peninsulas, in which many people seem to
lose themselves."

Our next-door neighbour, who imagined that we were
quarrelling, became suddenly and tactfully informative. The
settlers in those villages, she told us, were cut off by snow
and ice from the rest of the world for more than half the
year, and many were so ignorant that months after the War
broke out they remained unaware of it. They were poor, and
priest-ridden, and heavily over-taxed to pay for the upkeep
of their outsize churches. They were taxed for their front
porches and taxed for their doorway steps, so that most of
them were obliged to use only a back entrance in order to
avoid taxation, and the chief ambition of every villager was
to become sufficiently prosperous to possess a front door.
When I reached Quebec, said my informant, I must buy a

copy of Louis Hémon's *Maria Chapdelaine*, which told the classic story of the pioneers in the Province. Later, between those pathetic pages, I found concealed the bitter story of human adaptation when the enemy is not man but the recalcitrant earth, reinforced by the dividing hostility of empty spaces, by the deliberate sacrifice of contacts and culture, by solitude, by tempest and by cold.

As we moved slowly up the tremendous flood of the St. Lawrence, which reduced the remembered Danube to a rivulet and the complacent Thames to a pigmy stream, the harsh coast grew darker and more forbidding. Thickly and more thickly the spruce covered the hills; the younger trees, a pale terra-cotta, stood clearly outlined against the dense, older green. Cliffs with slate-coloured faces, deeply gashed by ravines running inland, shelved steeply into the water. Pockets of white cloud drifted like handfuls of ethereal cotton-wool above hills with blunt, rounded summits, which looked as though they had been made in gigantic primeval basins and turned out upon the uninhabited earth.

This land, I thought, has the naïve awfulness of the first chapter of Genesis; the watery evening sun streaming down upon the sharp-edged cliffs might well be the first response to a celestial command: "And God said, 'Let there be Light'." I had once seen an etching of the Deluge which resembled the clouds breaking above these stormy Canadian hills. It hung against the dark staircase-wall of my childhood's first home, and inspired all my youthful nightmares of the Last Trump and the Day of Judgment.

In this New World I should find, I felt certain, no human ghosts to disturb me as I had once been disturbed in Malta by the uneasy consciousness of watchful presences, surviving from the civilisations which had lived and died there. They were old, these presences, with the self-conscious age of humanity rather than the ingenuous age of natural phenomena, which have the simplicity of old men grown from childhood into senility without passing through the adult stage of reason. How wistfully I should long for those half-hostile, half-beneficent spirits when I wandered

about this new countryside, peopled only by the soulless
nature-deities of trees and rocks and streams! There would
be the hills, and the lights, and the waterfalls, and the township in the valley, but no historic memories to keep me
company when G. was away.

This empty continent, I concluded, reminds me of a
frigidly pure virgin; it desires to know nothing of the warm,
errant life of men, but remains austerely satisfied with its
own morose desolation.

The weather, throughout that unpromising journey, made
only one concession; it allowed Quebec to greet us from the
rose and pearl morning of a brilliant diamond day. As the
dominant outline of the Château de Frontenac emerged out
of the dawn mists, this Canadian Gibraltar towered suddenly above our boat like a shining cliff. Along the banks of
the narrowing river the maples had already turned vermilion,
and the water was grey silk shot through with the fire-opal
of the climbing sun. It seemed as though a fragment of old
France had drifted across the Atlantic to soften a tired traveller's first impression of sky-challenging New World cities.

Thankfully leaving the ship for half a day, the American
Professor and G. and I stumbled over the uneven paving
stones along the harbour, passed the incongruous grain-
elevator which resolutely advertised American civilisation
from the docks, and hurried up precipitous streets cobbled
like the old square round the Radcliffe Camera at Oxford.
We almost ran and almost sang upon the Heights of Abraham, where we looked down at Wolfe's famous landing
place of blue river and yellow sand and tawny autumn
bushes, and thought what a toy of a landing place it seemed
after the deadly steeps of Gallipoli. The Plains, we discovered, had become a public park, and the football matches of
young Canada were won upon the battlefields of Quebec.

With deep satisfaction I noted all round me the peaceful
mingling of British and French civilisation; in those
young, optimistic nineteen-twenties, when mankind was still
remorsefully contemplating the results of the last war

Cs

instead of cynically preparing for the next, it seemed an inspiring theme for a League of Nations lecture.

"Here," I recorded enthusiastically in my notebook, "there is sunshine, and spaciousness, and a sense of illimitable boundaries, within which international differences seem to evaporate into thin air. Here the two peoples share their languages, their architecture, their ambitions, and even, without a trace of retrospective bitterness, their heroes and their history. Monuments of Montcalm and Wolfe are scattered impartially all over the city, and the arch above the main entrance to the Parliament House is carved into twin niches, the one occupied by Montcalm and the other by Wolfe. In life they were enemies, but in death they are not divided."

Next day, when we landed at Montreal, sunshine and enthusiasm alike had evaporated. Battered by harsh winds comfortless as November gales, the beautiful climbing city looked as cheerful that Sunday morning as Derby or Nottingham on a wet English Sabbath. Under my feet the ground seemed to rise and fall, as it does to this day for a week after every rough voyage, and to my tired sea-stricken eyes the interior of Notre Dame Cathedral appeared as a dizzy panorama of black wooden pillars divided by dim points of swaying light. I felt intensely relieved when a banging, drenching thunderstorm drove us to spend the rest of the day in the Mount Royal Hotel. Late that evening we boarded the sleeping car which carried us from Canada into America, and I experienced for the first time that form of nocturnal transport described by Arnold Bennett as "men and women lying promiscuously on shelves under the supervision of a negro porter".

It has only been within recent months, after fifty thousand miles of American journeys and the gradual development of a philosophy of travel, that I have acquired a faculty for sleeping comfortably on American trains. Thirteen years ago, with apprehension, resentment and curiosity about the small town which was to be our temporary home making havoc of my peace, I was not disposed to regard with somnolent equanimity either the other female travellers whose sponges, combs and toothbrushes jostled mine in the communal dressing-room, or the occupants of the neighbouring bunks who snored in confident friendliness around me. I began to suspect, not for the first time, that my British individualism was going to suffer many shocks in the process of adjusting itself to American Rotarianism, Kiwanism, geniality, sociability, freemasonry, heartiness and general get-togetherness.

The American habit of settling down comfortably to the prospect of changing trains or crossing cities in the middle of the night was another which I did not acquire for years, and I had not slept when at 4.30 a.m. we tumbled from the Montreal express on to the dark platform of a large station and transferred ourselves to a local train. After an hour's run we were put down at a small town which was not yet our destination. The necessity of waiting there for four hours increased in my dismayed mind the sense that I was now half a world away from London, and should have to make a superhuman effort if I was ever to return there.

For most of the morning we explored that town in the back area of New York State, but discovered nothing more lively than street after street of wooden shanties and a number of new, improvised-looking factories. In the forlorn light of the cheerless September morning, the whole place reminded me of the Base in France; all the buildings looked as if they could be taken down and carried off on lorries during the night. Later I was to learn that the unfinished appearance of everything was in no way unusual; the greater part of inhabited America is always in process of being put up or taken down.

It was not a stimulating introduction to a new and mighty civilisation. When the second local train deposited us at the desolate station of the still smaller town towards which we had been journeying for a tedious fortnight, I was in no mood to appreciate the wild loveliness of the Iroquois country, with its lakes and forests and chasm-gashed hills where the white cascades tumbled thinly through deep dramatic ravines. Looking down from the University on the heights to the miniature city hugging the long valley two hundred feet below, I could only remember dismally that in Buxton, the home of my early youth to which I had vehemently refused to adapt my habits or my standards, the rugged grandeur of the Derbyshire dales had served chiefly to emphasise the fact that scenery is a poor substitute for living.

II

Looking back upon that part of my life which I have already fulfilled, I realise that its most valuable turning-points have always followed some refusal to accommodate myself to circumstances which I found hampering, uncongenial or oppressive. I have had constantly to choose between being disagreeable and becoming ineffective. In consequence I have acquired a number of critics—some of considerable eminence —who look upon me as an aggressive egotist deserving of no encouragement; but I have never regarded this adverse opinion as too high a price to pay for freedom from that sense of frustration which follows the loss of one's life work.

In one of the religious books which pious relatives were accustomed to present to girls of my generation at the time of their confirmation, I remember reading an injunction to the effect that we ought to cultivate "those virtues which grow at the foot of the Cross"—patience, meekness, self-effacement, the capacity for acceptance. I should like to ram that falsehood down the throat of the unctuous moralist who penned it. Nothing could be more destructive of character and more warping to vitality than a long course of abnegation and sacrifice. Were it not for this universal inertia of humble patient acceptance, the worst human evils—war, cruelty, poverty, the oppression of the penniless and the persecution of the weak—could be destroyed tomorrow. In the world as I have known it, I have come to recognise resignation as the deadliest of the seven deadly sins; to see it as a positive menace to the civilisation which only some tremendous renaissance of initiative can now rescue from doom. Resignation is the last vice of which that Renaissance country, the United States, can be accused. In proportion to my recognition of this fact, my affection for America has grown.

Small-town society, however, does not represent America or any other country at its best, and I had not long become part of it before I realised that I was in for another period of reaction against my surroundings.

It was unfortunate that this first experience of the United States should have been a provincial experience, for—as I have explained elsewhere—I have detested provincialism, and regarded it as the embodiment of all false values, ever since I was brought up in its atmosphere. In 1925, American provincialism was tinged with the complacency of the whole country during that boastful boom period. Most junior University teachers have a struggle to balance their private budgets and our community was therefore not a wealthy one, but national prosperity at that time represented a psychological super-investment in which everybody had taken shares. There was an exuberant satisfaction in being American, not so much because the United States was a grand, forward-looking country which would probably share with Russia the shaping of humanity's future, but because it seemed to have escaped the aftermath of the War, triumphantly solving its economic problems and shrewdly avoiding the grief and distress of Europe. Not only in the provinces, but later in New York and other cities, many of the Americans whom I met appeared to regard the poverty and despair into which half the Old World had fallen as a species of inefficiency that could easily have been avoided by a little forethought and commonsense.

Probably they were right; neither forethought nor commonsense was a conspicuous quality in the Treaty of Versailles. But I had seen and felt that poverty and despair for myself; I had known it in terms of the death of German children, the bitter helpless resentment of the population in the Occupied Territories, the undernourishment of whole peoples in Central Europe—and I had nothing but repugnance for a point of view which seemed to regard that suffering as negligible because it was due to mismanagement.

Ignorantly enough, I underestimated the great humanitarian work which America was doing even then in Europe, because of the indifference of Americans who had not gone; and, as the months went by, every instance of this indifference added strength to the antagonism already arising from personal discouragement. No sooner had I arrived in the country, than I was dismayed by the discovery that some of the wives of these small-town professors were as narrowly preoccupied with their homes, their children and their local scandals as the provincial Englishwomen whom I had known in my intolerant adolescence. Although I had been an Oxford student I had never actually lived in a University city, and it had not occurred to me that "Faculty wives" would fall as easily as any other kind of wife into the conversational traps provided by meals, babies, illnesses, and the delinquencies of the latest "help."

At first, realising that I must respond as gracefully as I could to the enthusiastic welcome which I received, I tried to stifle these critical reactions. With dogged conscientiousness I did my limited English best to meet each friendly gesture with the warm gratitude that I knew it deserved; but at home, once the wedding celebrations were over, my marriage to G. had caused no commotion, and I was overwhelmed and bewildered, rather than pleased and flattered, by the gifts and invitations which flowed into our modest apartment.

It required three visits to the United States to teach me that the very acceptance of America's lavish, spontaneous hospitality demands, on the part of an Englishman or woman, the deliberate cultivation of a saving graciousness which is not natural to our unresponsive race. In 1925, little English intellectual snob that I was, my manners were anything but gracious, and even the international outlook of which Europe's catastrophes had taught me the need, hardly helped to improve them. It was all that I could do to make the necessary adjustments in social etiquette demanded of me by the numerous luncheons, teas and dinners to which I was invited by the local élite. Nor was it always easy for a European to discover precisely who the local élite were.

The guests at these functions belonged mainly, but not entirely, to the University group. A party was really smart if it contained either the President of the University or a member of the municipal plutocracy, whose leader was the impressive owner of the local hardware store. It took me some time to learn the difference between English and American gradings in small-town society. In England, though a selective provincial hostess might still turn up her nose at "trade", she could safely invite any one of the local doctors, and unless she were a pacifist she would probably feel that a military or naval officer gave an enviable *cachet* to her party. In the United States it is "trade"—always assuming that the tradesman is successful—which provides the oligarchy. The doctor, if he belongs to an established local family, may also be welcome, but more probably he will be treated as a highly-skilled artisan who cannot expect invitations to his patients' parties. As for the Army, apart from the higher ranks it is a poor relation, admitted on sufferance and a little apologetic in the presence of the commercial hierarchy.

At the close of the first social function given in my honour, I was frankly disconcerted by the generous American habit of presenting guests with the flowers from the vases and the cakes left on the table. In England such an action would imply that the recipient of these gifts could not afford to buy flowers or cakes for herself. I felt astonished, too, when my hostess accepted with barely a criticism my use of my maiden name, but seemed disproportionately upset if I wore a hat when she did not expect it, or failed to wear one when she did. At London post-war cocktail-parties I had grown accustomed to appearing hatless or not, just as I pleased; and it seemed strange to return to a society in which the War had not destroyed these trivial conventions.

"It is all very amusing, like a play on a little stage with the wide world outside," I wrote to my mother, but I confessed that, with my thirtieth birthday recently past and the long story of the War and its aftermath behind me, I had been exasperated by the general assumption that I was an inexperienced young girl just down from the University, with a pathetic predilection for novel-writing. "Everyone here takes me for about 23—and suits their conversation accordingly. I am so bored with being described as 'our little English bride', and with being told 'my little daughter—she must be about your age—went to England last year when she left college'. . . . I have already been asked by Professor X. 'Are you going to write us all up?'"

By God, I thought, as youthfully resentful of patronage as if I had indeed been twenty-three, one day I will!

Almost before we had unpacked and settled in to our apartment, the callers began to appear. During the first week they dropped in one by one, but by the second they were arriving in platoons, and by the third in battalions. They started coming soon after lunch, and we could never feel certain of freedom for the rest of the day. Quite frequently they appeared late in the evening, when G. was preparing his lectures and I was trying to write a new book, entitled *A Honeymoon in Two Worlds*, which I had just begun.

It was a short book, combining travel impressions with unorthodox reflections on marriage. From the standpoint of style alone it was probably better written than anything I have attempted, since I had more time to give to the careful modelling of sentences during that year in America than I have ever had before or since. But though several publishers' readers subsequently praised the writing, the manuscript belonged to no recognised category, and nobody would risk its publication. At the moment the bitter disappointment of that rejection added to my belief—later to prove so illusory—that my first year in America was just twelve months of wasted time.

I began the book, however, with the usual excited hopes, and casual interrupters were by no means welcome. Having broken loose from it once in my life, I did not propose again to become the slave of that social calling system which is the bane of provincial communities in England, America, and every place where it is still maintained.

This system is usually justified on the ground that it brings people who would not otherwise meet into friendly contact, and gives pleasant occupation to women who have not enough to do. Both these excuses are idle illusions. The best way to make friendly contacts is through work; the atmosphere of an afternoon call is far more conducive to malicious gossip then to the development of agreeable friendships. Nor does the system fill empty lives with anything worth having. By offering something which mimics occupation, it prevents women with too much leisure from facing the futility of their days and finding a useful outlet for their energy. Worst of all, it provides those petty, self-important individuals who exercise their spitefulness by ostracising others with an easy opportunity for snobbishness, and threatens the peace of any woman whose gifts and training lead her to prefer work to social chit-chat. She has to choose between wasting her time day after day, and being labelled "peculiar" because she does not conform to the accepted routine. In a University community, where secret wheels of intrigue move complexly within one another, a young man may easily be denied promotion because his wife has failed to repay with punctilious promptitude a call by the wife of an older Professor.

Had G.'s welfare not been involved, I should probably have returned none of my calls, so ferociously did I detest the system, and so little have I cared for any reputation which depends upon social angling or the placation of self-importance. But I could not sacrifice him either to my principles or to my prejudices, so I made an ignoble compromise and returned the calls of those families who counted in the University. These visits were soon repaid and led to some pleasant acquaintanceships in households where G. was already known, but when I found that he had never heard the names of several later callers who presumably came out of curiosity, I put a drastic end to my previous efforts at social adaptation, and with defensive discourtesy concealed myself and my work in the University Library every afternoon between 3.30 and 7 p.m.

From each of my visitors, and from many of G.'s local acquaintances encountered in private houses, restaurants, shops, street cars and lecture halls, the same question greeted me. I had heard it for the first time on the station platform when I tumbled wearily from the last of the three trains which had brought us from Montreal.

"How do you like our country?" ran the anxious enquiry, or, still more eagerly, "What do you think of our town?"

Now this was no rhetorical question, as it would have been if put by an Englishman about his own country. In London we often ask our American visitors: "How do you like England?" but we seldom wait to hear the answer. Nationally complacent and individually self-sufficient, we really do not much care what other nations think of us. My new American acquaintances, however, appeared to care a great deal; they asked if I liked their country because they really wanted to know. My approval was not of the least importance, but because I was an English woman and a stranger, they waited with some impatience for me to give it.

Later I was to realise that this anxiety, even in America, is largely a provincial quality. Friends in New York, in Chicago, in New Orleans, have been interested to hear my impressions and pleased if they seemed favourable; only a few months ago, a New Orleans newspaper devoted a column to half a dozen appreciative remarks which I had made to its representative. But had my reactions to any of these great cities been uncomplimentary, it would have been my judgment and not their civilisation which would, rightly, have stood condemned.

In 1925, having brought across the Atlantic the typical British partiality for ignorant and patronising generalisations about America, I believed that in this very desire for the expression of a good opinion, my questioners were answered. It was precisely, I thought, in her eagerness for appreciation that America differed most from England, and after a few weeks in the country I proceeded, like other ingenuous new arrivals, to write an article on my American impressions which embodied the supposed explanation of that eagerness. The article was entitled "The Evils of Good Fellowship", and was one of several which I tried out—at first hopefully, then with increasing and always justified pessimism—upon *Harper's Magazine*.

"Only the uncompromising individualist can afford to be impervious to criticism," I began portentously. "Most English people are still uncompromising individualists; that is why they limit the number of their acquaintances, exclude one another remorselessly from clubs, and, when they go abroad, treat the inheritors of ancient civilisations or the founders of new as though they were illiterate aborigines. No one who longs for the good-will of his fellows is prepared to endanger the achievement of his object by such behaviour, and the American at home appears to be less prepared to do so than the inhabitant of any country through which I have travelled in Europe. His desire for approval is the outstanding symptom of a national gregariousness which eschews eccentricity, avoids intimacy and flees from solitude as from the plague."

It was not until years afterwards, when I had come to know those vast inhuman emptinesses with which America humbles the critical strangers from little crowded civilisations, that I began to understand the desire of most Americans with an hour or two of spare time to "get together", to be welcomed and appreciated, to be saved from the morose contemplation of personal problems forced upon men and women by loneliness. Now that I have crossed the frozen prairies of Wisconsin, travelled along the solitary three-hundred-mile stretch of the Mississippi between Savanna and St. Paul, and looked out from the man-made luxury of a Pullman sleeper upon the Ozark Plateau lying huge and deserted beneath the October moon, I recognise this impulse as the compensating resource of a pioneer community. It survives from days when the comforting warmth of human society was man's only refuge from storms, droughts, hurricanes, and floods, his sole consolation for the loss of his crops, the ruin of his handiwork, and the surrender of his frail wife or helpless children to Nature's ruthless hostility.

"This gregarious instinct," my article continued, "gathers intensity both at school and in college. It thrives in the companionable atmosphere of these admirable democratic institutions, which in so many ways put to shame both the English Boys' public school, with its traditions of class distinction and 'superior persons', and the exclusive English girls' school, whose main object is only too often to provide cold storage until marriage. An inevitable result of sociability and democracy is the reduction of the exceptional to the normal, and where the American school fails to achieve this completely, the Boy Scouts or their feminine equivalent step in and finish the process. I know a keenly intellectual American woman who is also an ardent traveller; a short time ago she took her small son for a holiday in Europe. The boy had linguistic gifts, and in a few months became reasonably proficient in two or three languages. When they returned to America he was sent to school, and joined the Boy Scouts. At the end of his first term his mother met the scout master, a young man of twenty, who informed her that Buddy was doing as well as could be expected considering his handicaps. Somewhat perturbed, the mother inquired what Buddy's 'handicaps' were, and learnt to her amazement that his fellow scouts were helping him to 'overcome' his knowledge of Europe and his fluency in foreign tongues.

"In the later years of adolescence, the spirit of good fellowship is approved and fostered by every form of American custom and social observance. The ideal entertainment, for both young and old, appears to be one which permits of the largest possible crowd at the same hour and in the same place. Where time and space are limited, the small group is the less effective but still desirable substitute. Both crowd and group provide opportunity for the usual robust courtesies, which gradually warm into heartiness, and finally expand into the typical explosions of boisterous geniality. Only once have I been invited to a meal at which

I was the only guest, and then the invitation came from a family who often visit England, and are consequently accustomed to the English habit of retiring into a spiritual corner."

Whenever G. and I were not being entertained at one of these functions, our habit, according to the current aesthetic description, was to "eat out". My article went on to describe how these expeditions to the town—a smaller and more homogeneous community than the numerous semi-industrial "Middletowns" with their thirty thousand inhabitants—put me in touch with yet further varieties of unfamiliar conviviality.

"Outside my immediate social contacts, there are groups which provide even richer soil for the seed of joyous companionship. In the town where I am living there is a large office building with a restaurant on the top floor, and beside the restaurant a spacious ball-room, which is also available for luncheons, dinners, conferences and lectures. If an English provincial town of the same size ever brought itself to construct such a room, it would be used perhaps once in three months, and the preparations for the event to be celebrated would keep a dozen people on the run for the whole of the previous week. In the top-floor ball-room, however, luncheons and dinners, conferences and dances appear to spring up almost daily without any preliminary perturbation on the part of anyone. Catering for large groups, gathering them together, and clearing away after them, seems to be part of the normal routine for which every American is prepared.

"Often, after taking my meals in the restaurant, I have watched the good-humoured assemblings of the Rotary Club, or the Student Luncheon Club, or the League of Women Voters, or the American Association of University Women. And always, when the meal or the meeting is begun and I glance as I go out at the cheerful group which eats or meets in radiant publicity, I marvel at the communicative vitality that seems to enable each member to be all things to every other. If the crowd is composed of men, they are often singing songs and clapping one another on the back in the unrestrained exuberance of appreciative affection; if the gathering is of women, they are talking together, or listening to speeches, in a spirit of fellowship less exuberant but no less absorbing.

"The town, as American towns go, is attractive; it is too much broken up with hills and dales to be wrenched into that pattern of geometrical simplicity which seems to be the architectural ideal of the New World builders. At one end it tails off rather untidily to the shores of a long lake, surrounded by low, desolate hills of the Scottish type, and everywhere it is full of immense, drooping trees, maples and oaks and sycamores, which now wear the orange and chestnut and vermilion of Joseph's coat, and scatter their lovely leaves in golden munificence over houses and paths and roads. The houses, mostly of wood painted green or yellow or brown, seem to have grown up haphazard like plants which spring from seeds scattered by the wind; they have an improvised, unsettled appearance, as though their builders had dropped them casually from above.

"Whenever, by day or by night, I pass one, the same neighbourliness that I found in the restaurant beams at me from its kindly and unshaded windows. In all directions from the main street these small, comfortable buildings have sprung up in rows, and each is divided from the next by that space of which the New World has still so much to spare.

"In England such unwonted roominess would instantly be used for the manufacture of privacy. Hedges would spring up; a garden, laid out with formal beds and borders, would fill the bare grassiness with occupants less garrulous than man; trees would be planted to hide the garden from the street, and to conceal the house from the garden. But to the gregarious American the largest space, like the five oceans after the days of the great discoverers, suggests not a division but a contact. The street is his link with the rest of humanity, and he desires no hedge to separate him from it. He does not wish to sit alone in his garden, so he plants no flowers to adorn his solitude; and if trees divide him from his neighbours, he cuts them down.

"The result is a mixture of astonishing incongruities, as though an immaculate gentleman clad in spotless underwear of the finest quality had arrayed himself in the outer garments of a tramp. I know scarcely an American house where I could not eat with perfect confidence off the floor or even the bath-tub, yet their unkempt, hedgeless 'gardens' are general repositories for tins, ashes, cigarette ends, old papers, and all the flotsam and jetsam which usually collects in the gutters of the local Whitechapel. As for their parks, an English Professor who has lived in New York tells me that sitting in Riverside Park in May is like sunning one's self on the municipal rubbish dump, and I can easily believe it.

"The community spirit is equally evident in the ball-room and along the highroad. At a dance I am, like other women, the victim of a cutting-in system which is evidently based upon the assumption that no conversation with a partner can be too intimate to be interrupted. When I walk into the country, my isolation is perpetually challenged by the poster-correspondence along the roadway, addressed to the drivers of automobiles from the club-rooms of a welcoming municipality. I am also the means of holding up a score of solicitous motorists, who cannot believe that I really do not want a lift. The American citizen's own notion of pleasure is to crowd a small herd of friends into his car, and to spend several hours in an atmosphere of speed and draughts and Go-gas, instead of breathing the autumn air full of the rich, poignant scent of dead leaves and sodden fields. On a golden afternoon along a country road, with frost-diamonds glittering upon tawny leaves, and the distant hills as dreamily and celestially blue as any poet could wish, I have been passed by a hundred automobiles, but never by one other solitary pedestrian. Even the dogs rush out of the houses and bark at me as I pass; and dogs, as everyone knows, are the embodiment of bourgeois morality. If a dog disapproves of your occupation, you may be quite sure that you are guilty of something which simply is not done."

I was not, I found, to have much contact with the University. Although they were popular with his students, G. sedulously discouraged such perfunctory attempts as I ever made to attend his lectures. One or two other discourses which I sampled, though an improvement on the normal performances of distinguished scholars at the older English Universities, gave no indication that the standard of academic lecturing which had first astonished me at Oxford would be dramatically reversed in America.

In any case, the University was not disposed to encourage the intellectual pretensions of its female appendages. It was one of the few coeducational institutions where the status of the women students was definitely lower than that of the men, and its Faculty had displayed from the first a resolute intention to keep its wives and daughters in their place. Wives were admitted by courtesy to its historical clubs and other small discussion groups, but whatever their qualifications for taking part in the debates, they were expected to retire to another room and talk Bridge or babies when the real business of the evening began. The Faculty Club frankly reserved its entertainments for "men only" as soon as they involved more stimulating ventures than music or tea-fights, and I once caused a good deal of embarrassment by concealing myself with deliberate conspicuousness behind the club-room curtain during a luncheon-hour address by Professor Harry Elmer Barnes which I particularly wanted to hear.

One reason for excluding women from the more intimate gatherings seemed obvious enough. I had not realised, until I actually entered University society, how much secret wire-pulling and continuous place-hunting goes on throughout the academic world. These carefully laid schemes and stratagems are doubtless no commoner there than in other professions, but their range is wider, and I was still enough of a naïve idealist to be disturbed by the discovery that a strongly-developed capacity for personal manœuvring could accompany a high standard of scholarship.

Ds

"This place," I recorded ruefully, "is Magna Graecia, full of sophists and with every opportunity, for those who like them, for glorious intrigues. Secret diplomacy, which has officially been turned out neck and crop from the Council Chambers of Europe, appears to have taken refuge in the Halls of Academe, and to have transformed them into a highly-organised international whispering-gallery. In California they discuss what the dons are doing in their apparently innocent gardens at Oxford, while in this Faculty Club we criticise next year's appointments at Cambridge or Tokyo or Calcutta. It is a very exciting game, especially if you do not happen to want any of the appointments yourself, but it must be rather nerve-wracking for the would-be elect to be perpetually trying to discover what is being said behind their backs on the other side of the world."

In so far as I was able to learn any facts about the University teaching system, its scholarly aspirations seemed as high as any cherished by the Old World, but its methods involved too rigid and too intricate a standardisation of courses, which led students to depend unduly upon the "spoon-feeding" of notes taken in class. Only a few of the students seemed wealthy; had we been living at Yale or Princeton, Vassar or Bryn Mawr, the proportion would have been different.

Nearly all the student body owned Ford cars, and the age of the Ford provided an index to the economic status of its owner. Never had I seen so many automobiles in such varied stages of disintegration; no degree of ruin seemed to matter provided that the contraption still went. One, attached to the tattered remnants of a coupé, drove up and down the steep hills with the announcement "For Sale— $50" chalked on the back. The most proletarian of all was a wooden box on wheels with a driver's seat and steering gear nailed to the front. Whatever the condition of these vehicles, their owners drove them remorselessly over level-crossings, tram-lines, bridges, or dirt-roads gashed with gullies and torn by deep ruts.

Occasionally the wealthier students entertained us at the

College Club or their luxurious Fraternity Houses—a manner of student living which seemed strange to me after the comfortable masculine shabbiness of Oxford and the bleak frugality of its women's colleges. Of the less well-to-do we saw little, though occasionally in the evenings we entertained a dozen or so from G.'s class in our tiny living-room, where they sat on the floor consuming biscuits, cream cheese and non-alcoholic beer. Most of these boys and girls were too busy working their way through college by acting as waiters and waitresses in local restaurants, or as part-time secretaries, or as domestic "help" in private houses, to have time for social contacts with their teachers. When I first came to the town they mistook me for one of themselves, and for three weeks I could not cross the Campus without being urged to purchase undergraduate journals, join dramatic clubs, "take" athletics, or buy an embroidered bag in which to send my washing to that most enterprising of money-making institutions, the student laundry. My local hair-dresser, I discovered, had a son who made two hundred dollars during one Long Vacation by working as a road-mender in Illinois. The following year, desiring to "see life", he acted as "watch" on the *George Washington* and worked his way across to Germany. In Germany, as in the United States, he kept himself by taking, without any sense of lost dignity, such casual jobs as the German students despised even in that era of poverty and inflation; like his fellows he was ready for anything from building a bridge to minding a baby.

When my "Evils of Good Fellowship" article had disposed, to my own satisfaction, of the local town life, it continued by criticising the University.

"In England, I have known both directly and indirectly a good many Universities. Each of these has provided its contingent of pugnaciously sociable students, but the majority of the undergraduates, especially in the older foundations, have been more or less solitary souls, who spent their working lives alone or in couples, and only joined a group of their fellows when the day's business was done.

"This American University, however, seems to me to be as gregarious as the town; within its precincts the isolated soul is suspected, pitied or blamed. The more popular the student, the less is his opportunity for solitary work. There are organisations for every kind of interest, as well as dances, smoking clubs and afternoon At Homes. No fortunate students live alone; they are gathered into Fraternities and Sororities, where from the age of sixteen to twenty-two young men and women are steam-rollered into the pattern approved of by their contemporaries.

"Quite recently I met a man who is an excellent amateur 'cellist, and who, when he was a University student, belonged to a Fraternity. At that time, one of the most flourishing societies in his University was a Mandolin Club, on which each Fraternity aspired to be represented. Mandolins, therefore, were the fashion of the moment, while 'cellos were regarded as unnecessary and undesirable. My acquaintance was one of the few musical members of his Fraternity, and he had in consequence to endure criticism and opposition from his fellows, who wanted him to abandon his 'cello for the mandolin, and represent them on the club. This, being a youth of some character, he steadily refused to do, and at length the attempt to persuade him was transferred to a less stubborn student, who was an organist. This student, in deference to public opinion, abandoned the organ and took up the mandolin instead. As soon as he left college, he naturally found that the mandolin was of little use to him, so he gave this up also, but never had time to recapture his lost skill on the organ. Thus, thanks to his Fraternity, he was deprived of expression for the musical talent which was his chief claim to individuality.

"The University Faculty have also their smoking clubs and their departmental clubs and their research clubs, and at meal-times they haunt those eating-houses which are frequented by their kind. Several times a year they repair to distant cities, to hold conferences with colleagues on every classifiable subject. Professors gather together from Boston and California, from Georgia and Montreal; they all pour into one hotel, pull strings, talk about their new academic captures and run promising 'discoveries' into quiet corners, safe from interruption owing to this concentrated interchange of learned information. An English visitor to America once told me that the noise of Niagara is greatly exaggerated; it is much less than that of these academic Associations at their annual gatherings. He could speak, he said, with authority, for he had heard both."

When I wrote those words, I had no personal experience of the peculiarly American phenomenon known as a Convention with which to test my informant's statement. Since that time, I have lived in the same hotel with Library Conventions to which I have been lecturing, and once, in Chicago, I had to hold my own against a Meat Packers' Convention for an entire week-end. But none of these fulfilled the description given me so closely as the Baseball Convention which recently thundered in and out of the largest hotel in Milwaukee, where I was putting in a spare half hour before a luncheon-lecture at the Women's Club. When I sat down at a desk in the lounge to write a letter, I felt as though I were trying to compose my correspondence in the midst of the rush hour at Charing Cross.

"If I had to sum up in a sentence," my article severely concluded, after rashly wandering down the casualty-strewn highroad of British generalisations, "I think I should say that a nation, like an individual, can never become mentally mature so long as it cultivates the habit of social dependence and the unthinking worship of the average. The fear of being 'different' is essentially the fear of a school-child, and especially of a school-boy; no creature in the world is so anxious to do the 'right thing' as the school-boy prefect of sixteen or seventeen. To stand alone, to defy public opinion and endure criticism—these are grown-up qualities, whose too perpetual discouragement may well produce a uniform society which is mentally aged sixteen . . .

"I cannot believe that this country will ever again put forth through a new Thoreau or a new Emerson the literature of lonely meditation, or produce a poet of solitude who will rightly be ranked with Wordsworth, or Thomas Hardy, or W. H. Davies. Life here is lived on the speeding circumference instead of at the quiet centre; it has become too much of a hustle for the slow, secret pleasures of watching for the first snowdrop, or gathering primroses, or sitting alone with a book in the sweet shadow of a laden rosebush. And it is only by cultivating the garden of his mind in the same leisurely peace as he needs for cultivating the garden of his house, that a man's ideas grow gradually but certainly to completeness and perfection.

"Solitude of such a kind proves what man is; gregariousness is only a test of what he says and does. Perpetual speech and action in common with others must surely at length produce the mental incapacity to form an original opinion. Is America to contemplate a civilisation in which no man's mind remains capable of conceiving and bringing to birth a complete thought, but where division of labour is carried so far that even an idea has to be the product of the community?"

I spent many more hours during that first visit to America in trying to estimate the vast philosophical differences between this genial, communicative modern society and that which long ago witnessed the supreme flowering of human reason, when Callimachus and his friend, old Heraclitus, "tired the sun with talking and sent him down the sky."

Dare I confess that even by 1937, when I spent a few days sunning myself in the warmth of established friendships before my second American lecture tour began, this contrast still perturbed me? Though every other aspect of American civilisation appeared in quite a different light from the remorseless glare of 1925, a letter written to G. from New York at the beginning of October, 1937, put exactly the same questions as my critical and pompous article twelve years before.

"As usual I have the heavy-headed, slightly dizzy feeling of being in a remotely nightmarish dream in which the floor is insecure and nothing quite substantial. . . . . It is a part of getting accustomed to the pace of this country and to the fact that one moves everywhere in crowds. The one thing about America, much as I adore it, which I can never get used to or like, is that people never seem to want to be alone together except for sexual or semi-sexual purposes. . . . You, I know, like it, and think one ought to like it—but I can't understand how people's minds or their personal relationships develop under such circumstances. . . . How would you like a married life in which you never saw me alone in the day-time? And I can't imagine how people think out anything—even a business proposition, let alone philosophical problems—unless they are sometimes by themselves, or with one other person who is prepared to examine and analyse as I do with you. . . . I can't quite get at the reason for this American desire to congregate perpetually. They are not (as we so facilely summarise it in England) really superficial, or like children, and they are certainly not afraid of looking situations in the face. But they seem to be perpetually escaping from something—as though the pre-occupation with self, with ideas, with the soul, with the Absolute (call it what you will) out of which thought arises, were somehow part of an old, bad, fettering tradition, which would keep them back from where they want to go. But where do they want to go? You know America so much better than I do, and are equally sympathetic to Americans, so do explain."

It was not until I had finished that second tour that I thought I began to get a glimpse of the answer to my own question.

III

At the end of our first few weeks in the small town, I sent home a time-table of my day.

7.30. Get up and go out to breakfast.

8.30. (or thereabouts). Clean out the apartment with vigour and rapidity.

10.0. (or thereabouts). Settle in to write till lunch.

1.0. Go out to lunch.

2.0. Continue to work (unless there are letters to write or shopping to do).

4.0 Return calls or go to some function or other (unless you are caught by callers yourself first, which involves getting tea and receiving calls instead of returning them. Returning them is preferable as it usually involves a long walk which provides exercise for the day).

6.0. Work till dinner, unless having had no exercise, in which case go for a walk with G., who always prowls about restlessly at this hour.

7.0. Go out to dinner.

8.0. Read papers—innumerable papers—not only *The Times*, etc. from home, but the *New York Times*, the *New Republic*, *Harper's Magazine* and anything else which gives one intelligent information about America.

10.0. Make cocoa (which G. really likes at 9.30!).

10.30. Do a little more work.

11.0. Bed.

Into the midst of this programme were also sandwiched At Homes, lectures, library reading, luncheons and dinner parties. It was perhaps not surprising that I commented in a later letter: "Always too much to do here—and not all

of it, alas, important. . . . I am in a perpetual state of
snatching time to write; I always seem to be getting dressed
to go out to something—a luncheon, a dinner, a tea, a
lecture, a University function—and coming back and
getting undressed again; or else going out for meals."

In spite of the hours snatched so feverishly for writing,
I was coming reluctantly to the conclusion, foreseen in
England, that attempts to acquire an American reputation
as writer or speaker were likely to remain futile when made
from a place as far from New York as Berwick-on-Tweed
from London. We were even separated by sixty miles from
the nearest large town—which was merely one of the
seventy United States cities with a population of 100,000
or more. Outside our own little community, American
audiences were not exactly impatient to hear lectures by
an unknown English girl whose insignificant youthful
exterior belied every experience that she had ever been
through, while the first onslaught upon *Harper's Magazine*
—a series of suggestions for articles on the state of Europe
—had produced the following characteristic reply:

"MY DEAR MISS BRITTAIN,

"I am afraid that vignettes of life and manners in
Hungary or studies of the zones of occupation in Germany would hardly fit into our present editorial scheme.
We are ruling out descriptive articles of this kind, and
devote most of our space to papers of a more dynamic
sort, which discuss current problems of living and touch
upon modern American interests. Perhaps you have other
ideas to propose, and if you will glance over recent
numbers of *Harper's* I think you will get our editorial
slant on possible magazine material."

In that overcrowded existence, so full of insignificant
events which led nowhere, one of the largest daily interruptions was the cleaning of our four-room apartment. This
small flat occupied the top floor of a typical frame-house
on the edge of the Campus, built from long timber planks

grown grey with age. Round it spread the usual patch of unhedged, untended grass which represented the forlorn American substitute for a garden, and two or three wooden steps led up to a sheltered verandah. Like the front door itself, the glass-panelled door at the top of the stairs which shut off our apartment always remained unlocked—my first experience of the American self-respect that so seldom descends to the petty pilfering, still common enough in England, which became the curse of Central Europe after the period of inflation.

The apartment provided us with two bedrooms, a living-room and a bathroom-kitchenette, which had no facilities for cooking except an electric grill standing on a marble-topped cupboard where I made tea. The four little rooms were comfortably furnished, but somewhat dark owing to their brown ceilings and olive-green walls. I soon discovered that dim rooms are customary in America, and have recently been surprised to find in Mary Ellen Chase's charming book of essays, In England—Now, the remark that English lighting is "woefully inadequate". Her comment seems to me even truer of American lighting, particularly in hotels, where my first action on taking possession of a room is always to pull back the curtains, draw up the blinds and throw open the windows. Recently, at a large hotel in Buffalo, a notice between the electric candlelights on my dressing table assured me: "The lighting in this room is certified as sufficient." It may have been sufficient for the male electrician who installed it; it was quite insufficient for me when I wanted to powder my nose and make up my face.

The window of our largest bedroom, where I usually worked while G. prepared his lectures in the living room, looked due south over a back lawn, shaded by tall, heavy trees, to the spruce-covered hills beyond the town. Soon after we arrived, the back of the house acquired a log-cabin appearance owing to a prolonged coal-strike, which induced our generous landlady to cut down one of her trees and chop it up into blocks for the furnace. On the top of another tree a tiny red squirrel with a huge bushy tail would run precariously along the thin, unsubstantial boughs, or scamper in ludicrous excitement round the iron railing of the Fraternity tennis court next door. His antics so frequently accompanied my writing that to this day the torn and discoloured manuscript of *A Honeymoon in Two Worlds* brings back to my mind the scarlet streak of animation which, even when snow covered the lawn and the trees, gave life to the empty, log-strewn garden.

We felt that we were living on a desperately extravagant scale because this country apartment cost us £4 a week, and another £4 went on the weekly food bill for the two of us. (In 1923, Winifred Holtby and I had rented a much larger London flat, with four rooms, a big kitchen and a fair-sized bathroom, for £60 a year; and the housekeeping bill for ourselves and a maid came to less than £3 per week). These prices did not include the charge made by the local laundries, which we were obliged to use for everything but the smallest articles since there was nowhere to wash and iron but our tiny bathroom. These laundries were both haughty and expensive; one would accept only personal clothes, another only household linen, and both were liable to refuse our washing altogether if I wrote politely to explain that a shirt or a towel had been mislaid. Our weekly bill for two sheets, two pillow-cases, four towels and three or four of G.'s shirts amounted to about 10s.

The restaurants which served this moderately-endowed community were also far from cheap according to English standards; $1 (4s. 2d.) was the usual price for a plain three-course supper, and on Sundays a midday meal could be obtained nowhere under $1.50 (6s. 3d.). We breakfasted very frugally at a typical American institution known as "The Pop-Shop", which sold ice-cream sundaes, hot chocolate, coffee, soft drinks, candies of all kinds, and the innumerable varieties of sandwich obtainable in cities at every drug store. I was impressed with the cleanliness of this modest eating-house, with its constantly washed marble-topped tables and fresh paper mats. An English "tea room" of the same economic standard would have offered its customers soiled cloths, stained tables, tarnished pepper-castors and fly-blown mirrors.

From a breakfast of coffee and a fried egg sandwich, I returned to the daily wrestle with our apartment. At first G. and I "did" it between us, he polishing the wooden floors with a mop and going over the mats with a carpet-sweeper while I made the beds, washed the bathroom, and dusted. But soon his work intervened, and the burden of such domesticity as we could not escape fell upon my shoulders. At first I engaged an Italian student boy to help me, but when I discovered that he was adept at spending half an hour upon shaking three mats in the garden, I decided that fifty cents (2s. 1d.) per hour was too much to pay for the privilege. Before long I was doing the whole apartment myself, and the precious morning writing period which has always been my best time for work began at 11.30 and ended at 12.45, when we dressed to go out for lunch.

Unlike the instructors' wives who could not afford even to "eat out", I had not much shopping to do apart from the purchase of afternoon tea and a few cooking and cleaning utensils, but even these small commissions taught me the different usage of many words which is gradually making American quite a separate tongue from English. When I set out to buy a kettle, I could not understand why I was always offered the equally homely but quite different implement known to England as a saucepan, until someone explained that what I wanted was evidently a "tea-kettle". For weeks, in attempting to provide the accompaniments of four o'clock tea, I was confused by the fact that the words "biscuit" and "cookie" are used in America to describe the commonplace luxury which England calls a "cake", while Americans refer to the English "biscuit" as a "cracker".

Even today, when I am so familiar with the American language that I fall unconsciously into its idiom after a few days in New York, I find myself inadvertently asking for the "Ladies' Cloak Room" and being led to a closet containing a row of hooks and those only, instead of to the still more necessary establishment which I ought to have described with greater delicacy as the "Ladies' Rest Room" or the "Toilet."

I have recounted in some detail these domestic aspects of our married life because it is precisely this burden of domesticity which, especially in small towns, impedes the forward march of America's highly-qualified and ambitious women. Though it fell lightly upon me I found its perpetual disturbances exasperating enough, for in spite of the practical efficiency taught me by my hospital war service, I have always detested domesticity as the unnecessary and too meekly accepted obstacle to woman's achievement, the final and fundamental explanation of sex-inequality. Only those who appreciate the different qualities of work produced by complete and by partial concentration, can ever estimate the extent to which women's performances suffer from constant small interruptions and petty, time-wasting tasks. The triumphant inquirers who put their hackneyed question: "Why have we never had a woman Shakespeare, Michaelangelo, Rembrandt or Beethoven?" need look no further than the ill-adjusted burdens of the average household for their answer.

Occasionally a Jane Austen or a Madame Curie transcends these besetting trivialities by sheer force of genius, but the callous wastage of human ability is likely to continue until the wealth, industry and intelligence now expended upon the mechanisation of the world's armies in order to obtain maximum efficiency in destructiveness, is applied more constructively to the organisation and mechanisation of the home.

The dreary, eliminable obligations of domesticity did not weigh upon me more heavily only because, so long as we lived in America, I deliberately remained childless. This decision was made before we left England, but had

I still cherished any romantic doubts, they would have vanished the moment that I realised the problems which afflicted the wife of a small-salaried instructor or assistant-professor, with two or three children, no income of her own and no opportunity of earning one, in a country where white maids and children's nurses charged $80 (£16) a month and refused to do laundry.

Later, in New York, I found that even some well-to-do relatives with whom I stayed at their comfortable Park Avenue apartment prepared and served their own breakfast, and kept no servant except for a superior being who swept and dusted from 11.0 to 1.0 at the rate of a dollar an hour. For households which could not afford full-time employees, domestic service in those prosperous days was so specialised that one maid came in daily to sweep and dust, and another weekly to scrub floors and bathrooms. One man appeared at intervals to use the vacuum cleaner, a second polished the windows and a third brushed and pressed clothes. That invaluable all-round treasure the butler-houseman-valet, who is the joy and mainstay of my English household and many others, appears to be quite unknown in modern America.

Since the seventy-five cents (3s. 2d) an hour usually charged by casual domestic labour was beyond the capacity of an instructor's wife struggling to make ends meet on a tiny income in an expensive country, most of these young women floundered along beneath their domestic load with no one but their husbands to look to for help. This was usually given as a matter of course; it would be, I felt, a salutary experience for some pampered English husbands whom I knew to see young college lecturers—and often their seniors as well—mopping floors, drying plates, clearing fireplaces, mending furnaces, bathing their babies and helping to nurse their sick children through measles and whooping-cough.

"Mrs. R. B.," G. once wrote me of an American acquaintance, "says that her brother-in-law's family were all brought up by their mother, girls and boys, to cook, sew, and 'launder'. Hence when she and her sister went in 1908 early morning peaceful picketing for the shirt waist workers' strike, Robert B. got breakfast for her, and Henry B., a vice president of the Metropolitan Life Insurance, ironed out her sister's white skirt before starting. *Ces Américans.*"

In recent years I have met many American men with sufficient means to afford an adequate domestic staff, but even they think nothing of clearing tables, washing up glasses, carrying buckets of firewood, heating saucepans of milk, and serving drinks after the theatre. America, with her thousands of business and professional women, has not yet overcome the disadvantages of ordinary family life; because she has created her civilisation by a series of short-cuts to efficiency, her love-in-a-cottage experiments still tend to smother the wife. But at least she has succeeded in abolishing the sacred immunity of the male from all forms of housework.

Owing to the absence of domestic help, the University children were reared exclusively by their mothers—for whom, as they reached adolescence, they seemed to lose all remnants of respect.

"My children have seen altogether too much of me," a middle-aged Professor's wife who had once cherished literary ambitions complained to me bitterly. "Every little thing that they required I have had to do for them, and now they think I am here for nothing else."

Nearly all these children, as in every American city, attended the local high school. Here they mingled with other American children of all classes and both sexes; they also came into close contact with the siftings of a dozen races from Poles and Slavs to African negroes. Problems resulted with which England, even in the East End of London, has nothing to compare. Theoretically, this arrangement implied that every American public school was a seed-bed of democratic ideals. Actually, owing to the incurable tendency of children to adopt the standards of the lowest common denominator, the University juveniles carried back to their homes the manners and language of the immigrant population.

Once, in a letter home, I described returning the call of a professor's wife whose four children, aged from three to fourteen, kept up a loud clamour for their mother throughout my visit. Conversation was impossible for either of us, but my hostess, too resigned even for embarrassment, wearily accepted what was evidently the normal situation without comment or apology.

"I want," my letter continued, "to publish two more books before embarking on a family. America—where nursemaids and servants are prohibitive to all but the very rich—gives one a dreadful idea of having children. No kind of independence or freedom seems possible for any but very well-to-do mothers; they are simply swamped by their families, who are brought up in a sort of hullabaloo, have the worst manners of any children I ever met, and are nothing but a trial and an anxiety to their parents as soon as they become old enough to know their own minds. . . . In children democracy seems to show its very worst aspects; of course the whole population gradually raises itself by this kind of communal education, but it goes through a very bad time doing it."

As I now recall those over-worked small-town mothers, the saddest fact of their lives seems to have been that steady narrowing of interests towards which, at the time, I was so intolerant. As soon as I recognised, unwillingly enough, that women who discussed babies, illnesses and domestic difficulties by the hour had come to regard literature and politics as "highbrow" and tiresome, I tried to avoid invitations to the numerous wives' tea-parties on the Campus; but I still have a record of one at which I behaved as badly as any supercilious intellectual who ever set foot in America from England.

I had gone with more than the usual reluctance, for I was obliged to leave G. in bed with a heavy cold, and when the conversation turned on to the usual topic of family ailments, I thought that for once I might be able to profit.

"By the way," I announced cheerfully, "I do want to know of a good doctor here. Can you recommend one, Mrs. Y.?"

There was a sudden tense, interested silence, and a ridiculous rage burned in me as I realised, even before I heard the answer, that though my companions did not want to know anything whatever about the book that I was writing, they were deeply concerned to discover whether I was or was not pregnant.

"Oh *yes*, Mrs. C.!" came the eager reply. "*I* like Dr. X. Manners not very good, of course, but—well—I had him for *my* baby, and he has the name of being quite the best baby doctor in the town."

I can still hear the malicious sweetness of my rejoinder.

"Oh, I wasn't thinking of myself, Mrs. Y. I'm very well, and I don't expect to need a doctor all the time I'm here. I wanted someone for my husband, and he's a *little* bit too old for a baby doctor, don't you think?"

Today I look back with shame upon the deliberate pettiness with which I responded to the subconscious pettiness of others. Pettiness, in any case, is a quality which merits pity rather than censure. It is usually the result of frustration, which in itself springs from the enforced acceptance of a life dominated by trivialities instead of the larger existence which its owner once desired. This sense of frustration is even more general in small-town America than in provincial England, for in the United States ambition and education are as normal for a girl as for a boy.

Of the women whom I met in my small University city —whether young women struggling, with no training in mothercraft, to manage their fractious babies, or older women wistfully watching their unruly sons and daughters, whom they had reared at such cost of tedious sacrifice, growing up to despise and evade them—it would probably be safe to say that ninety per cent had once ardently dreamed of becoming "best sellers", magazine editors, or University professors; of taking up politics, business managership or social organisation. And then they had married,

Es

and after resisting frantically for a time had at last been defeated—by having children too soon, by the high level of domestic wages compared with the low level of instructors' salaries, by the annihilating distance of small upstate towns from all sources of employment, perhaps only by that lack of ability to "stay the course" without which even the most exceptional talent will never reach fruition.

As the University community changed for me, with longer acquaintance, into groups of individuals, I came to know women who still secretly tried to write novels, who occasionally contributed little pieces to the local newspaper, who read in the library or attended lecture courses in the vague belief that they would lead to something. These turned to me, as to all newcomers, in the hope that I might perhaps suggest some source of encouragement which they had not thought of, or at least ventilate their restricted lives with a breath of fresh air from the outside world. More persistent than the rest, they were postponing defeat a little longer, but each of them saw it at the end of her road.

For me not the least of the University's tragedies lay in the contrast between its married women and its girl students, vital with the eager, confident youth which their teachers' wives had once possessed. Instinctively I compared the poise and charming maturity of these girls with the conscientious gaucherie of students still in the majority at English women's colleges. The garments worn by Oxford and Cambridge young women have brightened a good deal since "blue-stocking" days, but compared with the jumper suits and day frocks of their American counterparts, they are still as Balham to Bond Street. Complete with rouge, lip-stick and permanent wave, these American girls paraded before their male contemporaries in bright georgette or crêpe de chine "creations" half covered with loose fur-trimmed coats of orange or scarlet plaid, and never reflected that the very boldness of this gay sexual challenge might drag them, within a year or two, into the same morass of domesticity which had engulfed their elders.

It is not, of course, only married American women who suffer from the despairing, thwarting sense of isolation produced by the enormous empty territories of the larger or less developed states. Not long ago I received a letter from a girl reader in the Middle West, who implored me to suggest some method of escape from the small unprogressive community in which she lived:

"I have enough money saved to get out of this wretched place. I have an A.B. degree, can type fairly well, have a decent sort of even disposition, and at one time could take dictation. My present work . . . is all book-keeping done with machines. . . . Could I qualify in any way, shape or form to be of any help to you? I could look up statistics and data for some of your writing, or do just anything. I have to get out of this town."

She may well succeed in getting out, since, given the necessary persistence, there is always hope for American girls so long as they remain unmarried. It is these early romantic unions with graduate students or instructors—whose ultimate achievement, in a profession where promotion is inordinately slow, will probably be a $4000-a-year Professorship in a remote State University—which bring them slap up against the dead end of respectable poverty minus opportunity. Through lack of freedom and the means to travel, these young couples remain in each other's company year in, year out, until their marriage becomes a mere tedious habit, and they grow tired of each other before they realise it. It is not only the hope of anything better that dies young; the romance of which that hope was the price lies dead too, never to be revived. The whole conflict is frankly described in *The New Poor*, the first novel by Clarissa Fairchild Cushman—one of the few "Faculty wives" who have emerged triumphantly from small-town isolation to a successful career of fiction-writing.

This pathetic deterioration of eager, vital feminine ability is among the pressing social problems which America has to face. It is a problem even more urgent for America

than for England. In this country domestic help, though
difficult to find outside large cities, is still obtainable at a
price adapted to middle-class incomes, and so far we have
a much smaller proportion of educated, efficient and ambitious young women. As a Socialist I need not recapitulate
the advantages of that classless society which America,
especially in its small towns, is in process of evolving, but
since I lived a small-town life myself I have realised that
this equal society has also its penalties, and that it is the
woman who pays them. She pays heavily, in terms of
exasperation, disappointment, frustration, resignation and
boredom, followed by a gradual descent into censorious
pettiness and a bitter, critical jealousy of the handful who
escape.

A scientific approach to subjects usually discussed emo-
tionally was made by the short-lived "Institute for the Coordination of Women's Interests", financed by the Laura
Spelman Rockefeller Foundation, which I visited at Smith
College in 1926, but the work done here, like the experiments then being made with nursery schools, touched only
the outskirts of a complex social dilemma. No doubt
America, in her present mood, would resent the suggestion
that she has anything to learn from the sullen dictatorship
of the U.S.S.R., but the future of her own women is in the
balance, and any expedient that might save it is worth
examining. In Russia the universal state provision of communal kitchens, nurseries and laundries sets the industrial
woman free to contribute to Soviet economic resources. It
is not fantastic to suppose that the same system could be
adapted by the United States for the benefit of another type
of woman, whose potential contribution to America's
intellectual and social wealth is now thrown away.

Whenever I was not tidying our apartment, or paying
calls, or attending local functions, or trying to write, I went
out for the solitary walks which I had described in my article
on "The Evils of Good Fellowship". As G. was occupied
at the University nearly all day, I was obliged to explore

alone that high country of lakes and hills and forests eight hundred feet above the sea, where the Indian hunters and rovers of the Five Nations once reared their families and pursued their sustenance.

From a wide, gently-sloping road which skirted the edge of our rutted lane, the two main streets of the city branched sharply downhill into the town. The wide road ended in country lanes and woodlands whispering with wind and tiny streams, where I searched for the few surviving wild flowers. Here, when we first arrived in the early autumn, the white star-like woodbine still climbed over narrow, half-hidden watercourses, and meadow-rue and purple-pink steeplebush sprang from the swampy grass at the edge of the trees. Sometimes instead I crossed the wide tree-shadowed Campus, split into sections by deep ravines, and walked to the top of the highest inhabited hill, where a choice residential district overlooking the long narrow lake petered out, with the tentative untidiness of American cities, into bare, half-cultivated fields.

A letter home described the country as "sunny, cold, windy, very beautiful and rather boring—so isolated, so unstimulating, so far from the pulsating centre of things". As the year moved on into the late fall, the boredom, at least, was mitigated by a few superb days of Indian summer, when hillsides and forests suddenly took fire. After the temperate rust-brown of an English October, this challenging gold and flaming scarlet burst upon us like a voluptuous melodrama, emphatic, extravagant, overwhelming. One tiny lake in the depth of the woods seemed to have drawn all the vividest hues of earth and heaven into its encircling maples and sumacs, until I felt that the trees literally shouted at me with their hallelujah chorus of colour.

On the way home, when I glanced apprehensively downwards from the middle of the low-railed, swaying suspension bridge above the deepest ravine which I was always terrified to cross, the steep gorge two or three hundred feet below looked blood-red from the crimson shrubs at the edge of the rushing water. As the sun set, the University chimes, with their pleasant sentimentality of hymn tunes like a child's Kingdom of Heaven, rose skyward from the library tower, and the smoke from the little town drifted upwards in a blue haze against the hills until it vanished into a clear sky of orange and turquoise.

Slowly, beneath the first faint glimmer of stars, the wide velvet lawns of the Campus grew dark. When the moon rode above them, the giant trees flung their jet-black shadows across the damp grass to the steps of the majestic temples where the various Departments pursued their race for academic honours, regardless of the fact that if a man has personality they do not matter, and if he has not personality they do not count. When I first came to the United States I could see no useful purpose in the competitive passion of American universities for possessing what their pundits called "a fine educational plant", so that this university must have the largest library in the country, that the largest laboratory, the other a stadium beside which the Greek original would appear as a mere village playground. But now I recognise this ambition for monumental buildings as part of the ceaseless American quest for an ultimate perfection, which decrees that even white elephants must be whiter than any other elephants in creation.

By Thanksgiving Day the temperature had changed; before evening the ground was lightly powdered with snow. Already the gold and vermilion of autumn had vanished, and the brown leaves, poor withered ghosts of summer, flew crackling before the bitter wind. I do not recall how I spent that first American Thanksgiving, though both its successors are diamond-clear, but part at least of a day must have been given to a letter dated November 26th, 1925, which describes amongst other events a minor exasperation of local politics:

"We never get morning letters till 1 o'clock and the *New York Times* does not arrive till 5.0 in the afternoon! Recently most of the inhabitants of our avenue sent in a petition to the Post Office asking if letters could be delivered somewhat earlier. Now the minor Post Office appointments in this

country are political, consequently the P.O. is mainly
Republican, while the inhabitants of the avenue are mainly
Democrats. So in consequence of the petition we now
receive our letters even later than ever!"

As winter came nearer, the landscape turned to a study
in numberless shades of brown. The gales blew the last
dead leaves in our faces; racing torrents plunged dramatically down the gorges, and the air was wet with spray
tossed by the wind from the waterfalls. Soon the cascades
froze, and enormous icicles hung down the sides of the
ravines. The students put on skates and crowded to the
lake; "Faculty children" rushed up and down the steep
paths on skis or toboggans, and those of their elders who
did not care for winter sports turned to indoor amusements.

My letters home record a few small speaking engagements for local or University groups, and describe with
scorn a luncheon meeting of the local League of Women
Voters.

"I went to the lunch, and well! it was—elementary!
Good-people-love-your-home-do-the-thing-that's-nearest,
keep-your-feet-on-the-ground, don't-ask-impossibilities sort
of people! Their aim is simply to educate the woman voter,
but she must need a lot of educating if she requires the
kind of treatment we received from one of the after-lunch
speakers, who gave us a little sermon on the word 'Citizen'
(each of the letters standing for some quality we ought to
aim at—'courage', 'initiative'—you know the kind of
thing!) as if we (mostly Professors' wives) were children
at a kindergarten! After it was over Mrs. W., a contributor
to the *Saturday Evening Post* and our local authoress, came
up to me and apologised, and said, 'It's only because it's
the country; it wouldn't be like this in New York'!"

Just once or twice, ripples from the large political world
stirred with their wider sweep the little ruffled surface of
our municipal back-water. One evening during that winter
the Governor of New York State, Mr. Franklin D. Roosevelt, came to the town to address a political meeting.

State Governors meant little to me then, and I have always
regretted that I did not go. At the University itself politics
were discussed perpetually, and I sent to England an eager
account of one such conversation.

"X. was at the Peace Conference; he is a veritable mine
of information about Wilson, the League, and America and
world-politics. He says there is no doubt that Wilson had
some kind of minor paralytic stroke after the Armistice but
before he went to Paris, owing to the sudden relaxation of
tension. Apparently not only Wilson but all America got
the impression from the great German offensive of 1918
that America had gone in on the losing side, and apparently
this notion persisted here almost up to the end. So Wilson
half collapsed but rallied, and went to Paris with his brain
fogged; there he nearly died of 'flu, but this was kept quiet.
X. says that if he had sent two leading Republicans, such
as Hughes and Elihu Root, to Paris, and remained behind
himself, he would have won America for the League. As it
is, it has now become a purely party issue and is as unreal
and artificial as most party-issues are; the Republicans
oppose it whatever sort of action it involves or line it
takes."

Quite a number of English lecturers gave addresses for
University Foundations, and I listened to most of them,
ranging from Norman Angell—who drew the largest audience that I ever saw there with a talk on "Current Political
Illusions"—to nervous fledgelings from Oxford or Cambridge being "tried out" for academic appointments. The
volatile Professor of Romance Languages, who was one of
my pleasantest friends, managed the fund which brought
most of the "lions", and often asked me to his house to
meet them after the lectures. I shudder now to reflect that
on those occasions I must have made myself exactly the
same kind of nuisance to tired lecturers anxious only to get
rid of the clinging remnants of their audience and go to
bed, as similar ambitious "young marrieds" were to make
themselves to me years afterwards, when I had become one
of the harried performers.

As the thermometer descended towards zero, the cold dark evenings made lectures less tempting, and when I was not writing I spent the hours after supper in reading newspapers and journals or the "best-sellers" of that period— Margaret Kennedy's *The Constant Nymph*, T. F. Powys's *Black Bryony* and Sarah Gertrude Millin's *God's Stepchildren*, a novel based on the colour problem. Winifred Holtby, who was shortly going to South Africa to study the colour problem for herself, sent me a copy of *The Flaming Terrapin*, by Roy Campbell, the South African poet, and at a local book-store I purchased a copy of Beatrice Webb's newly-published autobiography, *My Apprenticeship*. G. and I were amused to discover from this book that the cause of Mrs. Webb's first drift towards Socialism had been a circular describing business opportunities in Egypt, "where living is cheap and labour docile".

At any rate, we agreed, it wasn't docile in America! No feature of the New World civilisation had impressed me so much as that.

When Christmas came we had thirty degrees of frost; a white blanket of snow covered the town, and the long lake, now the colour of steel, was frozen a quarter of a mile from its circumference. In the city club-rooms and the hall of the local hotel, scarlet and jade paper streamers festooned the synthetic oak rafters and the elks' heads so dear to the antiquity-loving Rotarianism of the festive proprietors. Appeals for contributions to the city's Community Chest Fund hung in the windows of the principal stores. At dark corners of the main street stood municipal Christmas trees festooned with coloured electric bulbs, a chain of rubies and sapphires and emeralds twinkling between the black branches to prove that civilisation had advanced some distance since the days of Good King Wenceslas.

There was nothing half-hearted, it appeared, about a North American Christmas. Our British one-day family functions, which we hold a little reluctantly and tidy away as quickly as possible, would seem dismally inadequate to the party-loving Yankee, whose capacity for celebration extends from the turkey and cranberry sauce of Thanksgiving to the final mince-pies and crackers of Twelfth Night. I carried away from that Christmas vacation a memory of glowing lanterns and cheerful faces surrounding the Yule trees beneath crystal-cold skies; of jazz music, and brilliant light streaming through unshaded windows on to hard-frozen snow. Somehow these simple festivities seemed to express, not only the gay soul of America, but the spirit from which all courage and gaiety springs. They brought back to me the recollection, already several years old, of lighted huts on the French coast in the last winter of war-time, and convalescent soldiers singing rag-time songs round the roaring Christmas fire.

I missed only the early spring flowers, dressed up in coloured bowls with bright satin bows and tinsel ribbons, which are so often sent as Christmas presents at home. Flowers in America are expensive luxuries, used chiefly for parties or as presentations to distinguished guests; consequently the flower-shops do not stock the inexpensive varieties so easily obtainable in England, or perhaps the growers do not find them sufficiently profitable for cultivation. Because I seldom saw vases of autumn dahlias or chrysanthemums in the small households where I returned calls or dropped in to tea, I assumed indifference when the actual cause lay in limited means. Subsequently I was to discover that, amongst those who could afford to buy them, no people were more ready than the Americans to "say it with flowers" whenever they wanted to make a gesture of gratitude, admiration or affection. Never, in any country, have I worn so many gifts of orchids, carnations, violets or talisman roses, as in this land where flowers are almost as costly as jewels.

Because I, too, could not afford the products of the local flower-shops during that first American winter, I craved for them all the time. Occasionally G. presented me with a few carnations costing $1.50 (6s. 3d.) for half a dozen, but I hesitated to buy daffodils or freesias at 1s. each flower, or pussy-willows at 1s. the spray. Even in present-day England—which seems an expensive country to us who can just remember the fairy-tale prices of goods before the War— a large bundle of pussy-willows can be purchased for 6d. (12 cents), a bunch of fresias for 1s. (25 cents), and a dozen daffodils or short-stemmed tulips for 1s. 6d. (37 cents).

As the bitter evenings grew colder and darker when the brilliant but short-lived midday sun had disappeared behind the grey snow-laden clouds, I spent more time than ever upon my abortive travel book, or in futile attempts at articles which were invariably returned by American magazines, and were now refused even by English newspapers because they had ceased to be topical by the time that the slow-going winter steamships had carried them across the Atlantic. In our dim, flowerless rooms, though the steam-heat kept them cosy enough despite the speed of the racing icy gales, my sense of isolation and frustration seemed to grow with the steady fall of the thermometer. On January 13th, 1926, the United States Department of Agriculture reported our small city, with its bleak lakes and hills, as having the lowest temperature in the whole country. The thermometer stood at —4 when New York was 14, Boston 16, Washington 14, New Orleans 36, Los Angeles 56, and even Duluth, Minnesota (of which a favourite American "chest-nut" relates: "The coldest winter I ever spent was a summer in Duluth"), recorded no more than —2. The icicles hanging from the edges of the ravines had grown six feet long; the small bushes above the frozen waterfalls were tangled skeins of snow. "Meals-out" became a time-absorbing problem when on each occasion it was necessary to put on long snow-boots, fur coat, hat, scarf and huge woollen gloves, and then walk for quarter of a mile along a slippery road where every step was dangerous.

Often I felt as though the interminable winter would never end, or the sun and the flowers come back. When the light, cold evenings of early spring began without bringing any appreciable change in the temperature or the outlook, the cumulative depression crept into my letters to England.

"This is a land of eternal winter—the grey north when all my soul longs for the blue and golden south," I wrote on March 13th. "Eternal winter—and we have just reached the deepest, deadest part of it, though in England now spring is already coming, and there are buds on the hedges and primroses in the Devonshire lanes. Here the snow still lies, frozen hard with all the winter frosts, fall upon fall, no longer pure white but instead grey and jaded. The winds are bitter, and it is as cold as ever—ten degrees of frost today. Where the snow has gone the earth is the dreariest yellowy-olive-brown, all the grass withered under the snow; it looks like the skin of an enormous dead lion. There is no other colour and no sign of life, and all the trees and bushes look like withered sticks. Half the students are down with grippe and measles . . . and in my most depressed moments I begin to associate winter and influenza and small towns with marriage—which is most unfair both to marriage and G., because all these things are temporary, and in three months from today I ought to be in London again."

A week later periodic thaws started, like small repetitions of the Deluge; everything dripped with water, and crossing the road meant negotiating the bed of a stream. It was now possible to have supper by daylight, but everywhere the sodden snow still lay in patches and there were no signs of spring, no buds and no birds. I was just beginning to decide that I could no longer tolerate this sombre protracted winter, combined with small-town isolation and the persistent failure of every minor literary experiment, when quite suddenly, like a burst of sunlight penetrating desolate fog, came the unexpected intimation of release.

IV

IN THE LAST week of March, 1926, G. was summoned to New York to meet a Committee of the Social Science Research Council. For some time he had been corresponding with its members, and now went up to discuss a scheme which held possibilities for ourselves that I had not realised.

The Council was then considering a large investigation into the effects of Prohibition throughout America, and was looking for someone who would undertake a preliminary survey of the sources of material in order to find whether sufficient data existed for further research. One or two of its academic members had already met G., and thought him very suitable for the work owing to his experience on the British Liquor Control Board as a temporary Civil Servant during the first half of the War. He had also the advantage of being an Englishman, which guaranteed a measure of impartiality less likely to be found in an American investigator. At the interview in March they offered him the job, which had to be completed in five months, provided that the University would allow him to give up teaching for the last half-semester of the academic year and set up a small office in New York or Washington.

With the characteristic generosity of American Universities—so much readier than our own to admit that experience valuable to scholars may exist in non-academic fields—permission was readily given. More profoundly relieved than I dared to admit even to myself, I packed up our now dusty collection of clothes, books, files and papers, and we moved to New York for the spring and summer.

"The five months will be a wonderful chance for me and make coming to America more than worth while," I wrote exultantly to England. "I gather from various organisers and editors that once I get on the spot in New York my lectures and articles will be limited only by my time and capacity."

This optimism—as always in those days—was quite unjustified, but while it lasted it was a wonderful tonic after the long dreary winter.

By this time G. knew New York fairly well, and even to myself it was not quite unfamiliar. We had been up there together for a few days in November, and heard Count Coudenhove-Kalergi and Dr. Lange of Norway debate the possibility of a United States of Europe at a Foreign Policy Association Luncheon.

"It was a huge meeting, held in the reception room of the Hotel Astor," a letter sent home recorded, "and 800 people were there, all by special ticket, like ours. I have never seen a reception room in Europe like it for vastness and luxury; the ceiling is made of dull blue-green glass behind a filigree work of light wood and gilt, and all around are galleries with gilded rails. The meeting was followed by discussion, and altogether lasted from 1.0 to 4.0! Imagine an English luncheon where people talked about foreign policy for three solid hours! Most English enthusiasms only lasts for $1\frac{1}{4}$ hours; our League of Nations Union luncheons used to end at 2.15 prompt!"

On my first visit to that incredible city of sunshine, wind and hustle, I had been overwhelmed by precisely those phenomena which overwhelm all newly-arrived foreigners —by the clean wash of the golden air upon the heights silhouetted above Central Park; by the arrogant sweep of Fifth Avenue across the paths of its poor relations the cross-town streets; above all by those Futurian monsters, the sky-scrapers, with which America sets her trade-mark upon the years to come. Believing myself intolerant of heights, I had been so much intimidated by the prospect of those giant altitudes that I had prevailed upon G. to take an overshadowed room on the first floor of the Pennsylvania Hotel. When I actually looked up from the canyon-like depths of Thirty-second Street to the yellow sun-drenched pinnacles resembling range upon range of mountains designed by Euclid, my sentiments matched those of the novelist, A. G. Macdonell, who arrived in New York just before I began my first American lecture tour in 1934. Going out with me late one September evening on to the balcony of the lofty ballroom at the Waldorf-Astoria, and seeing immeasurably farther above us the unexpected glowing eyes of still higher skyscrapers, he asserted with profound solemnity: "I don't believe it!"

As I tried to convey my initial impressions of New York to my family, the excitement which had infused my description of the Foreign Policy Association luncheon extended itself with equal fervour to the Pennsylvania Hotel.

"The ground floor is exactly like a busy outdoor thoroughfare. It has offices and shops of every kind—ticket offices, information bureau, post and telegraph offices, steamship office, bank, drug store, perfumery, hair-dressing shop, fancy goods and every kind of luxury store—magazines, candies, etc.—that you can think of. Also 6 restaurants —where meals range from 75 cents to anything you like to pay. (Fortunately I am being entertained by people to a great many meals or I should be ruined!) One could live a complete life in this hotel without ever going out. It has its own dentist, its own staff doctor, and the tenth floor (there are 22 floors) is a hospital staffed with fully trained nurses!

"Each room is equipped with its own bath, its own lavatory, its own telephone, little electric lamps everywhere, its own writing table and note-paper, and even its own coathangers! The hotel even issues its own magazine, and every morning a free copy of the *New York Times* is presented to each room. No wonder they charge! But the American conception of comfort is so high that no hotel could exist which did not provide these things. . . . New York is an amazing city; the skyscrapers on the picture heading are not at all exaggerated. At night it looks like one of the sinister worlds full of monsters as imagined by H. G. Wells. My room is on the first floor; here the higher you go the more you pay! The lower rooms are like perpetual night and you can't see without the lights on, but I shouldn't much care to be right at the top, even for the daylight."

Now, in April, with five months of living expenses before us, we had to look for something less impressive. We found it—or rather our co-operative and invaluable Park Avenue relatives found it—in a small apartment hotel on Morningside Heights opposite Columbia University, with the city lying far below us, and the Atlantic on the horizon. The front windows of the hotel looked across the wide quietness of West 116th Street to the domed University Chapel. From Riverside Drive at the end of the street we could see the majestic Hudson sweeping grandly northward towards Poughkeepsie, and the factories and Palisades of New Jersey on the opposite bank. Every evening a huge electric sign above one of the factories gave us the correct time, periodically sandwiched between scintillating advertisements.

Beautiful as London can be, its choicest positions fall short of that capacious loveliness which was so surprisingly accessible to our modest purse. It seemed as though London University and the British Museum had been lifted on to the heights of Hampstead and bounded by Chelsea Embankment.

The apartment hotel supplied us with a newly-decorated suite of two tiny rooms and bath on the eighth floor at the rate of $56 (£11 11s.) a week for the two of us, with service and meals included. This charge was very inexpensive for New York in 1926, but it seemed dear to us with our inelastic income, which had to take into account the living expenses of a third person and the cost of cross-Atlantic fares. I felt, nevertheless, that the little rooms and their blue-grey carpets, pale buff walls and gaily striped curtains of blue, black and yellow silk, were more than worth it. The sitting-room especially, with its French settee and comfortable arm-chairs, seemed bright and entrancing after the winter gloom of our country apartment. From its windows, on a clear day—and most days were clear—we could see the milk-blue water surrounding Manhattan on all sides but the south. At the moment I asked for nothing more spacious or more luxurious. After the small, constant, irritating demands of provincial domesticity, it was a relief such as neither G. nor even an American male could realise to have everything done and everything found.

No sooner had we dumped the few suitcases which we had brought in advance of our heavy luggage, than it became necessary to find an office for G. Being as impervious to heights as I myself have since become, he took a small room on the twentieth floor of the Knickerbocker Building in Times Square. He then set forth to engage a secretary and order some impressive-looking notepaper headed "Social Science Research Council", on which he was described as "Director" to the Committee "On a Preliminary Study of the Operation of the Eighteenth Amendment". The Committee list contained the distinguished names of John L. Gillin, the Chairman, Haven Emerson, Irving Fisher, Edgar Sydenstricker and Walter Thompson.

A day or two afterwards, G. brought me his first provisional list of "Institutions or Agencies from which it is suggested that data might be obtainable". It seemed—and proved—to be a formidable catalogue for a five-months' investigation, even when he was provided with assistants to cover specified areas of a country as large as a continent.

It ran as follows:

Homes for the Inebriate.
State Boards of Insanity or Insane Asylums.
Public Health Associations, especially Committees on Tuberculosis, Venereal Disease, Mental Hygiene, Child Hygiene, or Visiting Nurse Associations.
Hospitals and Clinics (Public and Private).
State or City Boards of Charity or Public Welfare.
Almshouses.
Municipal Lodging Houses.
Day Nurseries and Orphanages.
Voluntary Charitable Organisations likely to possess

Fs

significant statistics or data, especially Family and Relief Associations.

State Commissions of Prisons issuing a report.

State or City Registrars or Vital Statisticians.

Penal Institutions—Houses of Correction or State Farms.

After a few weeks of discussing G.'s work daily, I felt very well informed about the Volstead Act, and proceeded to castigate my family for their facile assumption that Prohibition was "a farce" in a long letter which I reproduce here (with apologies to my friends in the Middle West) for the benefit of English readers:

"Prohibition has to be considered State by State. There is almost as much difference between some of the States of U.S.A. as between the countries of Europe. When an Amendment is made to the Constitution, it has to be carried by a majority of all the States voting State by State. Now Prohibition was carried by what is known as the 'Middle West'—roughly all the States which are neither the South, the East coast nor the West coast. They include such States as Kansas, North Dakota, South Dakota, Minnesota, Illinois, Wisconsin, Ohio, etc. etc. Now these States in mentality are mainly agricultural, not very cultured, very 'moral', very narrow and bigoted; in fact you might roughly describe them as having the mentality of a Nonconformist temperance reformer. They are mostly Methodist and Presbyterian in religion.

"These States have always been 'dry'—i.e. pro-Prohibition. They are 'dry' still, and Prohibition is, as far as one knows, most successful there, being what they want. On the other hand, the coastal East, the coastal West, and the South did not want Prohibition. These areas (much smaller all three together than the huge prairie of the Middle West, but much better known to Europeans because containing the chief business and tourist centres—i.e. New York State in the East, California in the West, Florida in the South) never wanted Prohibition; they are mentally cosmopolitan, and they voted against it. New York State is the strongest

anti-Prohibition State, and in New York itself even the
police do not pretend to keep the law. The other evening
I went with the C.s to a French restaurant in the centre of
New York; we had a bottle of red wine with our dinner
and two liqueurs to follow. Everything was put openly
on the table, and except that the wine is more expensive,
we might have been in London or Paris. In the New York
towns the police actually protect the bootleggers from
assault. Why not? They did not vote for Prohibition or
want it.

"But because Prohibition is a farce in New York (and
perhaps in California and Florida) this does not mean that
it is a farce in vast America. English people spend a few
weeks—or days—in New York, see everyone drinking there,
and come home and sweepingly state that Prohibition is a
farce. But this is a matter of opinion even in New York
State itself. You cannot conclude that Prohibition is a
failure because you see a few rich people drinking in a
few expensive restaurants. You can only decide this when
you have, e.g., inquired in all the hospitals of all the 48
States whether diseases due to alcohol have increased or
diminished, and compared your results; when you have
inquired of prisons whether 'drunks' have increased or
diminished, of social workers whether there is less misery
in industrial areas, of Trade Unions whether unemployment has decreased or increased, of employers whether their
total output is greater since Prohibition, or less—etc. etc.
etc; you can multiply this type of inquiry in all directions. . . .

"Now when the Research Council begin in September,
they do not want to waste their time by inquiring at useless
sources or by collecting unreliable statistics. So what G. is
doing for them is to conduct a preliminary inquiry as to
where the material for an investigation is to be obtained;
which States provide the best, which hospitals, prisons,
asylums, social workers, research bureaux, temperance
societies, anti-temperance societies, Trade Unions, employers' associations, etc. etc., have kept records and

which have not. He has nothing to do with what these records prove. He has not either to be 'for' Prohibition or 'against' it. He has not to pronounce an opinion of any kind, but simply to make a report as to where the materials for forming an opinion are to be found."

Since G. had now an office to himself where he worked nearly all day, I was usually alone in our apartment on the Heights. But I did not care. In those first few weeks I literally basked in a sense of release from the gossip, the minor snobberies and the constant critical supervision of small-town society. At odd moments I made enthusiastic notes for a chapter on America which I had decided to add to *A Honeymoon in Two Worlds*.

"What matter that we are obliged to keep our boots under the bath, our books piled high on a table against the wall, our tables and chairs so completely inundated with pamphlets and papers and typewriters, that when we smoke our after-dinner cigarettes we have to sit on the floor? Each morning, when I throw up the eighth floor window of our sitting-room, breathe the cold, wine-sharp air of the heights, and look across the roofs of the smaller buildings to the blue-grey bluff where the Hudson turns inland, my city-loving heart sings like a bird set free from a little cage into the fresh air and sunlight."

Now that I was again in close contact with the main currents of life, my letters home became lyrical with satisfaction.

"I am drunk with delight at being in New York," runs one written on April 16th. "As soon as G.'s book is well under way I shall launch my introductions." (This book, *The Science and Method of Politics*, later published by Kegan Paul, had been temporarily laid aside while the work for the Social Science Research Council was discussed and organised. I had promised G. that if he accepted the job I would help him by revising and typing the manuscript.) "Being here is like being out of doors after living for 6 months in a stuffy parlour. The air, with the Hudson estuary almost at

our door, is just like the sea-side, and New York is always
full of sunshine which streams into our room at 6 a.m. . . .
I could sing for joy. And the buds are slowly, slowly beginning to uncurl."

Even when G. ignominiously fell victim to an attack of
measles, and I had not only to nurse him carefully for a
fortnight, but wash up his eating utensils, make his bed, tidy
his room, change my frock whenever I left it, and pretend
to the hotel clientèle that he was suffering from influenza,
my happiness remained undiminished. I interviewed his
secretary, dictated his letters, answered the telephone,
kept up the fiction that he was either at his office or out somewhere "investigating", and whenever I could, sat in the
sunshine in Morningside Park and watched the spring
appear. After the greyness of the Iroquois country, the clear
sparkling light seemed to wear a peculiar radiance, like the
glory shining upon the jasper and amethyst and chrysolite
of the Holy City when the first heaven and the first earth
were passed away.

I found no bathos in these alternating preoccupations,
and never lost confidence that I could so handle the situation that G.'s new job would not suffer nor his portentous
professorial superiors become exasperated by his misfortune.
The sympathetic young doctor recommended by Mr. Bruce
Bliven of the *New Republic*, to whom I confided our predicament as he was living for the moment at the same
hotel, assured me that I should not get the disease if I
believed myself impervious and spent as much time as
possible in the open air. Either his faith or my precautions
justified him, for I remained immune. My "contact",
however, provided a useful protection against those tiresome pickers-up of unaccompanied females from whom,
being small and defenceless-looking, I have suffered all my
life.

"You a Columbia girl?" inquired one tormentor, snug-
gling close beside me on a seat in Riverside Park.

"I'm not a girl at all," I answered firmly. "I'm a married
woman. What's more, I'm nursing my husband through

measles, and if you don't want to get it, I'd advise you to keep out of my way."

Never have I seen an unwelcome attaché cut and run with such instantaneous alacrity.

By the time G. recovered it was May, and the leaves in Morningside Park, unspoilt by smoke, opened golden-green and crumpled upon the trees. The country outside New York, where friends sometimes drove us on Sunday afternoons, shimmered yellow with forsythia and pink with apple-blossom. In those days of perpetual sunlight warm as an English June, the General Strike to which the New York papers gave long columns in the first week of May, seemed very far off. Later, at the English-Speaking Union, we heard an American woman traveller who had spent the spring in England give a talk on the Strike, and felt guilty because we had not been at home to lend a hand to Labour.

America had her own troubles that summer; we had not been long in New York when the discontent which culminated in the great strike at Passaic began to mutter sullenly through the textile mills of New Jersey. More recently I have understood better the root cause of those subterranean storms. In 1926, dollar-chasing America— the America of Big Business, of Wall Street speculation, of the secret manipulators of international finance—had become as confident, as boastful and as exultant as it was ever to be; riding inexorably over wage-slavery, racial discontent, and the worst manifestations of lawlessness under Prohibition, it set the pace at which the whole country pursued the golden bubble of Prosperity until its catastrophic explosion in 1929. Though the threat of economic thunder rumbling beneath the surface eluded me just as it eluded so many wiser and more experienced observers, my modest standards of expenditure were constantly outraged by the extravagances that surrounded me, by the readiness with which persons of normal tastes and upbringing daily flung away large sums upon drinking and dining, and most of all by the cynical shrewdness with which money could be extracted from those who, like myself, had little to spare.

As soon as I left our peaceful area round Columbia, I was intimidated by the speed of the traffic in the streets, and overwhelmed by the noisy mobs in the overcrowded stores. One morning I came home with an appalling hat and a pink Kasha frock which I disliked from the moment of purchase, because I had been struggling in the same store for over two hours, and in spite of the "take it or leave it" attitude of the brusque girl shop-assistants, had felt reluctant to go away without buying anything. Much alarmed by that everyday manifestation of Prosperity, I seldom left the cooler quiet of the Heights for the rest of the summer. Never, except on the subway, has the crowded rough-and-tumble of the metropolitan traffic seemed so oppressive in these later and saner years.

Throughout that crazy period of indiscriminate money-getting, New York was a terrifying city for a young married couple living mainly upon a research worker's pay. Though G.'s salary, as such salaries go, was generous, and all his travelling and office expenses were met, our carefully budgeted funds seemed to melt away when matched with prices half as high again as the small-town prices which had appeared so heavy in comparison with English standards.

"This wretched America," I wrote home later in the summer, "with the ocean journeys and the terrible cost of everything here, swallows up all my money and makes a big hole in G.'s."

Other letters protested against the disproportionate charges made for personal services such as hair-dressing, and one concluded with an enraged description of a hair-dresser's "racket" which trebled the price of a permanent wave.

"One of the things I hate most about this country is people's habit of trying to make money out of you whether you can afford it or not, by the simple method of arguing down your resistance. . . . The other day, when I went to have the sides of my hair rewaved so that it would last till I got home (they do permanent waving so much better in England) and said I wanted four curlers a side, the man (a reputable New York hairdresser) argued and argued with me until by sheer dint of wearing me down he had put ten curlers on each side of my head and I was too exhausted to protest; for this I had the privilege of paying 22 dollars, which I couldn't afford, when I had only meant to pay 8. . . . That's America all over."

But we had not been long in New York before I discovered that American civilisation had other aspects than the prosperous strident boastfulness so intimidating to strangers from less richly-endowed territories. That very boastfulness, I found, had its critics, such as *The Nation* under the editorship of Mr. Oswald Garrison Villard, who upheld the neglected cause of the underdog (later to be more politely rechristened "the under-privileged") with an upright disinterested passion unsurpassed by any journal of "the Left" in England. The longer I lived in America, the more fully I became aware that standards of culture and integrity existed about which the haughty Oxford whose product I was need feel no sense of superiority. A reply to a letter from my mother, in which she described a conversation with an acquaintance who had uttered one of those stupid generalisations about the United States so often indulged in by English ignoramuses who have never been there, produced an outburst of positively pro-American wrath.

"What exactly does Miss H. mean by the 'American Government', and how precisely is it 'corrupt'? Does she mean the President, who is elected every four years, and who is at the moment the dull, conscientious and very cautious Calvin Coolidge? Or does she mean the House of Representatives, who are *elected* every two years in much the same way as our House of Commons? Or does she mean the Senate, which consists of 96 Senators, two *elected* from every State? Or does she mean the Governors of the States, who are also elected? And how is it possible for all these people, who are all elected, and many of whom are bitterly opposed and only too anxious to expose each other's private lives, to practise deeply-laid schemes of corruption? What nonsense!"

Nevertheless, by the end of July, I was still confessing to "a fierce desire to flout America and its impertinent vulgarity". But I did have the grace to add: "I don't mean that *all* America is impertinent and vulgar, I mean the part of it that is."

V

AMONG THE MANY contrasts in national history and personal fortune which made the America of the nineteen-twenties so dissimilar, for me, from that of the nineteen-thirties, not least was the difference in the speed and variety of my impressions.

Between 1925 and 1927, the vivid kaleidoscope of experience which the United States was to offer me in the next decade seemed an adventure reserved for persons more privileged than I was ever likely to become. My contacts in that earlier period were limited mainly to two communities, one very small, the other as large and diverse as every capital city, which I had plenty of time to study in detail. But the series of short trips and longer journeys which G.'s new work required during the spring and summer of 1926 gave me—though I could so seldom afford to share them—at least a foretaste of the richer knowledge that lay in the future.

We had not been settled in New York for twenty-four hours when G. was summoned by his Committee for a conference at Madison, Wisconsin. Their object in requiring him to make this costly thousand-mile journey was apparently to urge upon him the strictest economy in spending the Rockefeller money provided for research. It was an injunction never repeated after he had pointed out that the expenses of his trip would have furnished the rent of his office for several weeks.

The Committee's summons involved us in a ludicrous predicament, for in their deep concern with their own need for economy, they had overlooked the fact that ours was even greater, and omitted to supply G. with any funds for the long expedition. As we had spent all our available cash upon moving to New York and paying deposits for our apartment and the office, he was obliged to borrow the fare from an acquaintance at Columbia University. I was left with $10 upon which to exist until the indefinite date of his return.

Fortunately for our solvency, he was only absent for a few days. From Chicago (about which an enthusiastic native had recently told us: "They haven't taken up culture yet, but when they do, they'll make it hum!") came a gilded postcard showing the arrogant engine of the Twentieth Century Limited by which he had travelled. A characteristic note in pencil was scrawled on the back: "The American will talk gaily from the depth of ignorance about theology or philosophy. But, does he pull himself together, grow serious and solemn, and put forth his best intellectual power —you know he is going to discuss Transport. And is this not as much 'Community' and a confession of 'the incompleteness of the Finite' as a theory of the Deity? The German talks about God and the American produces a railway train."

Later, to cheer the bewildered solitude in which I wrestled with trunks and packages continually descending from the country upon our miniature apartment, came a long letter describing that Middle Western territory which in after years was to become so familiar.

"Here I have crossed New York, the Empire State; seen Lake Erie from the Pennsylvania Corridor, the North-West corner of the Keystone State; crossed the Buckeye State of dreary, flat Ohio, with its interminable yellow fields of the dead stalks of maize and buckwheat, and then through Indiana, with its little townships in a low, undulating country. I remember . . . the wooden houses and wearisome station of Wawaka, with a little girl running from a little house to greet the train as it comes to a stop after miles beyond sight of the eye of geometrically level track. Nearer Chicago, that Birmingham-on-Mersey of the New World, appears a little more life. At South Bend, on the St. Joseph River, a confessional bell—the one quite human thing on the whole trip—rings somewhere back of the bright street lights. Then on to more changeful Wisconsin, the Badger State; low hills as of a vast league-long pancake blistered a little after baking; warm, bright sun, the last challenge to the winter snow. A clump of trees, yellowish snow-sprinkled fields, a white wooden farm house, farm buildings painted red, the inevitable corn-silo, an automobile, a road leading away from the farm. Ditto repeat *ad infinitum*. No villages; only townships. A great difference, this, though the number of inhabitants may be the same, for a township always expects to become a town and end as a city. Its very dirt-roads are laid out on a rectangular basis, in expectation of future traffic problems; there is the gasoline pump which will supply you with Go-Gas or Solite or what you will; there is the druggist, the hardware store, the dry-goods store.

"'A Good Place to Live,' reads the advertisement beside the station of a Wisconsin town—a brisk, bright enough little place, like most of these Wisconsin towns under the 'Socialist' rule of La Follette, and with a thrifty Scandinavian population.

"Here and there a reminiscent white church, spick in its painted wood turret and green roof, appears rather pleasing —the Catholic one with its Cross, *les autres sans idoles*. And so on to Madison, with its twin beautiful lakes, thirty miles round. Oh, the snare of these lovely, half-frozen, alluring harsh lakes, and the red, which tries to be rose, of the sunset, emphatic in colouring, turning to greenish dun, and gamboge, and most translucent light delphinium—not soft, but clear and pure and cold as porcelain. This is the land of 'Main Street'; a good land in its way, with good soil and good men, but something between the two is lacking, something that even in the flat Belgium of snow-bound January in war-time I did not notice as absent, despite the like straight roads and wind-bemoaned country.

"The hand of inhuman Nature still rules too much here; no benign *Menschengeist* has forced it back. A bad land for a belated traveller—but then, who travels on foot? The engineer rules in the countryside as well as in the cities; the land has been won by machine and railroad, not by horse and the hand of man. It lacks a blessing; the blessing that you and I have so often felt in the Oxfordshire lanes. I would that there were more confessional bells or an occasional Angelus."

Various shorter expeditions followed the long trip to Madison. From one, to Atlantic City, G. brought me back a black and silver musical box, with a demure lady in powdered wig and green gown painted on the lid. At the top was a space for powder and puff, and whenever the lid was removed the box played a plaintive, tinkling tune. I have never seen a similar musical box in England. The simple mechanism is still unimpaired; today, twelve years afterwards, the gentle little melody repeats itself as patiently for my children, whose onslaughts have failed to damage it, as it ever did for me. I have often thought it strange that a gift from the most boisterous of American cities should have turned into such a tender symbol of family affection.

On many of these smaller journeys I was able to accompany G., and I left New York for the first time when we went to Washington together at the end of April. In New York, and even in our University town, I had already been impressed with the excellence of American cooking, about which every English traveller writes ruefully home—without, alas! making any apparent impression upon the watery and tasteless vegetables served up by English cooks, or the unappetising cold beef and boiled potatoes provided at lunch-time by English inns. But now I realised that these high standards were a national demand, and could be equally relied upon in trains, station buffets, restaurants, hotels, and even private houses.

Looking back from more recent and wider experience upon the first-rate hotel dinners served me in small or unfashionable cities as far apart as Winona, Minnesota; Mason City, Iowa; Waterville, Maine; and Fort Worth, Texas, I reflect with shame that outside London and a few choice hotels in holiday resorts, American travellers in England cannot yet depend upon getting an appetising meal. As for those delectable everyday dishes which can be obtained anywhere in the United States—oyster stew, clam chowder, lobster Newburg, fried scallops, chicken à *la* King, Waldorf salad with Thousand Island dressing—our chefs do not know them and apparently do not want to.

I have found only one London restaurant, on the top floor of an Oxford Street fashion store, where salads made from permutations and combinations of peas, beans, dates, asparagus, cream cheese, pineapple, nuts and celery, resemble the imaginative American models. Even in our crack trains and brightest Bohemian restaurants, a "salad" is still the forlorn time-honoured conglomeration of sliced unpeeled tomato and sodden beetroot, artlessly mingled with damp bruised lettuce, and frigidly served with crude vinegar or sour bottled "dressing". Lettuce, it should be explained for the benefit of English readers, is not "salad" to an American; it is merely the substance upon which an exquisite mixture of fruit, vegetables, cheese, jelly and mayonnaise is deposited. Most Americans would as soon think of eating it as of swallowing the paper carton which contains an ice-cream. We have only one small cookery lesson to teach them— namely, that a good cup of tea cannot be made by placing a very small canvas bag of dry tea-leaves in tentative contact with half a teapotful of tepid water.

On an April day warm as English midsummer, I thought Washington the loveliest city I had ever seen. Here were no skyscrapers, no subways, no crowds in the streets, no struggle for places in buses and trams; the vivacious enterprise of the New World was softened by a touch of that leisurely mellowness which lies like an ancient benediction upon the President's Castle in Prague and the Fishers' Bastion at Budapest. Only the George Washington Memorial, like an immense candle on a very flat candlestick, challenged the beneficent peace of the even sky. At night the flood-lit Capitol, brittle as a white-sugared wedding-cake by day, hung suspended like a giant chandelier from a vault of black velvet.

Here, it seemed, I should find at last the tender brilliance
of spring colour which had not yet appeared in wintry New
York. In every street and public square, the saffron and scarlet of myriad debonair dwarf tulips shone candid and flawless. More gently, between their geometrical rows, beds of
pansies, hyacinths and periwinkles gleamed delicately blue.
Within the parks the Chinese purple magnolia had burst
into its softest, freshest bloom—not really purple but deep
magenta, shading to palest rose at the edge of the heavy
waxen petals. Along the banks of the Potomac the Japanese
cherry trees, past their zenith but still almost perfect with
the incredible perfection of a fairy tale, rained their pastel-
pink blossoms upon the mirrored surface of the smooth,
quiet water. The air was filled with the warm scent of
honey, and English wood-violets grew secretly in the long
grass beneath the trees.

Throughout our three days we worked assiduously, feeling very important each time we established one of the "contacts" so necessary for G.'s research. We attended meetings
of Congress and the Supreme Court; heard General Dawes
and Charles Evans Hughes speak at a banquet of international lawyers, and listened to bluff Senator Borah of
Idaho and ferocious Senator Reed of Missouri arguing before
the Senate. At a White House Presidential reception I
shook the cool, dry hand of Calvin Coolidge, who as I
approached looked over my head at the next-comer in the
long line of unimportant and fatiguing strangers. When I
re-entered the White House for the first time eleven years
later, I felt qualified by that earlier memory to estimate the
vote-attracting value of the Roosevelt smile, turned upon
me in intimate friendly greeting from the midst of agitating
diplomatic exchanges on the sinking of the *Panay*.

While G. pursued Congressmen and Senators who had
strong convictions on Prohibition, I called at the headquarters of the National Woman's Party with introductions
from home. Nine years earlier, these uncompromising
American feminists—the counterpart of the Six Point Group
with which I had worked in England—were still persistently

picketing the White House, waiting in long patient lines with their lettered banners for President Wilson to emerge. Their ranks had included young and lovely society girls such as Doris Stevens—now, in 1938, the chief international protagonist for an Equal Rights Treaty—and veteran suffragists like the Rev. Olympia Brown, a tough old warrior who died in 1926 at Baltimore aged eighty-nine.

In two respects the Woman's Party militants were unlike our own suffragettes. Under the direction of their founder and leader, Alice Paul, they had skilfully made political use of the War, which ended the British militant movement; they had also refrained from the more violent manifestations of "direct action". For this moderate defiance they had nevertheless suffered long terms of imprisonment, which involved penalties almost as drastic as the ingenious tortures inflicted upon our Pankhursts and Pethick-Lawrences. I had read the brave story of their campaigns in Doris Stevens' biographical *Jailed for Freedom*, and various newspaper articles had given me details about their intimidating leader. Their headquarters were established in an old house with dark, beautiful rooms, which had accommodated the American Government for a few weeks during the War of 1812. It should now, I thought afterwards, have had inscribed above its historic doorway a sentence from Olive Schreiner's *Story of an African Farm*: "Men and things are plastic; they part to the right and left when one comes among them moving in a straight line to one end." I went there hoping to receive enlightenment on the relative positions of American men and women—a problem which, like a dark undercurrent swirling uneasily beneath the surface of my mind, had disturbed me ever since my first uncomfortable tea-parties with the "Faculty wives" of our University town.

During this "prosperity period" in which I first knew the United States, the great majority of male Americans who carry on some form of business appeared to be universally narrowed and restricted by the frantic craving for money which possessed the whole country. Women, so numerous magazine writers asserted, were taking control of the arts and professions while men concentrated upon the grinding task of amassing the wealth on which social prestige depended. Often, during those early months, I compared the responsible part which professional women played in this urgent America with their still minor importance at home.

Almost every small American town with a population of ten to twenty thousand had its well-established woman doctor. The working managers of newspapers, editorial offices and literary agencies seemed as often to be women as men. Social work in the great cities had brought fame chiefly to women, such as Jane Addams and Lillian Wald. The best-known American poet was a woman, Edna St. Vincent Millay, and among the novelists, Edith Wharton, Willa Cather, Dorothy Canfield and Elinor Wylie had acquired as much prestige as any masculine writer. Even the legal profession—where at home it was still almost impossible for a woman to make a reputation or even scrape together a modest living—contained nearly three thousand women holding salaried posts.

Polite accomplishments, such as the minor interpretations of music and painting, and the maintenance of conversation at social functions, seemed also to be left more and more to women. Without their attendance, it was said, picture galleries, lecture rooms and concert halls might as well close down, since these strongholds of culture would not receive sufficient patronage to sustain them from dollar-collecting males severely tied to an intensive routine which permitted no "irrelevancies". Big business might be the most romantic and stimulating of pursuits, but the small businesses in which America's masculine citizens were mainly involved provided a very limited range of experience. They tended to develop ideas only about "shop", combined with a few conventional opinions on the overworked topics of automobiles, Prohibition and golf.

At small-town parties, I had found the social conversation of store-owners and "real estate" dealers limited to mono-

Gs

syllabic grunts, or to such brief and discouraging comments as "That's fine", or "I don't get you". There were even movements afoot for improving the general knowledge and conversation of business men who believed themselves too busy to read. Advertisements abounded of "Elbert Hubbard's Scrap Book" or "Dr. Eliot's Five-Foot Shelf of Books", which respectively undertook to supply the harassed realtor with predigested titbits of the world's wisdom, and to select a course of reading guaranteed to stock the less practical side of his intelligence with "all you need to know".

There seemed every prospect that women would capture America's cultural future . . . unless too many of the highly gifted got married and went to live in small towns. Even from New York, I had already informed my family that "I never tell the people that I meet for the first time that I am married now. Over here, when people meet you and think you unmarried, their first question always is 'What's your job?' or 'What are you doing here?' But when they know you are married they ask 'What is your husband?'"

I thought the whole subject well suited for discussion with the National Woman's Party, but when I met Alice Paul it struck me that she, at any rate, was unlikely to feel much sympathy for the problems of those women who had incompetently yielded to the promptings of nature and had fallen as a result into the slough of domestic despondency. Unlike Mrs. Pankhurst she displayed no sensitive femininity, nor appeared to desire it. Small, alarming, implacable, perhaps the clearest example of the one-track mind that I have ever encountered, she questioned sternly the pursuit of any interest which appeared to divert the attention of a promising recruit from the position of women. What was the purpose of attending a conference on international law? Why was I so much interested in the League of Nations?

"But surely," I protested innocently, "you want to prevent war?"

"Certainly not!" came the severe reply. "I don't care if there's another war, provided women get equal rights!" And she expounded to me her unshakable conviction that nothing which might happen to a nation, whether poverty or prosperity, peace or war, success or failure, should be permitted by the true feminist to deflect her from the pursuit of absolute equality, since this would only be achieved when privileges and disabilities based on sex had been repudiated in every sphere of human activity. She regarded the League of Nations as a useful international agency for raising the status of women throughout the world. To its other functions she was quite indifferent.

I remembered a sentence written by the Oxford historian, Professor H. W. C. Davis, about Simon de Montfort: "The world is moved in the first instance by those who see one side of a question only." Did the Alice Pauls get what they wanted, simply because they wanted nothing else? I dared not present my further series of feminine problems, with their too personal application. Husbands and children, I felt, would seem as irrelevant to Alice Paul as the frivolous cultivation of sex appeal. The only thing that mattered was to hammer, hammer, hammer behind the political spear-point until it penetrated the obdurate crust of masculine governmental tradition.

If I did not misjudge her on that distant April evening, I think that she perceived only one half of the battle. The future progress of women no longer depends, I believe, wholly or even mainly upon political measures, valuable as the success of these will be. It lies in the organisation and universal acceptance of a way of living which will allow the great mass of ordinary intelligent women to fulfil both their mental powers and their biological needs. This new way of life cannot be achieved solely by laws, however excellent; it will be the product of education, of social and domestic co-operation, of the development of a greater generosity in one sex and a more determined courage in the other. The enemy which we fight today is not political disability; it conceals itself more subtly in the unexamined prejudices and habitual assumptions so deeply ingrained in women as well as men.

Nevertheless, I carried away from Washington a keen

admiration for the single-minded purpose of Alice Paul and the dynamic methods of the Woman's Party which I retain to this day. They were one of the two political organisations (the other being the League of Nations Non-Partisan Association) with which I came into close touch during that first visit to the United States, and I still remember how graciously their workers at headquarters entertained an unknown English stranger. They were the last group that I addressed when, somewhat less unknown, I was about to leave their country at the end of 1937.

Before G. and I returned to New York, we had passed a windy Sunday in Baltimore, stayed the night at Philadelphia, and dined in Boston with Professor Manley O. Hudson, of Geneva fame, and Mrs. Sayre, the gentle sad-faced daughter of President Wilson. Philadelphia, with its wide squares of budding trees, its rust-red fringe of suburbs, and its Chestnut Street of skyscrapers towering above the little Hall which saw the Declaration of Independence, was busy celebrating its Sesqui-Centennial Festival.

"150 years of American Independence!" proclaimed the posters in the city to any abashed Britisher who might venture to appear there. No wonder, intimated G., pointing out to me the statue of Benjamin Franklin, whose benevolent countenance watches over Philadelphia like that of William Penn from the City Hall, no wonder that in America they raise Penns and Lincolns and Franklins to the heights of their public buildings, instead of patron saints with loin cloths and haloes. Not that, he added, the noble Benjamin would always have felt comfortable in a halo, since rumour whispered indiscreetly that he once grew tired of the monotonous "naughts" on the little daily table of catalogued sins which he kept for his moral improvement, and began to set Philadelphia an example of another and most regrettable kind.

When G. went to Michigan to investigate conditions in Henry Ford's works at Detroit, I was again left by myself in New York to read his comments on a conversation heard in the train between two young women *en route* for Chicago.

"They were what in England one would call the servant girl type or the less reputable shop girl, and there was really very little indeed of their legs which they did not show without my being in the least inquisitive. Snatches of conversation came across:

"'He was talking about Einstein and that; he was funny!'

"'I must show you a book I have . . .'

"'See here, all these medi-eval tales! You read this, isn't it wonderful for those old days; it's called the Romun of the Rose. Isn't it *cute*?'

"I cannot despair of a nation whose servant girls are interested in the Roman of the Rose. Not that I think it is a nation interested in the things of the mind; it isn't. That is, if we mean speculation. It is only 'objectively minded', it will tell you. But it is possessed by a devouring curiosity —which is the beginning of knowledge."

As summer reached its wearisome height, I spent more time than ever alone in our small apartment. The weather had become too hot for long walks, and I had no money left to squander on amusements. The last of several little lectures, which coincided with G.'s trip to Detroit, was a speech for the League of Nations Non-Partisan Association at a meeting in Long Island ("flat as a pancake and resembles one vast allotment," I recorded distastefully). This meeting, I wrote home, "was a surprise to me, as the people couldn't have been more frumpish or conservative if they had come from a little village in the middle of Shropshire or Buckingham; it was astonishing to find typical examples of the provincial mind within 30 miles of New York. I spoke on International Current Events, but half the audience hadn't heard of the smaller countries of Europe, and none of them could pronounce their names. They weren't working women either, but the usual 'good women' of the middle-class."

I omitted to relate that my view of this meeting was perhaps coloured by a crushing comment from the disconcerted organiser: "We're not used to speakers who look about sixteen." It was not, however, my final lecture for this humiliating reason, but because, as I could explain with less sacrifice of dignity, "here in the summer everything is at the dead end. The Non-Partisan Association tried to get up one lecture for me in Boston and two here this week, and had to cancel the arrangements for them all as everyone is away. America is soaked, steeped, saturated in lectures; and overdone, overwhelmed, indigestible with lions. The other day, at the dinner given by the Non-Partisan Association for Dame Rachel Crowdy, I met a certain Mr. L. . . . He has been endeavouring to get up meetings, lectures, etc. at the chief Universities to interest students and faculty in international and especially Asiatic affairs. One of the Professors in charge of such arrangements at one of the principal Universities (I think Yale) said to him: 'If you sent me Butler or James Harvey Robinson I might get forty people together. If you sent Lloyd George over I could perhaps just manage to fill the hall!'

"America will turn out for nothing less than Crown Princes; she still likes them because so few have been over here. E.g. the Crown Prince of Sweden, who is over here at the moment, is drawing crowds. I don't suppose we should cross the road to look at him in England."

By July such friends as we possessed had left New York; all public activities were over, and in the clammy summer warmth I could not sit for many hours on end typing G.'s complicated manuscript or wrestling wearily with the final chapter of *A Honeymoon in Two Worlds*.

"My honeymoon book is exasperating me," ran one intimate letter. "It needs so much revision; I drop so easily into the academic, 'leading article' jargon; find myself writing such atrocities as 'the domestic situation', 'racial improvement', 'a limited vocation for marriage', etc. etc. Good Oxford English, my dear, is the enemy of all true art. I am taking a diet of the best recently published novels to cure myself of the habit."

Of this contemporary fiction, the book that remains most clearly in my mind is Anne Parish's *The Perennial Bachelor*, which followed a somewhat tougher selection—Theodore

Dreiser's *The Genius* and Will Durant's *The Story of Philosophy*. I can still remember lying awake over it for the first half of a sultry night, haunted by the peculiar horror of failure, frustration and tragic futility.

"I finished *The Perennial Bachelor* in bed," I wrote to G., who as usual was absent. "A dreadful book towards the end, as everyone gets older and older, and poorer and poorer, and becomes more of a failure, and one sister commits suicide through sex-repression (so convincingly done that I longed for you to be there to assure me that I myself was not the character in the book!) and another dies of cancer. I don't like reading about failures. After all, so few people are failures as complete as that (though possibly Victorian women were, because if the chance of marriage didn't come to them there was nothing to do but wait for death). Most people, though they probably don't get everything they want, end further on than they started. But sex-repression is real enough. X's sister showed symptoms of it before she was thirty; she would have married anyone, anything—and did; and is happy. There ought to be clinics where it is wisely and discreetly treated. . . . Even work isn't always a remedy. However, I have got out *Helen of Troy* (John Erskine), which looks like a refreshing change."

For the first time since the enforced dilettantism of my Buxton youth, the days dragged and seemed empty. During the few cool intervals, I tried to refresh my jaded mind by acquiring information which I vaguely felt might "come in" some time. Letters from Winifred Holtby, who was then in South Africa lecturing for the League of Nations Union and studying the position of the African natives, spurred me to a similar interest in the American negro. "I have been investigating labour conditions a little *via* the League for Industrial Democracy," I was able to retaliate, "and have got quantities of literature, all about the textile strike at Passaic, the spy system for preventing organisation of the workers in the big industries, etc. The only negro Trade Union here is a semi-secret organisation of the railway sleeping-car porters."

After much travel I have acquired a real respect for these negro porters and the cheerful good nature which they bring to the tedious task of constantly making and re-making sleeping berths. In many thousand miles of train journeys I have only come across one who was at all bad-tempered, and I have never received a single protest against my inconvenient preference for sleeping with my face towards the engine, which often means the remaking of my berth after I have boarded the train. My knowledge of the agreeable negro temperament was more limited when I set out one Sunday morning from the eastern extremity of 116th Street, known as "Little Hell Gate", to explore the coloured districts of Harlem. But I had recently heard a story which pleased me about Florence Mills, the talented negro actress destined for premature death, who was then playing to crowded theatres in *Blackbirds*. Wishing to take an apartment in a fashionable quarter of New York, she went to see the agent to inquire about the price. With that insolence which among the ill-educated is still considered the proper attitude towards negroes, whether geniuses or not, the agent replied: "We don't let apartments in this block to niggers." Miss Mills meditated for a moment and then inquired innocently: "How much would it cost to buy the block?"

In Harlem, that city within a city extending on either side of Lenox and Seventh avenues from 125th Street to 144th Street, plenty of evidence seemed to exist that other coloured American citizens could afford "to buy the block". Dignified in white spats and grey Homburg hats on that bright Sunday morning, a procession of opulent-looking dark-skinned business men walked grandly into the Methodist churches. Their wives, perambulating proudly beside them in fashionable Fifth Avenue frocks of strawberry, primrose or periwinkle-blue georgette, carried their collection in large bags of bright-coloured beads. Others, less ceremonious though equally decorative, pushed up their windows to watch the speakers going into Liberty Hall, where a mass meeting was advertised "for the emancipation of our friends in Africa". Everywhere cinemas, soda-fountains and beauty-parlours abounded, the last offering to the wives and daughters of prosperous citizens a costly form of hair-dressing "guaranteed to take the kink out of your hair".

It seemed a strange investment when I considered how much I spent upon having the kink put in.

Except for the dark skins of its population, this prosperous, spacious district was indistinguishable from any other part of Manhattan. Nothing in its self-respecting solidity suggested the grim "coloured quarters" of South African cities which Winifred had described to me. Soon afterwards I learned from *The New Negro*, an anthology of negro literature published in New York, that the chief problem of Harlem's intellectuals was to find any cultured group with which they could associate outside their own community. The leisured and prosperous negroes also led lives very similar to those of leisured and prosperous classes the world over; they travelled, owned cars, played tennis and golf, yet if they ventured into a fashionable restaurant in some other district, the crockery that they had used would be smashed before their eyes.

"In New York," I reported to Winifred, "there is the same fear, and its same expression in resentment, as you find in South Africa. Restaurant-keepers endeavour to prevent coloured people from coming into the restaurants which white people use. . . . A little while ago a negro Yale graduate went into a restaurant in Greenwich Village (the Chelsea of New York) and ordered a meal. The restaurant keeper asked him to go and he refused. The restaurant keeper then brought out his negro cook to persuade him to go. The man still refused, and then the keeper, with the help of the waiters, turned him out. The negro brought an action against the restaurant and won it—there being no legal discrimination between white customers and black. So we go on. At one University two negro girl students claimed to be allowed to live in the women's dormitory. For weeks controversy raged on the matter, the leading history professor, a man of pronounced liberal and democratic views, espousing the cause of the girls. At last the matter came up before the President, and as a result the girls were allowed to live in, but were given a room quite away from the others with a separate entrance which the others never used!"

Like every other civilised society, Harlem had its own movements for emancipation. Apart from the money raised for African negroes, missions went out to educate the backward rural peoples in the derelict coloured communities of the South. There was even a feminist movement, though the struggle for sex equality seemed likely always to be second to the fight for race equality. One negro writer and social worker, Elise Johnson McDougald, described in *The New Negro* the special handicaps of coloured women:

"Even in New York the general attitude of mind causes the negro woman serious difficulty. She is conscious that what is left of chivalry is not directed towards her. She realises that the ideal of beauty built up in the fine arts has excluded her almost entirely. Nor does the drama catch her finest spirit. She is most often used to provoke the mirthless laugh of ridicule, or to portray feminine viciousness or vulgarity not peculiar to negroes. This is the shadow over her. To a race naturally sunny comes the twilight of self-doubt and a sense of personal inferiority."

In 1934, a few months after *Testament of Youth* appeared, a letter came from a negro woman reader in Pittsburgh to assure me that some coloured women have conquered this sense of inferiority in spite of adversities sufficient to intimidate a woman of any race. She was twenty-six, she told me, very poor, "a rabid feminist", and the fierce, unabashed mother of an illegitimate three-year-old son.

"I am a graduate of high school where rather than teaching us that war is outrageous, they glorify every conflict in which our country has taken part, always picturing America as the righteous nation. I had been out of school for years before I began to realise, from various books and magazine articles I had read, that every war was most unnecessary, but the most colossal stupidity in American history was the Civil War. We coloured folks would gradually have arrived at a state of freedom plus civilization without that terrible war, the aftermath of which was a sharp and abrupt estrangement between the two races in the South. The Civil War and the Reconstruction are the main causes of the lynchings and oppression in the South today. White Southerners are obsessed with the determination to 'keep the nigger down' and 'keep the nigger in his place'. In spite of which my people are really getting somewhere.

"Feminism is my chief interest. In America women still have numerous rights to fight for. One of them is to obtain birth certificates for illegitimate children. Recently Illinois passed a law granting certificates to *all* children. It is unbelievable that a difference could be made between children according to whether or not their mothers are married. I have often thought of the humiliation I should feel on having a wedding-ring placed on my finger, unless my husband would wear one too. Also, why should women change their surnames when they marry? Why should the father's name alone be of value to a baby? Why should married and single women have two different titles? I am sick and tired of all these outrageous indications of the double standard and I shall do what I can to get rid of and destroy them. I didn't know there were male feminists until I read your book, but now I want my boy to be a feminist and a pacifist, like me. Therefore, I think the law would be an ideal profession for him. . . . Hoping that you don't share the negro-fearing prejudice of many Anglo-Saxons and that we meet sometime."

VI

I COULD NOT accompany G. in mid-July on the last and longest of his expeditions, to St. Louis, Denver and Salt Lake City, for by that time I had exactly $30 left over from the sum set aside for my return fare to England in August. I could afford to buy nothing—not even some new summer garments, although, as I complained to my family, "my clothes are all crushed and soiled, and my hats look as if they had been jumped on! G. is not much better off at the moment, as the S.S.R.C. will *not* send his expenses; they must think he has private means, as they expect him to use his own money for these expensive trips, and get it all back in a burst at the end! I must needs write some articles."

The articles which I was considering were intended for English newspapers, for I had by now sadly accepted the bitter fact that I had made no headway whatever towards acquiring a reputation in America. Magazine editors had presented a united front against my onslaughts; literary agents had been verbally encouraging but practically ineffective; lecture agents were relentlessly interested only in Europeans with names already made. The New World, I realised, would have to be conquered from the other side of the Atlantic if it was ever to be conquered at all. Nothing had materialised except small speeches for local organisations—which materialise anywhere for any person known to have the slightest talent for public speaking.

"The most devastating blow dealt me by the Suffrage Movement," confesses Laurence Housman in his autobiography, *The Unexpected Years*, "was the discovery it forced upon me that I could speak . . . so that in later years I have given up much time to speaking which might have been better employed in writing". Housman is certainly right in his conclusion that any author who wishes to concentrate on

his work should beware of betraying that he possesses this
fluency, for it is the most remorselessly exploited gift in
creation. Once the world becomes aware of it, he will never
again be left alone to maintain the very reputation which
makes his presence on platforms desirable. Instead, he will
be besieged with perpetual invitations to take long journeys
at his own expense, and address innumerable small audiences
in support of a hundred different causes. For the rest of his
life he will have to fight for the right to do his own job,
and for the peace and quiet without which it cannot be
done. He will receive bitter protests, and even abuse,
because it is his own job that he wants to do, and not the one
suggested by somebody else. He may even be forced to
emigrate to the mountains of New Mexico or the Arizona
desert in order to escape from persistent and ruthless
interruption.

The more clearly I recognised the futility of my own
literary experiments, the harder I worked on G.'s book,
typing, revising and correcting in order that he might
simultaneously complete both it and his report for the
Social Science Research Council by the end of August.
Such lingering hopes as I still possessed for myself were
now confined to *A Honeymoon in Two Worlds*, and in the
midst of his deep preoccupation with the consequences of
Prohibition or the fundamentals of social theory, I tried to
persuade him to bring my book to the notice of various
publishers' representatives who came to interview him about
The Science and Method of Politics. In the end I gave it up,
since my most ferocious outbursts of irritable impatience
never produced anything more conclusive than the following
conversation:

"Did you mention my book to Mr. T.?"

"Oh, yes. We discussed it for about five minutes."

"What did he say?"

"Oh—he seemed interested."

"Yes, but what did he *say*?"

"Well . . . he put cogent questions."

Never, all the same, did I doubt his genuine sympathy

with the sense of frustrated endeavour which had descended upon me like a mid-summer miasma. This sympathy had, in fact, reached the point of suggesting that he should return alone to his University post at the beginning of the academic year, while I spent six months in London recapturing the lost positions. When, in the autumn, I actually carried out this proposal, we were naïvely astonished to find some of our scandal-scenting acquaintances assuming that it was the inevitable preliminary to a permanent separation, so ludicrously inconceivable did any such catastrophic parting appear to us. Now, just before leaving New York to spend a week with our relatives at their Massachusetts farm during G.'s absence, I wrote to him in St. Louis ruefully describing that dry-rot of disillusionment which periodically attacks every writer.

"I have finished the revision of my book and tomorrow begin to type; I am anxious to get rid of it, and am beyond the stage of being able to judge it at all; things I thought wonderfully good ideas when they first occurred to me now seem as dull and conventional as rice-pudding. . . . The revision mentality is in itself rather dangerous; one can get into a state of mind when one is dissatisfied with anything one hasn't altered, even though it was much better the first time."

After the heavy petrol-saturated atmosphere of New York, the farm in Massachusetts seemed a refreshing oasis, though the dry maize and tobacco fields surrounding it shimmered and sizzled in the relentless heat. A long, low house, painted white with green wooden shutters, it was backed by rolling hills and thick woods dark with firs and pines. This New England country, old as America reckons age, looked friendly and familiar—a mingling of Oxfordshire and Hampshire with the rocky, indented coast-line of Dorset; it had traditions quite other than those of the bare, raw territories which I had seen even in New York State. Below the woods ran the Connecticut River, a silver streak between the hills. Although, as usual, there were few flowers in the garden, wild roses with pink petals and a sweet scent climbed in the forest. Butterflies clustered thickly amongst them; for the first time I watched, fascinated, the big black and yellow Tiger Swallowtails of North America and the rarer Silver-Spot Fritillaries with their blue-speckled brown and orange wings. Above the little swimming pool at the bottom of the garden, where bull-frogs croaked hoarsely at night in bass voices, huge blue dragon-flies with wings of dark grey lace darted like tropical humming-birds.

As my cousin was in New York throughout the week and his wife and her sister were pleasantly occupied in small duties required by the upkeep of the farm, I wandered alone through the hot lanes or the cooler trees, contented enough except for the continual conflict between G.'s claims as a husband and the demands of my writing, which seemed so unimportant to everyone else but was the mainspring of life to me. Could I really take advantage of his generous offer and leave him to endure small-town isolation alone for an entire autumn and spring? Yet if I did not, I knew that I should have to make, without hope of revocation, that final surrender of the claims of the human intelligence which I had always felt that no woman, as no man, should be required to offer on the altar of marriage. I should be forced to repudiate, once and for all, that struggle of creative intellect and artistic imagination for worthy expression, in terms of which—despite family prejudice, and war, and death, and the harsh set-backs of perpetual postponement—I had always lived and moved and had my being.

I was not conscious, during those sunny somnolent days, that I had made any decision, yet letters written home during this period suggest that the decision—like all decisions which rest upon some indestructible vital impulse—had already made itself.

"America has been experience but not achievement; it has involved too much moving about, squashing into small spaces (and you know how tiring this is—one gets into a habit of not writing an article because one has to look for the material among piles of papers), sudden spasms of urgency for us both which have left me a little flat and disinclined to settle to anything. . . . I want to get out of the academic atmosphere for a time. . . . Professorial society is an excellent intellectual tonic; it raises one's standard of mental exertion and exactitude, but after a time it is a little oppressive to be always with people who think that no work is worth while unless it is associated with a university appointment, and no book worth writing unless it contributes a meticulous iota to the sum of human knowledge. Art is nothing; learning is all. . . . I am naturally resistant to 'atmosphere', but I have noticed that wives and daughters of professors—and sons too—who do anything on their own (alas! not many do) develop a kind of inferiority complex about their own work because it is not academic."

One afternoon during my short holiday, the worst thunderstorm that I have ever experienced burst upon New England. Throughout the previous suffocating night, the grass and trees surrounding the farm had been alight with fire-flies, like baby falling stars. Early in the morning, we could hear the storm muttering in the distance; by midday it had become a sullen booming, like the guns in France heard from Étaples during the War. All afternoon a growing crescendo of sinister sound caused us to move, restlessly expectant, up and down the house. At tea-time came a sudden hurricane of wind; all at once the world went black and the air was filled with whirling dust. In a moment the full blast of the storm was upon us, thunder and lightning banging and flashing through a solid waterspout of rain. We huddled together in the pitch darkness of the downstairs living-room for fear that the farm might be struck; the trees in the garden seemed to clash together, and the Spanish cook shrieked when a dagger of lightning smote one of the kitchen utensils into a burst of flame. For two hours the storm bombarded us, till our ears were deafened and our nerves on edge; then, quite suddenly, it ceased, and in the eerie quiet that followed we could hear the heavy drip-drip-drip of raindrops from the garden shrubs.

After dinner, my cousin drove us into the grey saturated twilight to inspect the damage. The woods might have been the scene of an air-raid; broken trees, blown over by the wind or struck by the lightning, had fallen against one another or crashed into the undergrowth. On either side of the main road, the maize and onion and tobacco crops of the Polish farmers lay soaked and flattened. Telephone, telegraph and electric light were out of commission for miles; in one village a huge tree-top had brought down the telegraph pole and wires in front of it, just missing a house not many feet away. All that night we had no telephone, and no light but candles.

Back in New York, I described to G. this melodramatic tempest, and received in turn the vivid story of his journey to Colorado and Salt Lake City. As he talked I pictured the city street cars with their cheerful legend "Opportunity— the only knocker in Denver", and the view from the city park of the distant snow-crowned Rocky Mountains stretched like an arrogant rampart across the American continent, as though to bring to an arbitrary end the civilisation continuously established from the shores of the Atlantic.

Yet somehow that civilisation, silent, persistent, invincible, deaf yesterday, today and for ever to the dull sound of the word "defeat", had penetrated to the other side of the gigantic barrier, carrying its railways through the permanent night of deep river-worn canyons, and its roads across thousand-mile deserts of sterile sand and salt-encrusted rock. The indomitable American had marched, delved, constructed, blasted his way through cliffs and gorges, left his bones to whiten in the wilderness and disintegrate into dust blown to oblivion by the wind—until at last he stood triumphant upon those strange heights which were to carry the temples of Salt Lake City, and saw, as G. had seen, the blood-red sun set sullenly over an empty universe of red rock and desert sand.

When August replaced July, only a week was left of our life together in New York. Already, on June 27th, we had celebrated the first anniversary of our marriage, and G. had bought me from Saks a turquoise-blue enamel powder box

Hs

with two appropriately affectionate love-birds in silver filigree
on the lid.

Our return, originally planned for June, had been postponed until the late summer by G.'s investigation. At the
end of August he was to present his Report to the Social
Science Research Council at their Conference in Hanover,
New Hampshire. As soon as this Conference was over, he
had arranged to sail for the brief fortnight in England
which was all the time left him for a holiday before the new
semester began at his University.

I was leaving before him because I could not, in any case,
have gone with him to Hanover, and I wanted to reach
Geneva in time for the admission of the German delegation
by the League of Nations Assembly at the beginning of
September. Today it seems a poor reason for abandoning a
husband to three weeks of solitude, but at the time we
believed that Germany's membership of the League would
symbolise the final ending of post-war conflicts and usher in
the hallowed dawn of a brave new world.

In New York the thermometer now remained steadily at
98°, and in the Middle West it had risen to 113°. Terrifying
thunderstorms battered round the skyscrapers, and even
upon Morningside Heights not a breath of cool air blew
from the glittering Hudson. The little apartment which had
seemed so fresh and charming in the spring, I now described
as "this terrible room, where the books and papers have
overflowed from the tables to the chairs and the chairs to
the carpet". Perhaps it was the exhausting, annihilating
heat, perhaps the task of packing, with hands perpetually
sticky and a forehead always wet, one steamer trunk, one
hat-box, three suitcases, three book-boxes, a package of
china and a typewriter in the few feet of space left over from
the accumulation of our possessions, which led me to
embody such critical conclusions about America in my
final letter home.

"America is the kind of experience you are immensely
glad to have had once, but hope you'll never have again.
Or, if you have it again, that the circumstances might be so

different that the place would seem different. . . . America is terribly noisy, terribly tiring psychologically, and terribly lonely. The noise consists not only in the automobiles and a peculiar kind of terrible iron drill which is part of the apparatus of building a skyscraper (they have been building one almost opposite to us since last week), but in the voices of the Americans themselves. . . .

"And it is tiring in many ways. For one thing, one leads a singularly arid life with regard to things that are small in themselves, but immense when added together. There is no early morning tea and no afternoon tea; one either makes it and drinks it with tinned milk and a biscuit that has lost its first crispness (you can't buy a tin of biscuits here, they are all sold in paper packets), or else one wanders down street after street looking for a restaurant that will condescend to serve it. Then there are no fires in winter; one stares at a black radiator that makes one stuffy rather than warm, and has to choose between keeping the windows shut and getting a splitting headache, or opening them and shivering with cold. Then it is tiring because one never 'gets' the psychology of the people. Every second person you deal with in the ordinary matters of life—shopping, eating, travelling, taxis, servants—is a foreigner, and a different kind of foreigner. In France you adapt yourself to the French, in Germany to the Germans, and so on. But in America you go into three shops, and are served by, first, a Polish Jew, secondly an Italian, thirdly a Chinaman. You are waited on by negroes and driven in taxis by Germans or Filipinos. And somehow all this adds to the loneliness as well as to the interest of life. No one understands you the first time; you have to say everything twice to all foreigners, and even then they don't understand because your English is not American-English. You also live in very small rooms with everything crowded on top of you. Even in the country the accommodation was inadequate, and here the squash is unspeakable. Half the clothes I brought out I have never worn because they are in drawers with others piled on top of them, or left in trunks; and half the papers I brought I have never looked at for the same reason. As for loneliness, one makes lots of acquaintances, but gets intimate with no one. At first I thought that, being English, one was suspected and distrusted a little; now I think that intimacy is not a characteristic which the American cultivates or needs. His life is a rush; he doesn't like leisure because he doesn't want to think; he likes living in public, has no locks to his doors and no hedges to his garden. . . .

"If one is to enjoy America, two things (and by no means easy things) must exist. First of all, one must be a 'lion' already; America is so surfeited with lions that you must bring your reputation over ready-made, and even then you mayn't be successful. . . . In the second place, you must have a host of friends who are prepared to push you for purely personal reason. The only other reason people will do anything for you is if they think they are going to get any money out of you. The people who are interested in impersonal things (like my nice League of Nations people) are a mere handful, an infinitesimal fraction, in the crowd of sensation-mongers, dollar-chasers, baseball readers, and the vast, complacent indifference of the Middle West, the land of Main Street. . . . One is so far away, so alone, so overwhelmed. . . ."

Late in the evening of August 7th, G. took me down to the *Majestic*, which sailed at midnight.

He told me later that after he left me, he sat up till 3 a.m. in the little disordered apartment finishing his report. The next day he moved over to the East Side, and spent three weeks at Union Settlement.

His report indicated that ample material existed for a wider survey and suggested a budget of $450,000, including $25,000 for two investigators abroad. The Council at Hanover accepted his suggestions almost in full, but decided that the cost of research was too great for anything less than a government investigation. When such an investigation was carried out by the Wickersham Committee in 1930, they used G.'s report as a basis for their work.

The White Star docks were quiet that night; the boat, so late in the season, was not quite full. In my small second-class cabin G. helped me, almost in silence, to stow away my suitcases under the berths. I did not tell him that I had already discovered my cabin companion to be an unwashed-looking lady with an odoriferous dog, or that I proposed, as soon as I could get hold of the Purser next morning, to exchange my carefully chosen upper berth in a room with a porthole for one of the few empty inside cabins in which, though I suffocated, I should at least be alone. When he cut his hand on a nail protruding from beneath the lower berth, I nearly broke down and wept, for the tiny mishap made suddenly acute the sense of guilt which had oppressed me all day.

Whenever, even now, I leave my family temporarily to do a job of work abroad, this same unhappy compunction afflicts me. Once I allowed it to influence and even to alter my decisions; today I merely accept and endure it as part of the heavy cost which has to be paid, especially by women, for any worth-while achievement. I recognised it long ago as a product of the feminine conscience of my generation, directed by early training towards persons instead of work or ideas, which in moments of crisis reverts to type even amongst those of us who have fought against it all our lives, and whose plan for living is shaped by intelligence rather than by instinct.

I was glad, just before the *Majestic* sailed, that my cousin came down to the boat to say good-bye. At least I could reflect, as we slid from the river into the cooler quiet of the midsummer sea, that I had not left G. quite alone in the sultry darkness of the docks.

A sense of guilt lingered uneasily in my mind all the way across the Atlantic, but nothing else mitigated the profound relief with which I returned to England.

II

(1934)

"Sweeter was loss than silver coins to spend,
Sweeter was famine than the belly filled;
Better than blood in the vein was the blood spilled;
Better than corn and healthy flocks to tend
And a tight roof and acres without end
Was the barn burned and the mild creatures killed,
And the back aging fast, and all to build:
For then it was, his neighbour was his friend.
Then for a moment the averted eye
Was turned upon him with benignant beam,
Defiance faltered, and derision slept;
He saw as in a not unhappy dream
The kindly heads against the horrid sky,
And scowled, and cleared his throat and spat, and wept."

—Edna St. Vincent Millay,
Epitaph for the Race of Man.

"To talk about the Depression is needless. It's like talking about the Flood. From 1929 to 1933, it surged. It took years to hit everyone, but it hit. From much to little, from little to less, from less to relief—and so we took prosperity in reverse, an Alger story turned upside-down. And the great problem became 'Can we take it? Can we solve this problem? Can we save something? Have we learned our lesson?' It will take another twenty years to answer all but the first question. We know we can take it."

—Letter to Vera Brittain from Izetta Winter Robb of
Duluth, Minnesota, January 19th, 1938.

I

At the end of March, 1927, I rejoined G. in America for the remaining three months of the University year.

Throughout that period I lived in the same small town, met the same people, and learnt nothing new. Prosperity was still raging on every front; outside our community the whole United States seemed buoyantly affluent while we remained unfashionably impecunious. G.'s *Science and Method of Politics* had brought him prestige, but was not the type of publication which ever creates wealth, and though I had re-established my contacts with magazine editors in England, I had not succeeded in publishing *A Honeymoon in Two Worlds*.

This brief American interlude would not even be worth recording except for the fact that in New York, during that spring, the tiny bit of human protoplasm which at Christmas time became my son, first stirred into life.

I did not see the United States again until 1934.

In those seven years the world had changed, both for America and for me. On October 23rd, 1929, Prosperity crumpled up with the annihilating suddenness of an over-inflated balloon; on March 4th, 1933, a further collapse of credit took the American nation to the rock-bottom of the Depression. Before the end of that year President Roosevelt, elected the previous November by a panic-stricken people to replace "Prosperity President" Hoover, had inaugurated the New Deal. Soon afterwards, Prohibition followed the fallen administration into the inglorious limbo of discarded experiments.

My own trivial affairs now wore a brighter face than these cataclysmic crashes and agonising recoveries. Between 1927 and 1934 my children had been born, and I had written

Testament of Youth. Although, a year after its publication, I contemplated with apprehension the American lecture tour which my New York publishers and an American lecture manager had persuaded me to undertake, I no longer feared to feel "so far away, so alone, so overwhelmed" as in 1926.

There would not, at any rate, be the same unequal struggle to guard every penny against the stampeding onslaughts of national prodigality, for our economic resources were now sufficient for persons without extravagant tastes. Although *Testament of Youth* had not made the enormous fortune naïvely supposed by the uninitiated to be the agreeable consequence of every "best-seller", the royalties, articles and lectures resulting from it had removed us a comfortable distance from those assiduous economies which made extensive travel impossible for me in 1926. Whenever, during that earlier period, we had taken nocturnal journeys together, I had been obliged in order to keep down expenses to share a sleeping berth with G., but now I could treat myself to a "single occupancy section" and get a really good night. Thanks to a substantial contribution from my lecture manager towards the cost of the voyage, we could even afford the daring luxury of a first-class cabin on the *Berengaria*.

Our permanent home was now in London, for after our son's birth G. had exchanged his full-time University appointment for a part-time Professorship which kept him in America only four months out of every year. In mid-September he was to sail with me for his annual American semester, while Winifred Holtby nobly took charge of our household during my fourteen weeks' absence.

The night before we sailed, I went upstairs at least four times to look at my sleeping children. Now that the eve of departure was actually here, the reasons which had persuaded me to leave them for the first long interval since their birth seemed ludicrously inadequate. Looking from the train next morning at the soft contours of the Hampshire fields, serene and lovely in the autumn sunshine, I wondered wretchedly why ever I had agreed to the rash

experiment of a lecture tour in a country where I knew
that audiences were immense and standards exacting. During
the fifteen months which I had already spent there, nobody
had seemed particularly interested in anything that I
wanted to tell. How did I know, in spite of the American
sales of my first successful book and the confident assurances
of publishers and agents, that my present reception would
be more enthusiastic?

At Southampton a distinguished company boarded the
Berengaria. Lord Lothian was among them, and Harold
Nicolson, and Captain Victor Cazalet, and Mrs. Wintring-
ham, but the reporters and photographers—to whom authors
and politicians are birdseed when film personalities are
travelling—ignored these dignitaries for the *Man of Aran*
cinema company, which the producer, Robert Flaherty,
was taking to Hollywood to make another picture. With
Winifred, who had accompanied us to Southampton, I
explored the enormous lounge, library, palm court and
promenade decks. The bewildering size and magnificence
of everything provoked, like our orderly embarkation,
an irresistible comparison with the hurried scramble of
departure from Liverpool as humble second-class emigrants
in 1925. This time not only the Cunard-White Star Company
but the American Consulate itself had embodied the very
spirit of co-operation, which aroused uncomfortable speculations on the disproportionate claims to courtesy of a "name"
and a little spare cash.

When at last the *Berengaria* sailed I remained for a long
time on deck, forlornly waving a scarlet handkerchief to
Winifred until her tall slender figure, and the tiny mirror
which she used to catch the brilliant reflection of the mid-day
sun, disappeared behind the swinging bulk of the boat
as we turned into Southampton Water.

"It reminds me of the War," was all that I could say to
G., as I remembered with sudden emotion how exactly
eighteen years before, on just such a calm, beautiful day of
mid-September, I had sailed down the Solent on the hospital
ship *Britannic* for active service in Malta. Then I had been

a very young and obscure V.A.D. nurse, apprehensively journeying to perform the humblest duties on a small Mediterranean island; now, incredibly enough, I ranked as a mature and sophisticated "best seller" going to lecture in America, but my sentiments on this second occasion remained disconcertingly similar to those of the first.

Why, I wondered repeatedly throughout that voyage, did the feeling haunt me that I was going out to a new kind of warfare, constructive and adventurous instead of destructive and tragic, yet also imbued with some indefinable spiritual significance? It persisted in spite of the normal accompaniments of luxurious travel—the epicurean meals eaten at night amid the glitter of costly jewels on expensive evening gowns, the conscientious spasms of exercise in the gymnasium or on deck, the conducted tours round the Tourist and Third Class quarters. I carried away Third Class programmes for breakfast, luncheon and dinner, and discovered with agreeable surprise that they offered a selection of fare far more elaborate than any meal consumed by my family at home.

The luncheon menu for Wednesday September 19th provided quite a series of attractive alternatives:

Consommé Vermicelli   Scotch Barley Broth
Boiled Cod—Egg Sauce
Sauerkraut and Frankfurt Sausage
Grilled Lamb Chops and Tomatoes
Green Peas
Baked Jacket and French Fried Potatoes

Cold Meats
Roast Beef   Wiltshire Ham   Boar's Head   Ox Tongue

Salads
Lettuce   Mixed Pickles
Beetroot and Onion   French Dressing

Oxford Roll Pudding

Cheese   Rolls and Butter
Tea   Coffee   Iced Tea   Iced Coffee

The end of the voyage ran to cocktails, dancing, and conversations until 3 a.m. with film experts or politicians. Nevertheless, the sense of some unspecified yet predetermined objective possessed me again with invading force on the evening before we landed, when the huge black mast of the *Berengaria* dipped gently against a burning sky as she sailed straight into the West. Behind us the sea, a rhythmic mingling of flame and opalescent blue, swung away from the boat with the shining ripple of shot taffeta silk. In the far distance a heavy bank of purple cloud, so deep as to appear black beside the smouldering sun, looked like fast approaching land.

It had been a calm, pleasant voyage, so different in its equable dignity from the tossing misery of my first Atlantic crossing, and I had not spent much time in the palatial cabin selected for me by my American publisher on his annual visit to London the previous June. Even by the end of the voyage, I found intimidating and incongruous its superb beds, colossal wardrobes, elegant dressing tables, comfortable armchairs, capacious trunk room and white-tiled, porcelain-fitted bathroom. They all seemed a very odd result of *Testament of Youth*.

But odder results were still to come.

In New York my publisher and contemporary, George P. Brett, Jr., the youthful-looking President of the Macmillan Company, met us at the docks with his friendly, hospitable wife. This time, as we moved up the Hudson, the full panoply of New York had burst upon us through the vanishing mists of a brilliant September morning, but from the moment we landed there seemed to be no time to rediscover the city's magnificence or even to think about it.

As we drove from the docks to my publisher's house adjoining the Macmillan building at the corner of Fifth Avenue and West Twelfth Street, I noticed in many office windows a poster, crowned by the mysterious letters "N.R.A." above a symbolic blue eagle, which righteously asserted: "We Do Our Part." Later I was to meet enthusiastic

Democrats only too anxious to explain to me that the National Industrial Recovery Act was a superb and unique instrument, devised to increase employment, raise wages, shorten hours, abolish child labour, end exploitation and generally inaugurate the New Jerusalem. But as soon as our taxicab reached its destination, a series of unforeseen and overwhelming demands so persistently beset me that my capacity for absorbing facts remained in abeyance for several days.

Once more, as I wrote home afterwards, I had "the kind of day which reminded me of the War, because one never had time to wonder if one was going to be able to get through it; one just went on". Outside the Macmillan offices my publisher, justly pleased with his tactful gesture, showed me that their book window was filled with the scarlet-jacketed ninth edition of *Testament of Youth*, which had come off the printing press only that morning, but alarm eclipsed my sense of gratification when we passed through the offices themselves. Apprehensively observing the army of elegant typists, the elaborate network of compartments, and the impressive Board Room, I recalled a comment made by Louis Golding to Phyllis Bentley when the Macmillan Company of New York took her novel *Inheritance*: "Being published by Macmillan is like having a knighthood conferred on you."

In the Bretts' pleasant living-room a few moments later, I felt temporarily reassured when the Company's Vice-President and chief editor, Harold S. Latham, who had accepted *Testament of Youth* in London the previous year, graciously appeared to greet me; but my spirits sank again at the sight of the secretary who followed him, bearing a large and portentous-looking mail. It was now past midday; we had breakfasted at 6 a.m. and landed at 10.0, and I felt quite incapable of reading and assimilating the contents of twenty letters. But as everyone seemed to expect that I should not only do this, but dictate the answers then and there to the secretary thoughtfully provided, I realised for the first of many occasions that authors who were rash enough to undertake American lecture tours must resolutely ignore such human embarrassments as hunger, diffidence, and fatigue.

The letters contained a bewildering assortment of disturbing requests. Would I make an appointment with my lecture manager immediately on arrival? Would I consent to be interviewed by the representative of this, that and the other newspaper on war and peace, the position of women, my impressions of America, the European situation, war and peace? Could I meet an "ex-Waac" living in New York for a few minutes' conversation about active service in France? Would I contribute a reply to the question "How Can We Prevent a New War?" for a high school magazine which hoped to publish a symposium of answers from "a selected list of leaders of thought"?

The strange shipboard consciousness of some waiting unforeseen experience came elusively back to me as I read this last request.

"We hope," it ran, "that the answers contributed will centre their attention on direct and practical activities which average citizens of the democratic nations and particularly young people in their high school or college years can undertake *now* with some prospect of influencing the course of international events and reversing the trend towards war which now seems so inevitable. . . . You have undoubtedly thought seriously upon these questions and have some convictions about them which you can quickly phrase in a few sentences."

My correspondent was right. I *had* thought seriously on those questions and possessed quite a number of convictions, but the task of "quickly phrasing" them in a dictated message to a secretary, who sat with her pencil expectantly poised before me in an apparently rocking room where G., my publisher, his wife, and two or three members of the Macmillan Company were all discussing whether I should see my lecture manager that day, and if so when, was by no means so simple as he supposed.

I had just succeeded in composing a two-hundred-word

reply at the conclusion of the other letters when lunch was announced, preceded, to my infinite gratitude, by an "Old-Fashioned" whisky cocktail, of which I was more than in need. I drank it with a silent salutation to those forces of American opinion which had brought Prohibition to its ignoble end.

"And now," said my publisher, with a kindly determination which admitted no argument, "we'll go right along to L.'s office and find out how he's fixed your tour."

Reluctantly I dragged myself from a pleasant post-prandial dream, rendered even more attractive by the whisky cocktail, of taking two or three hours' immediate sleep to compensate for going to bed at 3.0 a.m. and getting up at 5.30. My publisher, accompanied by the Macmillan sales-manager, brought round his car with indefatigable promptitude, and we plunged from the comparative peace of Washington Square into the roaring, sweltering, mid-afternoon activity of central Fifth Avenue.

In the lecture manager's sumptuous office, looking from its huge thirty-seventh floor windows over the shimmering Hudson between the sun-drenched pinnacles of the lower skyscrapers, I listened to a conversation which sounded so appalling that my immediate speculation, as I recorded later, "was not *whether* I should break down, but simply *when*".

My tour, it seemed, already included thirty-four lectures in twenty-five cities, many of which, from an English though not apparently an American standpoint, were immense distances apart. The final list of engagements, I learnt, would run to between forty and fifty lectures, but these represented the mere scaffolding of an intensely complicated and exacting performance. As soon as they began to discuss it, my publisher and my manager resembled two very determined dogs contending over one small bone.

I heard their arguments with growing amazement, since on my previous visits to America I had not been, as a commercial commodity, of the least value to anyone. The talk, gathering in emphasis as it continued, ebbed and flowed round bookstores, autographs, sales, audiences, fees, and the incomprehensible idiosyncrasies of lecture organisers, which "the depression" seemed somehow to have intensified. Two sentences emerged from the general atmosphere of intimidating bewilderment.

"But surely," urged my publisher persuasively, "if she took the night train and got to the city in the morning, she could visit the bookstores before the lecture begins?"

"Impossible," declared my lecture manager firmly. "The organisation which has purchased Miss Brittain would never stand for that. The engagement was booked on the understanding that it would be her first and exclusive appearance in Z."

I left that terrifying office with my mind—which was by now incapable of absorbing chronological or geographical details—in a whirl of alarmed confusion. During my ambitious youth, when I wanted fame so badly and it seemed so far away, I had innocently imagined that, once success came, the rest would be easy. One would sit on the golden throne of one's prestige, high and lifted up above the less fortunate crowd, do exactly what one liked, and be regarded with distant awe while one produced a new book for an eager, reverent public.

I now learnt, with increasing consternation, that the real thing, especially in America, was utterly different. Far from honoured and elevated peace, it meant going down into the arena amid the dust and heat generated by one's readers. It was not a matter of enthroned security, but of railway time-tables, perpetual journeys, incessant correspondence, competitive bookstores, and the constant invasion of one's privacy by the organisers of public meetings.

Henceforth one would not be the master but the slave of that public which, at long last, had accorded its favour. There would be no way of escape except by death, or by deliberate withdrawal from the position which had been captured at so high a cost of determination and perseverance. Even then, one's freedom would not be complete.

Is

Never again could one return to the entrenched obscurity of those whose names possess only private value, and have never become the property of publishers, lecture organisers, literary agents, book-sellers and book-buyers.

It was a sobering thought, which savoured too much of Dead Sea fruit for my peace of mind. Perhaps I wilted under it somewhat conspicuously, for though I was later to find my alarm thoroughly justified, I was first offered a delicious interval of peace without which I could never have faced the weeks that followed.

"You look just about all in," said my publisher late that night, after a performance of Sinclair Lewis's *Dodsworth* to which he and his wife had taken us. "Now, your tour doesn't begin till October 5th, and the Macmillan party on September 29th is the first thing you have to be in New York for. What about a week at our shack in the country first?"

I never learnt whether this generous suggestion arose on the spur of the moment or had been a prearranged plan. I only knew that, early next morning, G. and I found ourselves being swiftly driven from the clamorous heat of New York to the lovely, wooded tranquillity of Fairfield, Connecticut. G., who had to leave the following day for the beginning of his semester, adapted himself to the situation with his usual imperturbability, but my own head still ached and whirled from desperate speculations about my lecture tour and the endeavour to select, at top speed that morning, suitable clothes for an unfamiliar destination from the unutterable chaos of my luggage. Inevitably, as I wrote home, "I brought two suitcases here full of masses of things I didn't want and hardly anything I did", and was obliged to appear quite unsuitably clad at the various functions which already seemed, like most American parties, to spring up through some miraculous premonition wherever I appeared.

At first the hospitable procession of luncheons, teas and dinners suggested that the programme in the country

would differ little from the hurricane time-table in New
York, and I began—as always during the first two weeks
of every visit to America—to realise acutely the leisureliness of the ancient civilisation which had produced me. There
were times, and this was one of them, when I thought
resentfully of my Staffordshire ancestors, those staid Mid-
land yeomen established for two hundred years on the
borders of the Potteries, who for generation after generation went to bed at 9.0 p.m. If only, I lamented, they could
have bequeathed to me their tranquillising stolidity, as
well as their inconvenient preference for early hours and
long unbroken nights!

Then, with the conclusion of the week-end and G.'s
departure for his University, the healing quiet which I had
been brought to enjoy descended like a gift from benevolent
gods upon the "shack" and its surrounding untrampled
glory of autumn lanes and woods. My publisher's wife, well
acquainted with the inexplicable vagaries of authors, proved
to be the least formal hostess with whom I had ever stayed;
she left me as free as in my own home to walk alone or go
to bed early. When I had overtaken the lost hours of sleep,
I lay awake peacefully enjoying the delicious scents which
drifted from the garden through the open window in the
warm September darkness, or listening to the oddly sooth-
ing chorus of innumerable crickets and small frogs, like
the quacking of a million miniature ducks.

The so-called "shack" was a long, low bungalow, cheerfully painted and furnished in clear delicate shades of yellow
and green. Its front door opened onto a wide verandah,
where I sat in the sunshine each morning and answered my
mounting correspondence. The half-wild flower garden
which stretched from the house to the surrounding woods
was now a brilliant tangle of giant magenta dahlias, pink
and purple asters, orange nasturtiums and flaming gladioli.
Already the gamboge tints of autumn had crept over the
beeches at the garden's edge; the sugar maples were turning
golden, and the scarlet oaks wore their passionate October
dress. Beyond the woods the mountain ash with its red-

stemmed leaves climbed the slopes of the rolling uplands, and the antlered candelabra-like branches of the sumacs glowed orange and purple and vermilion in the sun.

Although this part of Connecticut, being only two hours' drive from the city, had become a favourite country house district among well-to-do New Yorkers, their large estates or smaller farms seemed to leave almost unchanged the profuse spreading wildness of hills and woods and streams. Different as it was from the dramatic Iroquois lakes and gorges, and even from Massachusetts with its comforting English landscapes, I had the same consciousness that vast virgin acres of soil and forest surrounded humanity's trivial habitations with their squandered luxury of space.

The verdant overgrown lanes and steep meadows of lush grass brought back memories of the Cotswolds, but this country was damper, warmer and more mellow than Gloucestershire. An exquisite excited happiness, such as I had rarely known in America, intoxicated me when the sunlight flooded the fertile banks where the Black Swallow-tails, with orange or red-spotted wings as large as the wings of bats, poised quivering upon clumps of goldenrod or wild purple aster. These tangled mauve and yellow clusters sprang from a riotous undergrowth of smaller flowers—heartweed, ragged robin, the feathery grey stone clover, and the cream-coloured evening primrose with its thick stem and abundant leaves. Above the green ribbon of warm grass which bordered the lanes, vivid smaller butter-flies—Meadow Browns, Bronze Coppers, Azures with gos-samer wings as blue as jewels—flitted lazily from pink-white milfoil to rough patches of yellow hawkweed or trails of climbing nightshade with backward curving violet petals.

In the afternoons my hostess walked with me through the ochre-shaded woods, and late in the evening, when the sun had gone down amid a celestial tumult of topaz and ruby and clear vivid turquoise, my host would re-appear from New York, to plunge for a twilight stroll into the thicket at his gate, or motor us after supper to his yacht on Long Island Sound five miles away. Under the full moon the deep indigo sea spread smoothly round us like a tropical lake, and the harbour lights blinked blue and red from the dark outline of either shore. On Long Island, eighteen miles across the Sound, tiny golden pin-points made a bright delicate pattern against the velvet sky. When we returned home at midnight, a shrill chirping greeted us from the warm damp grass: "Katy did! Katy *didn't*! Katy did!"

At first I had imagined the ardent amateur yachtsman to be as American an American as I was likely to meet, but now I realised that he inherited many qualities from his English father, George P. Brett, Sr., one of the greatest publishers of his generation, who founded the Macmillan Company of New York in 1896. The son, I discovered, actually preferred, like any Englishman, occasional quiet holidays with his wife and boys; he also enjoyed long walks, and took me for strenuous week-end tramps over briar-bestrewn fields, or through woodland swamps, thickly grown with underbrush, which put even my considerable walking powers to the test. On these expeditions I gladly discarded my inappropriate party clothes for a white shirt blouse and a pair of linen shorts borrowed from my hostess. Clad in this practical fashion, which somehow obliterated fifteen years overnight, I was able to do all that my ener-getic host expected in the way of climbing walls, leaping streams, and striding over the deceptively beautiful red-gold patches of poison ivy.

One long Indian summer afternoon I spent with his father, then living in retirement on the parent Fairfield estate, and devoting the energy which had once built up a great business to collecting new specimens for his pine plantation (portentously known to America as a *pinetum*). Although he had reached his middle seventies, the tall old man in leather jacket and brown leggings still appeared as straight and vigorous as his own young saplings.

As he escorted me with royal dignity down his long drive between dogwood bushes with waxen scarlet berries, which blossomed in spring like a cloud of pink-tinted

snow, he related how he had gathered from every corner
of the world the four hundred varieties of pines, firs,
junipers and spruces which composed his private forest.
Tramping through the thick swampy grass between the
trees, he showed me pines from Scotland, Canada, California and Japan; spruces with silky, spiky or lacy foliage,
green, golden and blue-grey; firs that soared ambitiously
skyward or clung assiduously to the ground.

Listening to his proud description of his adventures in
the search for them, I caught something of the fire and
determination which had once made his rival publishers
fear and respect him. He was to die two years afterwards,
before I returned to the United States, but he lived long
enough to see his Company, piloted by his son, triumphantly survive the depression which swept so many old
business houses from the American scene.

II

THE DEPRESSION WAS not, for the moment, conspicuous when I returned to New York, and with conscious effort transformed myself from a pseudo-juvenile in shorts to a velvet-gowned guest of honour at a Macmillan reception.

Officially I shared that exacting position with A. G. Macdonell, who was coming over to collect material for his travel book *A Visit to America*, and Sean O'Casey, whose play *Within the Gates* was about to appear in New York. But when the party began Archie Macdonell's boat, which was late, had not yet arrived, and Sean O'Casey, who symbolised his robust contempt for functions by appearing in a sweater, performed an immediate vanishing trick in collusion with his fellow-countryman Padraic Colum.

Desperately resolving that the situation demanded more graciousness than I had ever exhibited in the nine-year-old past, I stood my ground and for four hours shook hands with two hundred and fifty strangers, while the temperature in the crowded room soared up into the nineties, and my clinging velvet dress aroused wistful recollections of the hatless and stockingless days in Connecticut.

Since the long succession of guests appeared to contain exclusively celebrities, my right to be guest-in-chief seemed to grow less and less as their numbers became more and more. In sex, I remarked—and now remembered observing the same proportion at American parties in 1925—they were evenly divided between men and women.

"One of the things you notice the moment you enter this country," I told my family, "is how many men of your own age there seem to be compared with England. I suppose other English generations have been like America in this respect. She lost so few."

At last, to my intense relief, A. G. Macdonell arrived from his belated boat. Immediately the limelight transferred itself from my orchid-adorned diminutiveness to his imposing stature, and I was able to slip thankfully away to a sofa and a highball amid a group of newspaper correspondents in the Board Room. Neither they nor the other guests showed any disposition to leave for another two or three hours. As I. M. P. of the *New York Herald-Tribune* remarked later in her column: "Sean O'Casey had to leave in the middle of the party for a rehearsal. Everyone else stayed and stayed; we did go home finally, but the rest are probably there yet. . . ."

The week continued as it had begun. A postcard to Winifred recorded a three-day programme of seven newspaper interviews, three visits to editors, two to agents, two to photographers, one to an artist, another to a film producer, and a correspondence requiring a hundred dictated replies. It should also have included three dinners, two theatres, two luncheons and a hurried midday visit to New York's latest architectural phenomenon, the Empire State Building.

I found myself momentarily deafened by the roaring wind as the lift rushed us past one hundred and two floors to the observation tower twelve hundred feet above the city. Clinging ignominiously to my companion, I looked dizzily down over New York; the experience was a twentieth century version of being transferred to the top of a high mountain and shown the kingdoms of the earth and the glory thereof. For the first time I saw Manhattan as upon a map, lying between the Hudson and the East River. With serene deliberation a scarlet four-funnelled liner— the *Aquitania* or the *Berengaria*—left the docks and drifted slowly downstream towards the Statue of Liberty. Immediately below us the smaller skyscrapers, mere unambitious trifles of fifty stories or so, seemed already to belong to ancient American history. How many years would pass before they gave way, as out-dated structures, to new giants competing in the astounding national race to scale the walls of heaven?

"This life would be quite incredible," ran a scribbled letter describing the first rush of formidable work, "if one weren't living in it and knew it to be true. I thought I knew New York. . . . I *never* have time allowed me for such minor details as getting dressed, or packing, or unpacking, or reading my letters (even business ones have to be gone through at express train rate), or for changing into the elaborate toilet expected of one at the hotels or restaurants to which I am invited. When I first arrived a maid partly unpacked for me; the rest of my trunks are still half packed. I don't know where she has put all the things she has unpacked and have never had time to look; I don't clearly know what I have got in Connecticut and what in New York. When I do have to change (always in three minutes or less), I hopefully seize the nearest gloves, stockings, bag that I can find—and never yet, I think, have worn all together the etceteras so carefully chosen to go with each get-up! . . . Wednesday's interviews were terrific; each of them took an hour and it was worse than giving three lectures, because in a lecture you do know what you are going to say, and in an interview you have to make it up as you go along."

The newspaper correspondents who came to see me, even when they represented journals from the smaller cities, never resembled the cub reporters to whom lesser English newspapers sometimes entrust the responsible and tact-demanding task of describing personalities and estimating their significance. Some of them—like Dorothea Lawrance Mann of the *Boston Transcript*, and Lillian T. Genn, whose long syndicated interview appeared in the *Florida Times-Union* of Jacksonville, and several other newspapers—were distinguished and experienced journalists with claims to prestige which easily overshadowed my own mushroom-grown reputation. The feeling that it was I who ought to be interviewing them finally implanted in me a persistent scepticism, which perhaps saved my sense of proportion. The more flattering their interviews appeared when in print, the less I believed a word that they said.

These amiable impressions had no real reference to myself at all; they simply described a figment of the American imagination temporarily labelled "Vera Brittain."

Some material foundation for this figment had nevertheless to be supplied. With my head aching from the unremitting necessity of marshalling my thoughts in a city temperature mercilessly addicted to the eighties, I sat in the Macmillan Board Room (which, in addition to a first-class secretary, had been generously lent to me as my private office), and tried to answer their intelligent questions without revealing the ignorance of which I was only too often conscious.

What changes had I noticed in America since my last visit before the depression? Had I formed any opinion yet about the New Deal? What did England think of President Roosevelt? Was our depression comparable with theirs? How did the young people of England react towards the idea of another war? Did I believe that such a war was near? Ought the United States to join the League of Nations? Was the League's influence increasing or decreasing in Europe? Were women doing all that they could to bring about world peace? Would not the continuation of careers after marriage make for greater female intelligence? Was it desirable to legalise trial marriages? Did I feel that the easier divorce laws of the United States brought more domestic happiness or less? Had I any views on the future of Anglo-American relations?

I struggled to compose rational replies to this encyclopaedic avalanche, incidentally clarifying my own thoughts in the process. The last inquiry, especially, caused me to remember—for the first time with gratitude—the fifteen months that I had already spent in America. After all, I now recognised, they had not been utterly thrown away. That year and a quarter had given me an intimate knowledge of American life as lived both in great cities and in small towns; it had taught me those national details of habit and etiquette which can lead a visitor more hopelessly astray than the large international complications with which he is familiar. Knowing the country and its people as I did, I might perhaps hope to avoid those errors of tact by which foreign lecturers had done more to embitter Anglo-American relations than the politicians who defaulted on the Debt.

The more I reflected on those former visits to the United States, the less able I felt to take in the astonishing contrast of the present. Life could hardly have fulfilled with more disturbing thoroughness the bitter desire expressed in 1926: "America is the kind of experience you are immensely glad to have had once, but hope you'll never have again. Or, if you have it again, that the circumstances might be so different that the place would seem different."

By their belief in me and my work, the directing minds of my co-operative publishers had created for me a new America of which I was becoming slowly and incredulously aware. But this new America was composed of outlooks and psychologies very different from those of 1925; the comparison with the earlier period would have seemed less dramatic had not America herself changed profoundly in the interval. The half-considered replies which I had been obliged to give to the first question put by my interviewers now induced me to formulate more clearly my own impressions of America in 1934, and to search beneath the still swift and vivacious surface of American life for the implications of those changes that the depression had brought.

Already I knew, from books and newspaper articles, the skeleton tale of the disasters which had transformed the strident, efficient, self-confident nation that I remembered into a chaotic society undermined by bewilderment, humiliation and fear. Two years later, these facts were to be summed up in a Presidential campaign speech by one of the ablest young women in the State of Minnesota:

"The longest and best policed breadlines in history were formed. Men and women tramped the streets in the black years following 1929 while commissions futilely reported on the situation. The Hawley-Smoot Tariff Bill raised

walls so high that nations could not trade; and in consequence our total exports fell from a little over 5 billion
dollars in 1929 to about 1½ billion in 1932. Our farmers
were ruined as farm exports fell one billion; so we went
to 48-cent wheat, 6-cent cotton and 3-cent hogs. Our
national income in 1929 was 81 billion dollars. It sank to
39 billion in 1932. . . . But money is not the whole story.
The loss of courage, the threat of insecurity, the hysteria
of broken, beaten men and women gripped this nation
in 1932. This way was madness."

I learnt that the national debt, which had been over 15
billion dollars in 1930, stood at 20 billion plus in 1933. In
October, 1934, when I sat in the Macmillan Board Room
with my interviewers, and tried to be intelligent about the
National Industrial Recovery Act which a mercurial people
expected to achieve immediate salvation, the number of
unemployed in the United States was greater by nearly
quarter of a million than that of the year before. Counting
children and other dependants, eighteen million persons
were on relief, an increase of four and a half millions within
twelve months. They included 600,000 farm families in
addition to over eleven million industrial unemployed.

We, too, I told my questioners, had our unemployment
figures; since 1929 they had more than doubled, and now
represented about 22 per cent of our insured working
people. We too had our depression and our economic crisis,
which had driven the 1929 Labour Government out of
office in the General Election of 1931—the first that G. had
been free to fight in the Labour cause. . . . But neither
crisis nor depression had brought us so close to the verge
of panic and hysteria as the American depression had
brought the United States.

Why not? Well, for one thing we had experienced little
else but crises and depressions and slumps following temporary booms, from 1920 onwards. The inhabitants of post-
war Europe lived in a shadowed world where even the lights
were dim; like children brought up in a darkened room,
they had no knowledge of midday sunshine with which to

compare their faint illumination. In Britain—as Arthur Henderson wrote shortly afterwards in the *Christian Science Monitor* for December 26th, 1934—"a condition of crisis has existed since 1921, with a volume of unemployment far in excess of the pre-war average. . . . Except for brief intervals of apparent recovery, the records reveal a continuous worsening of the situation."

I might have added that our social philosophy was more complex and less optimistic than America's; it had also, during the course of history, been qualified and restated until its axioms were impervious to the fiercest calamities. Ever since 1914, we had been accepting the fact that the tranquil, secure age of Victorian prosperity would never return in the lifetime of our generation. For twenty years we had adjusted ourselves to catastrophe with a developing adaptability which America, unnerved and dismayed, had been obliged to acquire in a quarter of the time.

The longer I compared America's response to her depression with our more phlegmatic British reactions, the more clearly I remembered the belief I had met everywhere in 1925 that the United States, by some inherent national superiority, could avoid the post-war suffering which burdened Europe, and conquer, with the identical overriding efficiency that conquered nature, the destructive economic forces which had laid the Old World low. Now that she was compelled to recognise in herself the same fatal symptoms, the uncritical confidence produced by a century of spectacular progress had met with a sudden and violent reverse.

Had I been asked, in a lecture or an interview, to describe from the standpoint of a European that process of disillusion and its consequences, the attempt would have run something like this:

"In a hundred years your nation, leaving its original settlements for a new series of adventures, took possession of a vast and recalcitrant continent. Absorbing or sweeping aside the original inhabitants or earlier settlers, it crossed deserts, climbed mountains, drained swamps and forded rivers. By establishing cities, towns, farms and villages, it brought the finest material civilisation yet attained to virgin territories which offered every conceivable obstacle to human initiative. With a superb instinct for political and economic co-operation—the lack of which periodically drives Europe nearer and nearer to the verge of self-annihilation—your people welded the incompatible conglomeration of races, religions and languages which its experiment had incorporated or attracted, into a society whose common interests overshadowed and diminished its internal dissensions.

"It is not surprising that in this process you developed a belief that the steady rise in your standard of life would be perpetual, a faith in the unique impetus of your own destiny, a confidence that you alone could remain impervious to international chaos and world-wide disintegration. What the depression hit, even more than your pockets, was this fundamental confidence in your invincibility.

"To a European whose disorderly area of the earth's surface has known continuous failure and tragedy since the outbreak of the War, the deep mortification and vehement apprehensions that your depression has inspired seem pathetic and even disproportionate. But I believe that this very violence of reaction is playing its part in forging a new American spirit. By means of it America appears to be learning, as Europe from its numerous ordeals by fire has learnt again and again, that the human capacity for courage and charity is a spiritual treasure house which neither economic calamity nor political death can destroy."

Not only did the country seem different; I soon found that it was different. The American people, once so callous in their contempt for Europe's tragedies, had become humbler, kinder, less ostentatious; they understood now what chaos and sorrow meant because they had shared them. The brash optimism of 1926 had been purged away by the intensity of national suffering, and with it had vanished the only excuse for antagonism that I and others had ever possessed.

Already, as I went about the daily business of talking, shopping and travelling, it struck me that New York had become a far easier city for persons of moderate means to inhabit without discomfort or humiliation, than the clamorous wealth-intoxicated metropolis of eight years ago. One agreeable change I noticed was the disappearance of that pitiless shrewdness in extracting money from moderately endowed customers which had infuriated me among shop-assistants in 1926. The money was simply not there to be extracted; throughout the depression, hairdressers, beauty parlours, fashionable dressmakers and other dispensers of luxuries were fortunate if they could retain enough business to carry on. Sheer economic necessity had developed the habit of soliciting custom instead of challenging, brow-beating and swindling it.

It was a salutary change, and it had come to stay. Everywhere prices had dropped to meet the limited demands of fallen investments and truncated incomes. Prosperity and Prohibition—those twin devils decked up by national pride and self-deceived morality to look like angels—had both gone their way, taking with them the wilder sybaritic extravagances of New York in the nineteen-twenties. Meals were cheaper because, during the Prohibition epoch, hotels which normally made profits on wine had been obliged to raise all other prices to compensate for the vanished revenue. The "crowded rough-and-tumble" in the shopping areas which I had once described so critically was now less hectic because fewer people had money to spend, and more courteous because a community reduced to a lower financial level had developed the tolerant readiness to give and take characteristic of those whom life has belaboured. Crowds, heat, rush and discomfort are inseparable accompaniments of poverty, which become supportable only through the patience and self-restraint of those who must endure them.

Living and working in this politer, more subdued society, I realised that the top-hatted, cigar-smoking, dollar-pocketing Uncle Sam beloved of cartoonists was now no more typical of the ordinary American citizen than the

heavy, pot-bellied, beef-eating John Bull was representative
of the ordinary Englishman. He had not even been typical
in 1925, though a foreigner then visiting the United States
might have been forgiven for crediting the whole population
with the characteristics of that dominant "stereotype", since
it appeared willing to be included. But now that so many
of the gilded hierarchy had swayed ingloriously on the edge
of doom and had lost their prestige if not their money, the
hard-working incorruptible millions of the American people
—kindly, generous, lively, enterprising, and infinitely
courageous—had emerged from economic obscurity to
determine the temper of daily life.

I soon perceived that neither our small-town frugality
in 1925 nor our New York economies in 1926 had been
peculiar; America even then was the sum-total of hundreds
of such modest towns and thousands of such small-salaried
families. "Prosperity", I learnt, had mainly benefited about
half a million persons, of whom perhaps forty thousand
acquired large fortunes, but only about four hundred—in
a country with a population of one hundred and thirty
millions—had made spectacular profits and retained control
of national finance. The aggressive ambitions of the few
had been imposed upon the quiet conflicts of the many.

The business men whom I met in 1934 seemed to have
changed with the changed outlook of the country. No
doubt they were mentally better endowed, and geographically
more widely distributed, than the stock-brokers, realtors
and local store-owners whom I had encountered in New
York and New England between 1925 and 1927; but even
allowing for this difference, the masculine sense of proportion
was more evident. "Business" had unexpectedly failed its
promoters, and in the sorry years when innumerable
offices did not provide their owners with a full day's work,
the men who once slaved in them from dawn till dusk
now turned for consolation to newspapers, books and
even lectures. Apart from the ubiquitous women's clubs,
almost as many men attended my lectures as women. In
1937, the proportion was to become still larger.

"But do you mean to say," asked incredulous acquaintances after I returned home, "that the Americans went to lectures even in the depression?"

The answer was that they went even more. Though the spectacular fees paid to many lecturers in the swaggering epoch of the "New Era" dropped abruptly, to recover only partially later, the number of lectures, "forums" and discussion groups increased. Everybody wanted to have the cause of the depression explained, to know if it could be cured and its return prevented, to be told whether capitalism had failed, was doomed, must give place to a new social order, and if so, what that social order should be. The wizards of Big Business had let America down, so she sought a new collection of magicians in educators, scientists and "national planners", whose heyday coincided with the brief, booming hour of Technocracy.

"The real contribution of education at this time, when failure was still individual failure and a disgrace," wrote Lucy Wilcox Adams in the American *Journal of Adult Education* for January, 1935, "was to restore the uprooted person to community life. The sick anxiety of many of those who attended the forums and study groups was painfully apparent, but they found respite and regained self-respect in the contemplation of international chaos, which shifted the burden of failure from individual shoulders. Education could and at its best did create a new world of ideas to bring companionship and restoration of courage to men and women stunned by personal disaster."

In this particular department of national rehabilitation, I was now to become involved.

III

My LECTURES THAT autumn began and mainly
continued in the Middle West, which I had once dis-
paragingly pictured to my mother as "mainly agricultural,
not very cultured, very 'moral', very narrow and bigoted".

But when I actually arrived in that comprehensive region,
I found that it was even less possible to generalise accurately
about the "mentality of the Middle West" than about
an England which contains London, Plymouth, York
and Stoke-on-Trent. Two of the finest college audiences
that I have ever addressed came from Western Reserve
University at Cleveland and the American Association of
University Women at Columbus, Ohio. From Columbus
the president of a student association wrote to me afterwards: "We want you to know that many of us who are
college students of America, accept the challenge given
us by those from whom the War took life and happiness,
and pledge ourselves to the building of a world of peace
and harmony."

The librarians' conventions at Akron, Ohio, and Des
Moines, Iowa, proved exceptionally intelligent and appreciative; the women's clubs at Evanston and Kansas City
gave me a welcome such as no foreigner could forget. As
for "morality", when I lectured in 1937 on "Youth Morals
Today and Yesterday", no audience seemed better able to
appreciate what I was trying quite frankly to convey, than
the Town Hall audience at Toledo, Ohio.

On the evening of October 4th, 1934, I left the comforting protection of Macmillan hospitality for my first
lecture at Wheeling, West Virginia. In the sleeper I tried
to stifle my lively apprehensions by re-reading a letter
received from my lecture manager earlier in the year:

"It is not often that I give a lecturer any inkling of my
plans, but I am so sold on you as a person who will make

good in America that I am giving you the highest references. . . . We anticipate one of the most successful tours
ever booked for a European writer."

But this flattering testimonial was now quite useless. As
the train hurried me south-west from New York, I could only
wish forlornly that I was equally "sold" on myself, for I had
suddenly lost confidence that any success which might have
been mine on English platforms could possibly be repeated
in this alarming country which I had to learn all over again.

At Wheeling early next morning, when I took possession
of the handsome suite overlooking the giant Ohio River
which had been allocated to me for the unexacting sum of
three dollars a day, I felt temporarily cheered by the
illogical reassurance that comfort always brings. The reassurance seemed the greater because the comfort was solid,
middle-class and commercial, and therefore more consistent
with my inborn standards of living than the alluring Manhattan dazzle which even the depression had failed wholly
to quench.

"In appearance," I wrote to England from Wheeling,
"the hotel is much what you might see at Hull or Stoke
or Derby, but how different is the plumbing and the food!
At what provincial English hotel would you get, for four
shillings, the dinner I have just eaten? Fresh shrimp cocktail,
accompanied by celery, olives and a lemon-flavoured
radish on fresh lettuce and served with crisp biscuits, cheese
and plain; fried chicken on waffle with sauce, served with
potatoes hashed in cream and cauliflower; tomato, celery
and lettuce salad with mayonnaise, accompanied by freshly
cooked soft rolls and butter; chocolate ice-cream followed
by coffee with cream. The helpings too are so colossal that
I only seem to take a few spoonfuls from each, and the
receptionist asked me quite anxiously if I hadn't enjoyed
my dinner! Apparently the commercial travellers (here
known as salesmen) who frequent this hotel expect colossal
dinners at a minimum price."

Unhappily the hotel's reception of myself was not an
augury for the audience's reception of my lecture, which

fulfilled my apprehensions by turning out the most unmitigated failure that I have yet had to acknowledge. The
organisation which I addressed had asked me to speak on
Testament of Youth, but my assumption that its members
would therefore have read the book proved quite unwarranted; I did not in fact see a single copy in any shop window
of that industrial town. Nor had I yet acquired the technique
of adapting my English pronunciation to American ears, and
the expectant but highly critical audience only half understood me.

As the lecture season had barely begun, my next engagement (at the Ohio librarians' banquet in Akron) was for
October 9, and the intervening three days in Wheeling gave
me plenty of time to meditate on my unsuccessful start.
From the sitting-room window I could see a dark design
of smoking chimneys, and watch the long flat-bottomed
barges, laden with soft coal from the Appalachian slopes, or
with clay from Georgia and Florida to replenish the Wheeling
potteries, go hooting up and down the Ohio River by
day and night. Yet scarlet cannas and purple convolvulus,
their rich colour undimmed by soot, made bright patterns
in the public squares, and across the river the evening sun
descended flamboyantly over thickly wooded hills.

Having more time to record my impressions than the
tour was again to allow me, I described the city in a long
letter home.

"It looks like a combination of one of the less black
northern English manufacturing towns, and the Danube
just outside Budapest. . . . Today, in addition to writing a
two-thousand-word article for the *New York Herald Tribune*,
and four other letters, I have been for three solitary walks
—to the hills above the town, to an island over one of the
bridges in the middle of the river, and round the town
(an ordinary American provincial town, with everything
built for use and not for beauty). I dare say, fascinating
as the place is, I shall have had enough of it by Monday. . . .
The outskirts of the town have the same unfinished, shacklike
appearance that you get in every American city, as though

they were perpetually engaged in extending it. The effect is rather like the Wembley Exhibition before it was finished; whenever you get off the main street, you are never sure whether you are on a side road, or a temporary path leading to a brickyard. It is astonishing how long a day can seem when you don't speak to a soul, but after New York I am revelling in the quiet. . . . Tonight, looking out into the darkness, the lights on the river and the bridges remind me of the Rhine at Cologne."

Before long I was to discover lecture tours to be essentially lonely affairs, involving the constant alternation of thronging strangers with complete solitude, until the peripatetic lecturer begins to crave passionately for an intimate companion with whom to discuss all the exciting, amusing, exasperating and depressing occurrences that happen without cessation. I soon understood—though so far I have rejected it—the temptation to dissipate the profits of a tour by taking round a wife, husband or secretary as travelling companion.

"S.," I wrote home of a fellow-lecturer, "is bringing her little husband with her to act as secretary; even Mrs. W. on her brief tour is accompanied by a friend; I am one of the few going round alone. And God knows I could do with an accompanying secretary; every day flocks of letters follow me about some of the forty lectures, and have to be read, noted and filed, to say nothing of fan-mail and people who want to entertain me!"

My manager, I related, wished me to stay until January to take a number of lucrative lectures which had suddenly been offered from California. But already, after only a fortnight of the limelight, I had concluded that "not for ten thousand dollars would I extend my tour or abandon the attempt to get home for John's birthday. If I get through this tour all right I shall have all the cash I want for the present, thank you, and after the few spring lectures are over I go into cold storage, quite definitely, for at least a year. . . . A quiet life is *much* pleasanter than anything else in the world, really, though I suppose one needs to have been a 'celebrity' at least once to find it out, and that is why misguided people hanker foolishly after fame."

On the way to Akron I stopped at Pittsburgh for a luncheon given by my publisher's married sister. Shaken though it was by the depression, I had expected this iron and steel city so conveniently situated on the Allegheny, Monongahela and Ohio rivers to be the American equivalent of Sheffield or Birmingham, and was surprised to see rich woods and autumn-tinted valleys clearly vivid through air unpolluted by smoke. No doubt, I thought, remembering how I had stood on the Yorkshire hills above Halifax and looked down upon its silent, smokeless factories in the autumn of 1932, the inhabitants of Pittsburgh would gladly sacrifice this unsullied glory of Indian summer to see all their chimneys smoking again.

I had just alighted from the Wheeling train, and was walking across the Pittsburgh platform to deposit my luggage, when an unknown young woman stepped directly into my path.

"You are Miss Brittain, aren't you? Do you think the happiest marriages are made in youth from passion, or in later life from community of tastes?"

I had hardly recovered sufficiently from this surprise attack by the Press to murmur an incoherent reply, when I was hurried to the steps of a very dirty engine and photographed shaking hands with my long-suffering hostess. The shock interview, when written up, began as follows:

"IT'S BETTER TO MARRY FRIEND THAN LOVER!

"Plunk into Cupid's quiver, Vera Brittain, English author, dropped that bombshell . . ."

At the end of the day, walking warily through the station at Akron to pick up a taxicab from the outer darkness of the unknown city, I expected every shadow to turn into an enterprising reporter who wanted to know my opinion on the next war, companionate marriage, President Roosevelt, or birth control. Publicity, as I was beginning to learn, has one dominant characteristic peculiar to itself. When you have never had it you desire it passionately, but once you have acquired it you spend the rest of your life running away from it. And the faster you run, the more it comes after you.

The taxi carried me through a large, flat industrial town of the size and type of Coventry; its factories, I learnt, made more than half the rubber tyres and tubes produced in the United States. The airship *Akron*, which broke in two in a storm, had been constructed there; from the top of the highest building its huge hangar was still visible, like a clearly defined symmetrical grey cloud.

My impressive hotel, according to its notepaper, provided "Four Hundred and Fifty Rooms with Bath—4-Station Selective Radio in Every Room". A sound like all the selective radios being turned on at once led me to the librarians' convention on the second floor, where I saw— greatly to my relief after the experience at Wheeling—a stall on which a brave display of scarlet and white advertised the presence of *Testament of Youth* and its modest month-old successor, *Poems of the War and After*.

A letter home described the next day's all too typical programme:

9.0.   Breakfast with Miss H., the young local librarian who was acting as my hostess.

9.30–10.30. Simultaneous interview with three reporters representing different newspapers, and two photographers. Questioned on marriage and career, children, domesticity, marriage and career, lecture tour, size of family, husband, marriage and career.

10.30. Sign books at Library Convention stall on second floor of hotel.

11.30. Sign books at O'Neil bookstore on Main Street.

12.30. Lunch with young woman who runs Polsky bookstore on Main Street.

1.30. Hasty dash up to Polsky beauty-parlour to get limp hair shampooed and waved before evening affair.

2.30. Sign books at Polsky bookstore.

3.30. Go out for a drive to country and half-hour walk in woods, followed by tea at country club given by a librarian's married sister. This walk was lovely, in a really wild wooded "Reserve", and quite saved my life. The colours of the trees—varying from a purple-crimson to brilliant orange and gamboge—are quite indescribable; all the hillsides are aflame with colour; can't think why anyone chooses to lecture in the spring.

5.30. Get back in time to change for banquet (gold and blue frock).

6.30. Banquet began—huge affair in enormous hotel room; 500 librarians and about 300 people from outside. . . . The banquet and clearance lasted till 8.45; I then spoke for an hour—the same lecture as I gave at Wheeling but this time it was listened to with enthusiasm. . . . Afterwards much hand-shaking and more books to autograph with affection-ate messages; then dragged off with a very eager group of young librarians. At 10.30 escaped to my room, changed into travelling clothes, packed and caught midnight train to Chicago, fell into it more dead than alive and slept like a dead dog. Like a fool I didn't realise the time changed from Eastern to Central time, giving an extra hour, and got up this morning at 6 a.m. instead of 7!

That exasperating mistake—repeated more than once, and always with the same sense of being malevolently tricked by Fate instead of punished for my own inefficiency—at least gave me an early morning glimpse of Chicago, which I found "as lovely, scintillating and altogether stupendous as one has always imagined. Just after breakfast in the train we suddenly turned the corner from Gary, Indiana, to the shore of Lake Michigan, and there, an hour's journey away on the other side of the Lake, I first caught sight of the skyscrapers of Chicago's water-front, like Titans in

white shining armour. . . . Imagine Regent Street placed
on the English Channel, and you get a Lilliputian idea of
what Chicago is like."

In the great spreading city one of my publishers' many
representatives, who seemed to spring from the earth like
benevolent genii wherever I appeared, took me in charge
and gave me a second breakfast. All of them, I found,
assumed that I should have to be accompanied everywhere
until I described my previous American experiences, and
emphasized my years of discretion by talking firmly about
the War. But I was not sorry to have an escort, just before
it closed, through the Chicago World's Fair, "A Century
of Progress", laid out in a gigantic jigsaw puzzle of white,
scarlet and canary-yellow advertisement palaces between
the lake shore and Michigan Avenue. The riotous Sunday
afternoon medley of crowds, megaphones, noise and colour
suggested that a magnified Coney Island had married a
glorified Wembley and was now on honeymoon.

At my hotel overlooking Lake Michigan in a quieter
section of the city, I had already been greeted by a pile
of letters and telephone messages, and a box of choice pink
roses from Harold Latham, who was in Chicago on one
of his periodic quests for literary talent. Two days later, a
Macmillan luncheon arranged for me at the Blackstone
Hotel brought together a group of Chicago writers and
critics whose sophisticated effervescence reminded me how
inadequately heredity and environment had equipped me
for the part which I was striving conscientiously to play.

It was a grand affair which again flouted the depression,
for it started off with sherry and caviar, and the presentation to myself of two lavender orchids as a "buttonhole".
In spite of these pleasant preliminaries I was hardly a
success as a talker, for a return of the disturbing reflections
which had come to me in my lecture manager's office
temporarily subdued such conversational powers as I
possess.

Does every writer, I wonder, experience these moments
when he is suddenly intimidated by the contrast between

the inconspicuous solitude in which his best work is done, and the lavish public welcome which overpowers him as soon as it succeeds? My next-door neighbour, who was discreetly trying to draw me out on American impressions, evidently found the attempt more arduous than he had expected, for the *Chicago Tribune* tersely reported next day:

"Miss Brittain was amiable but not talkative over her luncheon . . . she tactfully avoided answering a guest who asked if she were going to do an E. M. Delafield, author of *The Provincial Lady in America*."

Across the luncheon table, conversation sparkled on topics more appropriate to the lively atmosphere than my own incongruous misgivings. One of the chief guests, the novelist Margaret Ayer Barnes, vivaciously described the astonishment of a contemporary woman friend when she saw the "layout" of *Years of Grace*. Recognising the author's name, her friend read the summary of the plot on the cover and cryptically remarked: "It couldn't possibly be the same person." This tale reminded Harold Latham of a similar story related against herself by a still more famous American novelist, Willa Cather, of her English professor at college. "Willa Cather. . . . Willa Cather. . . . Unh-unh—she didn't write this. Why, she was the dumbest girl in my class!"

That evening I lectured at Oak Park Community Centre, one of the Chicago offshoots of the American forum movement, and afterwards took a midnight train for a series of engagements in Iowa. When I returned to Chicago a few days later, Archie Macdonell, who was on his way to Nebraska, met me at the station. We spent the afternoon and evening together, walking for two hours along the shore of Lake Michigan until the sun set in the vehement vermilion of that amazing autumn and turned to blood the crests of the tiny waves. After dinner at a gay jazz restaurant, known as the Blackhawk, we both left Chicago by night trains, he for Omaha, Nebraska, and I for St. Paul. He was enjoying his trip, he said, except that he felt solitary in the evenings—a reaction with which I sympathised profoundly whenever I had a free enough evening to consider how I felt.

Journeying the previous week to Cedar Rapids, Iowa, I had perceived that in the Middle West it was possible to travel all day and still be passing at sunset through the same flat fields of dried maize-stalks which one had observed at sunrise. Like G. during his Prohibition investigations, I began to realise America's immensity, and the problems, as well as the authority, which this created.

At Clinton, on the border of Illinois and Iowa, I felt the thrill of excitement which surely comes to every traveller who first crosses the Mississippi. But once in Iowa I ceased to notice the miles upon miles of dull yellow prairie parching in the sun, for I compelled myself to read the *Chicago Tribune*, which I had opened that morning to find an account of the assassination at Marseilles of Alexander of Jugoslavia and Louis Barthou.

A day or two later, a cartoon in the *Des Moines Register* showed a smouldering bomb, labelled "The Assassination of King Alexander of Jugoslavia", lying in a puddle of water surrounded by anxious and perspiring national prototypes armed with buckets. In the background towered the disgruntled giant War with his load of unused bombs. The cartoon was entitled "One That Seems Likely Not to Go Off", but no such optimism mitigated the world's first gasp of alarm.

To a solitary European travelling through that sparsely inhabited agricultural area known to New Yorkers as "the sticks", Marseilles seemed only too likely to prove another Sarajevo in a continent darker with inflammable resentments than the Europe of 1914. What if civil war broke out in Jugoslavia between the Croats and Slovenes on the one side and the Serbians on the other? Suppose Italy "intervened", and thus drew France and the other powers into a general conflict? Two weeks afterwards a letter from Winifred Holtby, written on the same day as the political murders, told me that I had not been alone in my apprehensions.

"This assassination in Marseilles," she wrote, "is hideously reminiscent. I heard the news as I was going to take the chair at a women's mass meeting of protest against the Sedition Bill at Whitefield's Tabernacle. When I came in, sick at heart and apprehensive, I found the loud-speaker braying dance music in my room, and as I entered a crooner was wailing: 'Oh, don't let it happen again!' It was the unspoken cry of a thousand listeners that night, I imagine."

At supper in the coffee room of the Cedar Rapids hotel, I was still haunted by despairing thoughts of my helpless children and the width of the Atlantic, when my middle-aged neighbour at the next table—a midwestern farmer travelling to buy stock—stared hard at me for a few moments and then inquired: "Mind if I come over and join you?"

"By all means," I said, for in that mood of apprehension any society, however unselected, was welcome. Urgently I sought, without waiting, for the comfort I wanted. "I've been reading the paper. Isn't it terrible about these Marseilles assassinations?"

He regarded distastefully the startling headlines.

"Huh!" he ejaculated scornfully. "Don't care who they murder over there and who they don't, s'long as we're not dragged in again!"

Though I hadn't received much comfort, I felt some sympathy.

"The political murders of the past few months," I wrote that night to Winifred, "make one realise why Americans say . . . that all they care about is to avoid getting involved in the complications of Europe. It seemed strange today to be in the sun in beautiful, bright, eminently civilised Chicago—which we think of as so dangerous and full of gangsters—and read about the newest instalment of assassinations in the 'safe' Old World!"

By the time that I left Cedar Rapids for a tedious train journey to Des Moines, I felt reluctant to quit the clean sun-washed city where the white cylindrical chimneys of the Quaker Oats factories stood out like ramparts against the azure sky. Later, in New York, I was surprised to find some acquaintances who had never been to Cedar Rapids regarding the place as typical of Main Street at its gloomiest and worst. Throughout my two days there the sun never ceased shining, and the whole town, with its golden trees and friendly people, was pervaded by the warm comfortable smell of a gigantic breakfast perpetually cooking. Immediately I arrived the hotel manager presented me with a basket of flowers, and the ticket clerk, a plump good-natured man who spoke in a unique Yorkshire-American dialect, welcomed me like a long lost relative on the ground that he came from Sheffield.

My lecture, on "The Youth Movement in England", also appeared to please the audience, though a student journalist wrote afterwards in the local paper that it seemed "kind of silly" to hear a lecturer compare the benighted British traditions of her youth with the present enlightened standards of the Middle West. . . . A question period of half an hour followed the hour's lecture. When this was over, a group from the local university accompanied me back to my hotel for a further hour of political catechism.

"The organisations 'which have purchased Miss Brittain' certainly make her work her eight hours a day," I reported to Winifred, but I also described one of those small picturesque actions which spring from the imaginative graciousness of American hospitality. Before the lecture, the organiser's sister took me out to dinner. From publicity paragraphs in the local newspaper she had learnt the names of my children, and beside my plate had put two slim silver vases, each containing a red rose and labelled "John" and "Shirley" on tiny cards in the handwriting of her thirteen-year-old daughter. I have the cards still, and the silver vases—so conveniently small and slender—decorate our dining-room table at home.

Before I drove to the station an amiable reporter acted as my guide to the outsize white Memorial Coliseum, which dominates like a titanic toy the compact bridge over the Cedar River. Its stained-glass window, she told me proudly, was one of the largest in the world, and the figures protected by a huge symbolical deity presiding over equally symbolical skyscrapers represented the six historical types of American soldier. Beneath these figures ran an inscription:

"May the wreaths they have worn never wither,
    Nor the star of their glory grow dim."

Reading it, I meditated—as once long ago at G.'s university—upon the American passion for material embodiments of spiritual emotions which I now mentally christened "white-elephantism". Why did this hard-headed, efficient people spend immense sums upon erecting memorials—a costly trail of civic extravagance stretching across the world from California to the colossal granite pillar overlooking the Argonne from the heights of Montfaucon—to commemorate the dead who represented such a tiny proportion of their population, in a War which so many now remembered only to regret?

If the money so frozen had been spent on rehabilitating the live "underprivileged", would not one major problem of the depression be partly solved? But perhaps, I reflected, if wealthy donors had not been persuaded to contribute to these impressive symbols of municipal pride, the gilded minority later to become notorious as "America's 60 Families" would merely have given more gala dinners or doubled the floral decorations at their débutantes' balls! In that event, it was better that American wealth should be transmuted into civic temples of granite and marble which put to shame the many unsightly public buildings of the lethargic Old World.

THANKS TO THE Iowa railways, which compelled me to travel six hours in order to cover ninety miles, the trip to Des Moines, the capital of that agrarian state, was not the least uncomfortable of several similar expeditions.

An accident on the line, causing two of the few Pullman car deaths of the past five years, had disorganized the whole Rock Island system just in time for my journey. Halfway to Des Moines, my train crawled cautiously through the gruesome wreckage of the damaged sleepers, their framework and berths a twisted mass of buckled metal which I resolutely refused to remember the next time I travelled at night.

"The railway system in Iowa is atrocious," I told Winifred, "though the people there say you should see what it's like in South Dakota. . . . You go through miles upon miles of maize-filled, slightly wooded prairies, with hardly a house or settlement to be seen in between the small towns great distances apart. I had to change at a ghastly little junction in the middle of a huge rolling prairie, called West Liberty, but the only liberty I could see was freedom to carry my own suitcases! There was no porter there, and the railway men watched with interest and chewed gum while I lugged my quite considerable hand-luggage down an enormously long platform in the sweltering heat of an Indian summer afternoon. Finally the conductor of the train I had just got off took pity on me and carried the largest."

Afterwards, when a Rock Island Railway official appeared at Des Moines to inquire solicitously after my comfort, I told him very firmly exactly what I thought about the arrangements for handling passengers' luggage at West Liberty. He left me protesting that the situation should be remedied, and in fact it was, for on my next change at the

place described in my letters as "that damned little
junction", efficient help was promptly forthcoming. When I
used uncompromising language to my manager on the
subject of train routes in Iowa, he told me that I had a
"West Liberty complex". Perhaps I had; subsequent
experience in the South during 1937 was to teach me that in
the Middle West I had by no means plumbed the depths
of discomfort which a primitive train service can inflict.
But if, by my complaints, I persuaded the Iowa state
railways to treat travellers stranded at West Liberty less
like the tiresome scum of the American transport system,
my Iowa engagements were not made in vain.

In consequence of the railway accident and the long wait
at West Liberty, I descended frantically from the train at
Des Moines with only ten minutes to spare before the
lecture was scheduled to begin. The representative of the
Iowa state librarians, who had been waiting quite as
frantically at the station, saved a few moments by addressing
me immediately I set foot on the platform. Her efficiency
was explained afterwards by a paragraph in the Iowa
Authors Club Magazine.

"Mrs. Frederick W. Weitz, who was to meet the visiting
author on her arrival at the station, had been warned previously to pick out the traveller with the largest piles of
luggage—and truly enough by this means readily identified
Miss Brittain. En route on a lecture tour of forty engagements, the lecturer was feminine enough to wish to carry
plenty of costumes along."

As I dashed to the hotel to drink some soup and change
into a dinner frock while an amateur soloist entertained the
waiting audience, a female reporter, to my dismay,
materialised from the empty air. With the characteristic
pertinacity of American reporters, she refused to allow such
minor considerations as my hunger, fatigue and urgency
to deflect her from her job.

I was asked, I reported afterwards, "most intricate questions . . . about what I thought of the American insurance
system, although I kept telling her that I knew nothing of

American politics from the inside. When we got to the hotel she stuck to me like a leech, came with me up to my bedroom and stood about and asked me ridiculous questions while I tried to think in a hurry what I wanted to wear and where all the things were packed, unpack, wash myself, change, and swallow some dinner. I could gladly have killed her; for the first time since I came to this country I felt thoroughly irritated, and I quite expect an adverse 'write-up' as I couldn't prevent the irritation showing in my voice. Feeling thoroughly dishevelled and angry, I went downstairs to lecture to 600 librarians on 'Should Autobiographies Be Forbidden?'"

By one of the incalculable contradictions of fate the talk was a success, though I did not know this until I found, on my 1937 lecture list, a return engagement with the Iowa librarians. At the end of the evening they carried me off to a private house where I was surprised to discover several admirers of *Mandoa, Mandoa!* Winifred Holtby's brilliant satire on British Imperialism. This audacious novel did not reach so many American readers as her posthumous *South Riding*, and I had not expected to find enthusiasts for it in Iowa. I soon learnt that Des Moines was an oasis of vitality in the midst of Middle Western isolationism. From its numerous discussion forums, progressive schools, intelligent preachers and enlightened newspapers, its sociable inhabitants had acquired a better understanding of events in Europe than the students at many American universities.

In the *Des Moines Register* for October 12th, I found that Harvey Ingham, the author of an article entitled "Where the Next War is Likely to Break", quoted a contribution to the *Christian Science Monitor* by the Marquis of Lothian, with whom we had crossed on the *Berengaria*. In his article Lord Lothian had described the freedom of the seas (one of the questions, like the Debt, on which I was most often catechised), as "the hidden serpent which lurks in the middle of the Atlantic waiting suddenly to poison the relations between the two countries and even to bring them to the

Ls

verge of conflict unless its existence is recognised and its power to harm is sterilised."

The *Des Moines Register* writer concluded with truth: "Britain and the United States had the opportunity at the close of the war to put English-speaking democracy over the world by common consent, and the British and American navies could have policed the world into a decent regard for the new order. Does anybody believe that any of the things that have happened in the last fifteen years would have happened if Britain and the United States had gone together at the end of the War?"

It is a reflection which has often occurred to some of us during these sorrowful days of 1938. A juster and stronger League of Nations, with America as a member, could have saved Germany from post-war persecution, checked the growth of Fascism, defended Manchuria, protected Abyssinia, and rescued Spain.

Before I returned to Chicago next morning, a drive round the city showed me that the autumn exterior of Des Moines was quite as agreeable as its eager inhabitants. In the still undiminished sunshine its ecstatic trees shone like celestial mops turned upside down, and the gilded dome of the State Capitol gleamed with the burnished arrogance of a pagan temple. Round beds of cannas and salvia in the public gardens made bright circles of yellow and scarlet upon an orange carpet of fallen leaves.

My escort—the librarian who had met me at the station—supplied the Iowa Authors Club Magazine with personal impressions of our tour.

"Driving the visitor around Des Moines was quite a pleasure, according to Mrs. Weitz. Frankly enjoying our Middle West, Miss Brittain inquired about the capitol buildings which had been pointed out to her in every state capital and wondered what in the world went on inside (a point occasionally mysterious to the rest of us, too). She thought it strange that the state and federal governments didn't get mixed up, and was curious as to the nature of the strictly American 'Funeral Home', of which Des Moines offers a number of fine examples . . ."

Since that day I must have passed several hundred "Funeral Homes" and "Funeral Parlours", with their arresting illuminated signs hung out to persuade the bereaved that even mortality need not be a gloomy affair. They are, I believe, "strictly American" institutions because most Americans are so busy living and planning for tomorrow that death does not normally enter into their picture of the universe, and when it occurs they prefer to pretend that it is not so stark a fact as it appears. Talk to an active, vigorous American about death or serious illness, and he will change the subject with every symptom of evasive discomfort.

The women, perhaps, run away from the topic less anxiously than the men, for women, except in war, live closer to death, and are constantly brought face to face with it by the basic facts of their physiology. But even the small-town wives of my first America, though some of them discussed minor illnesses by the hour, stopped short of the morbid conversations habitual to English "mothers' meetings", where it is only necessary to mention that some acquaintance has died of cancer or appendicitis to start the whole assembly debating symptoms, operation procedure, last words, death agonies and burial rites for the rest of the afternoon.

The American attitude is healthier, no doubt, yet somehow the uncompromising word "mortuary" calls up in my mind less gruesome an image than the euphemistic "funeral parlour", which suggests the process of human corruption beginning amid the indoor stuffiness of heavy window draperies and china vases filled with wilting flowers. One does not really escape from the crude facts of dissolution by this solemn pretence. Running away from death may be due to a superabundance of vitality, but it may also argue the lack of a philosophy, since no philosophy of life is complete which does not include a clear-eyed acceptance of the fact of death. This acceptance is a function of maturity, impossible to children; perhaps it is also impossible to a young country still in process of working out its scheme of values.

For us in Europe—where the future, if the present threat of war fulfils its dreadful possibilities, may well be so much shorter than the past—our dead are constantly with us; we live looking back towards the long ages from which those whom we have lost still speak to us. But America, with her eyes upon her illimitable future, is disinclined to let her thoughts dwell upon the men and women who have departed and can no longer co-operate in the great vital experiment. Her living citizens are unwilling to discuss them, or to visit their graves more often than etiquette demands; there is even a prejudice against publishing a book by a recently dead author unless the illusion can be maintained that he is still alive. But as though lavish expenditure could compensate their dead for this reluctance of memory, the Americans put up inordinately extravagant tombstones, and even in the smaller cities turn their cemeteries into beautiful parks.

In the middle of October I began, for the first time since leaving New York, to wonder if I really had sufficient stamina to continue my tour. That week had included six lectures and five night journeys, culminating in a fifteen-hour trip to Mason City, Iowa, after my address at the Oak Park Community Centre.

Early in the morning I changed at the inevitable West Liberty for a one-car "local", which jogged for five hours from north to south Iowa. No meals were served on either train, and I should have had nothing to eat between a six o'clock dinner in Chicago the previous evening and a belated two o'clock luncheon at Mason City, had not my kindly negro sleeping porter run out to the buffet on Rock Island station at 6 a.m. for a carton of coffee and a fried egg sandwich. The temperature of the one-car train made me acutely conscious of the drastic physical adaptability required of English visitors by the American heating system, for the steam pipes raised it to boiling point in sublime disregard of the fact that we were travelling across the sun-blasted Iowa prairies at the height of the unremitting heat-wave.

After I had squirmed miserably for the first two hours upon a burning red plush seat which suggested the presence of an open volcano immediately beneath, a typical Middle Western dust storm blew up, filling the miniature train with so much black grit that everything I was wearing had to go next day to the cleaners. From the junction at which I alighted, hot, late and dirty, I had to drive ten miles to my destination, gulp down a hasty lunch, and appear on the lecture platform without having time to change my travelling dress or get rid of the grit filling eyes, nose, mouth and hair.

Blind with dust, heat and fatigue, I delivered the lecture as one in a nightmare and hardly realised what replies I gave to the numerous questions from an audience composed of the local women's club and a number of college students. I was the first English lecturer that the inhabitants of Mason City had ever heard, and as they can hardly have derived a favourable impression of the British race from my grubby and exhausted person, I was probably the last.

Travelling on to St. Louis that evening by yet another night train, I lay in my berth dismally reckoning up the extraneous disadvantages of American lecture tours for English lecturers. Forlornly I contemplated the perpetual rush of engagements, the overwhelming speed of living, the superheated rooms and trains, the absence of afternoon tea with its pulverising effect upon evening work, the gathering snowball of correspondence which each day's programme left no hour of leisure to answer. This burden of letters still seems to me the most terrifying obligation of a tour. They pile up and up . . . until late hours which should be devoted to sleep, or long train journeys which would otherwise provide a welcome rest between engagements, are desperately used to dispose of them somehow.

Do the generous correspondents who write so fully and charmingly of a lecturer's appearance, voice, clothes and character, realise the difficulty of finding time even to read these letters, let alone reply? Do the hospitable admirers of the lecturer's writings, who invite him to spend weeks in places far distant from the cities where his lectures are booked, feel snubbed because his answers are so brief? When I re-read my correspondence after a tour is ended, my inadequate replies fill me with shame, yet I can understand why some speakers abandon the hopeless task in despair and make no reply at all. Before my first tour was far advanced I was leaving most of these letters to my tactful Macmillan secretary, who disposed of them with an efficient cordiality to which I could never aspire.

By one of those strange coincidences which so often happened in our correspondence, a letter from Winifred Holtby awaited me at St. Louis, describing an unnecessary operation on a friend whose life was miserably dominated by nervous fears.

"After reading your letter," I wrote in reply, "I was at once reminded how much better it is to take risks with one's health . . . than to be a slave to the fear of doing one's self harm." The first thing to discard on a tour, I told her, was every attribute of invalidism; even the few practical instructions given me by a doctor before I left England were usually impossible to fulfil.

"You have no idea how ludicrously idealistic all Dr. H's rules and regulations appear! I never have a meal at the same hour two days running; I seem to feed either off banquets or snacks; the things I am supposed to take before or after meals are always either packed or else miles from where the meal is being held! In any case all meals are too large, and too infrequent, and too indigestible—and yet I have so far felt none the worse. . . . *Quite* the worst part of this queer existence is that as well as being the star performer one has to be one's own maid, secretary and laundress. . . . I'd give worlds to have someone to find the dress, hat and shoes which I invariably have to find and fling on as soon as I get to a place, straighten up my boxes and put things away, as well as wash my stockings and

gloves, and last but not least help with the vast correspondence from fan-mails and organisers of the remaining
lectures which follows me round. I haven't yet dissolved
into tears once, even from fatigue, but I never feel so much
inclined to do so as when I open my boxes and see the
ghastly condition of my clothes on which I spent so much
time and money. . . . In a queer way this tour reminds me
of the War, or rather, what I felt like during it. One's
utmost is continually being required of one—and yet all the
time there is a sort of stimulus, a queer excitement and
anticipation, that carries one through."

St. Louis delighted me; its urban immensity guaranteed
main-line trains and other advantages of metropolitan
civilisation. The women's club to which I lectured was
friendly and appreciative, but far more clearly than the
club or the lecture I remember seeing, for the first time, an
American blue jay. A vivid cerulean streak with white tips
to his tail, and black and white bars across his beautiful
wings, he flapped, as Audubon has painted him, against the
thick boughs of a flowering shrub in Forest Park.

Three days later, in Terre Haute, Indiana, my spirits
again descended to zero, and I began to realise that even if
a lecturer is fortunate enough to bring an even disposition
to his undertaking, the ups and downs of a tour will soon
endow him with as many moods as the most temperamental
film star. This time neither failure nor fatigue explained my
despondency, but the sad aftermath of the depression in
that black, dejected town. The American equivalent of
Wolverhampton, its chief claim to celebrity lay in the fact
that it had been the birthplace and political training-
ground of the great American Socialist, Eugene Debs.

"I could hardly see for headache when I arrived," ran
another letter home, "but successfully got rid of all but a
vague feeling of neuralgia in taking a walk—though there
was nowhere to walk except through rows upon rows of
grimy parallel streets between tumble-down frame houses
with the paint peeling off them, and their front 'gardens'
hidden beneath piles of fallen leaves and scattered paper. I

imagine that one would learn more about the depression from a few days here than from weeks in New York and Chicago."

When I discovered, in the main street, a "Labour Temple" dedicated to the memory of Debs, I thought it might prove an appropriate place for acquiring that further economic knowledge. Going in, I found a small office in charge of two stalwart guardians.

"Good morning," I began politely. "I'm an English Socialist, and I'd like to know more about the Labour Temple and this town."

"Eh?" inquired one high priest, while the other scratched his head. I repeated my question, and my fellow Socialists made replies to what they believed it to have been, but our respective languages were so reciprocally unintelligible that five minutes failed to enlighten them on the purpose of my visit, or myself on the origin of the temple. We parted with gestures of friendship and esteem, but had they or I been speaking Hungarian, our mutual understanding would have been no less.

On October 27th, at Cleveland, Ohio, I gave the last lecture for nearly a month in the Middle West. The railway line which passes through Cleveland between Chicago and Buffalo has now become one of the most familiar journeys in the United States, but whenever my train crosses Lake Erie—an American time-saving method which has never ceased to fascinate me—I am still enthralled by its beauty. On that first occasion the wind was blowing the water into wavelets, which reflected—like the waves on Lake Michigan ten days before—the vivid fire of the late autumn sunset.

Cleveland also was full of wind; it tore round the skyscrapers and tugged at the tall, high window of my bedroom in the Wade Park Manor Hotel. Since I entered the city after dark and was unable to take my bearings until the next morning, it was here that I first awakened with the bewildering queries which were to repeat themselves again and again during the next few weeks.

"Where am I? What's this hotel? Which city have I slept in this time?"

But half the night seemed to pass before I could even begin the process of going to bed. After four annihilating days in the Twin Cities, and eighteen hours' travel of which I had spent nine in answering accumulated correspondence, I arrived at Cleveland to find seventeen more letters full of problems, and a large pile of books sent for autographs by a local store.

One of the letters was from Storm Jameson. It contained the laconic and appropriate comment: "Your tour sounds just like hell opened."

V

WHEN THE CLEVELAND lecture was over, I turned with a sigh of relief to the next series of engagements:

October 29th. Toronto, Canada. Metropolitan Church.
October 30th. Toronto, Canada. Empire Club.
November 1st. Boston, Mass. League of Nations Association.
November 2nd. Wellesley, Mass. Dana Hall Schools.
November 5th. Fall River, Mass. Women's Club.
November 6th. Worcester, Mass. Clark University.

At last, I thought, I shall get ten days' respite from the driving energy of the northern states and the Middle West. In Canada, and perhaps even in New England, I can lean back for a short time upon the jog-trot leisureliness of British civilisation.

No illusion could have been more complete.

With the possible exception of Dallas, Texas, I found Toronto the most energetic city that I had yet visited on the American continent. I left it with the consciousness that, in Canada as in the United States, my background was too deliberate and my hereditary pace too slow for the robust vigour of New World standards.

My coming, I learnt, had been preceded by a long Press campaign. The Empire Club, where one of my feminine predecessors had been Lady Snowden, announced that I was only the third woman in its history to address it; and on the day after I appeared from Cleveland to find the Indian summer abruptly ended and the first winter snow powdering the railway tracks, the Toronto *Mail and Empire* devoted a leading article to my arrival in the city. The result, as I confessed later to Winifred, was "thrilling to the spirit, but rather devastating to that ass, the body."

"In the 3½ days," I wrote her at the end of my visit, "I not only gave my two big lectures, but did a broadcast interview with a perfectly charming young man, on *Testament of Youth* and my pacifist and League of Nations ideas; was given 4 luncheons, 3 dinners and 2 big teas; was interviewed 4 times by star reporters on 4 different papers; photographed 3 times; answered (by dictation, thank God, to a Macmillan secretary) about 100 letters written me from all parts of Canada; held a seminar with the Canadian League of Nations Society, answering their questions; visited a pioneer nursing centre and made a (seated) speech to the Canadian P.E.N. Club. . . . I was deluged with flowers; my room was full of orchids and roses of all colours; the Canadian Authors' Association made an official presentation to me of a bouquet of pink and cream roses at the Macmillan office; I got more from Macmillan themselves, and *dear* G. got them to present me on his behalf with a huge bouquet of orange and gold roses when I had just finished the Empire Club speech. It was all so exciting and exhausting that in a few minutes at my hotel between engagements the second morning, I found . . . that tears were pouring down my face—partly from tiredness, partly from a feeling that I hadn't got the right sort of impressive presence for all this publicity and could never live up to it."

Winifred's reply was characteristic.

"The Toronto episode reads more like the Prince of Wales having allied himself with the Salvation Army than anything else! The mixture of enthusiasm and prestige, hustle and discomfort, with moments of what must be very real enjoyment and satisfaction."

After only three days in the city, I began to realise how incorrect were some of the assumptions held about one another by British and Canadians who had never crossed the Atlantic. Many Englishmen picture Canada as a rough-and-ready country whose inhabitants practise crude methods of agriculture and industry, and live under wretchedly primitive conditions; yet the material sophistication of urban Canada made London seem medieval in its chilly discomfort, and agricultural Canada, so far as I could learn, rewarded best those pioneers whose open-minded empiricism was ready to test the latest scientific theory. Many Canadians appear to regard England as a proud, stubborn, ultraconservative Motherland, who endangers her world prestige by obstinate adherence to antiquated traditions; yet the little I know of Canada suggests that some of her inhabitants out-England even England in their passionate allegiance to the external symbols of respectability.

Comparing Canada, the one Dominion that I have so far visited, with Winifred Holtby's impressions of South Africa, I suspect that many conventions die even harder in some parts of the British Dominions than in the Mother country, and a great deal harder in both than they die in the United States. I doubt whether, with the possible exception of a few communities in New England and the South, there is any American city in which a newspaper editor, to whom my publisher had supplied a photograph of "Miss Vera Brittain and her two children", could have been rung up, as he was the next morning, by an indignant lady righteously inquiring why a portrait of "this notorious woman and her illegitimate children" had been allowed to appear in his respectable pages.

Physically an American city, Toronto showed itself only the more determined to maintain inviolate its respectful allegiance to the customs and social assumptions of the British Empire.

A fragment of paper surviving from this Toronto visit contains a scribbled "Programme for Monday", with "Programme for Tuesday" on the back. "Programme for Monday" ran as follows:

10.0. Macmillan office. Interview R. E. Knowles and Mrs. Howard.
11.0. Visit School of Nursing.
1.0. P.E.N. Club luncheon.

3.0. Photograph by Violet Keene.
7.0. Dinner, Government House.
8.30. Lecture, Eaton Auditorium.

The Toronto School of Nursing—one of the few institutions, among many that I was invited to visit, to which
instinct and the quality of a preliminary letter guided me—
had been described by its Director, Miss Kathleen Russell,
as "a little new nursing school . . . tucked under the wing
of the University (of Toronto) for administrative purposes".

In it, she told me, every one of those "unimaginative
stupidities" of the nursing profession against which I had
protested in *Testament of Youth*, "is being attacked roundly.
It is not possible that you could know anything about us
but it is a fact that we have here a training school for
nurses that might have been planned by yourself."

How could any erstwhile crusader resist such an appeal?
I went to the little school, sat amongst the comely young
students for an hour answering their questions, and came
away convinced that Miss Kathleen Russell had lighted one
of those small significant candles of progress which would
ultimately illumine a still backward profession.

At the P.E.N. Club luncheon and other functions, Mr.
Hugh S. Eayrs, President of the Macmillan Company of
Canada, who was my host in Toronto, supplied me with a
list of "those present". It was an efficient gesture which I
would gladly have seen repeated everywhere, for the guest
of honour seldom discovers the names of all the other
guests invited to meet him, and often learns too late that
he has been within a few yards of someone whom throughout his life he has wanted to know. The invaluable list
showed me that I was meeting a distinguished group—Lady
Willison, the President of the Canadian P.E.N.; Morley
Callaghan, the novelist; Professor Pelham Edgar, Canada's
most famous critic; Dr. (now Sir) Charles G. D. Roberts,
nature study writer and poet; and Professor G. M. Wrong,
the historian. But even this eminent gathering represented
a mere foretaste of what was to come a few hours later.

I had never experienced a more terrifying evening. Nothing on the American continent was to alarm me so much as my lecture at the Eaton Auditorium, and the State dinner at Government House which preceded it, until I lunched with Mrs. Roosevelt at the White House in 1937. I soon learnt that my host, the Lieutenant Governor of Ontario (the Hon. Dr. Herbert A. Bruce, the first medical man to hold the position), was to take the chair at the lecture. My fellow guests, amongst whom were the editors-in-chief of the Toronto *Mail and Empire*, and Toronto *Saturday Night*, probably found me less amiable and no more talkative than I had been at the Chicago luncheon party, though the Governor and his wife—who were so strangely linked with my war-time past—did their kindly and courteous best to mitigate the formality of the occasion.

"He is a perfect darling with penetrating blue eyes and curly white hair," I testified gratefully afterwards. "During the War he was in France as an operating surgeon with the R.A.M.C. of Canada, and curiously enough I remember seeing him at Étaples, as the Canadian Hospital, 26 General, which he used to inspect, was next door to ours. His wife, much younger than he and very charming, was an English V.A.D.; he met her at Wimereux, though how he was ever allowed to see enough of her to marry her is an unexplained mystery! He made a delightful little speech to introduce me."

Before the lecture, I was warned that the auditorium would be packed. Every seat had been sold, chairs were placed in the passages outside, I was supplied with a microphone, and the Metropolitan Church, which had arranged the lecture as part of a rebuilding campaign after a disastrous fire, made a considerable profit.

Trembling with terror lest my speaking powers should suddenly desert me after all this preparation (does the same periodic fear of being stricken dumb assail all lecturers, I wonder), I followed the Governor on to the platform. At once, upon my intimidated eyes, burst the most awe-inspiring vision of dress clothes and sparkling, beflowered evening gowns that I had ever beheld. I was accustomed by now to the vastness and elegance of American audiences, but this imposing tribute to the Old Country through my inadequate person opened up a new vista of experience, and I only wished that I possessed the dignified proportions to live up to the expectations of my listeners. As it was, I blessed the forethought of my host and publisher, who had given me a double spray of purple orchids, and urged me to make the best of my insignificant stature (though he put it more politely) by appearing in my best evening gown.

I realised the value of his advice the next day, when a leading Toronto newspaper omitted any report of the lecture, but gave a paragraph to the description of my frock—a flamboyant affair of gold tissue and sapphire velvet—and enthusiastically commended me for possessing "dress sense". Not for the last time I realised that what New World lecturing really demands, especially from a woman, is neither the fervour of an artist nor the intelligence of a scholar, but the histrionic endowments of a film star.

On the back of the crumpled fragment of notepaper, I can still read the pencilled details of "Programme for Tuesday":

11.30. Discuss broadcast with Mr. W. Strange.
12.30. Luncheon and address for Empire Club of Toronto.
3.0.   Photograph by Jay.
3.15. Prepare broadcast speech.
4.0.   University Women's Club tea.
6.30. Rehearsal of broadcast.
7.0.   Broadcast from CFRB.
8.0.   Dinner, Empire Club Chairman.

As the broadcast had been thrust at the last moment into a time-table already overcrowded, and the University Women's Club tea—which I had been assured was a small affair to meet the executive committee—involved a hand-shake and a few moments' conversation with each of its two hundred members, it was perhaps not remarkable that I collapsed in the midst of the dinner party which concluded the day, and spent the rest of the evening ignominiously lying on my hostess's bed instead of playing the expected rôle of honoured guest. But even when I returned to my hotel, humiliated, sick, and shivering with cold, I could not go to bed, for the numerous functions which I had attended had used up my entire wardrobe, and Wednesday's arrangements left no adequate interval for packing before I caught the night train to Boston.

Somehow I survived, for my letters show that early next morning, though rather shaky about the legs, I managed to continue the programme.

9.30. Correspondence in Macmillan office.
11.0. League of Nations Union discussion.
1.0. Lunch Lady Willison.
Afternoon. Visit 4 bookstores.

I conclude that I must have rested and recovered in that evening train. There certainly seems to have been no other opportunity.

Although the broadcast interview appeared, at the time, to be a heavy additional burden, it was probably the most effective of the Toronto engagements, for it was relayed over the Province of Ontario and adjacent areas of Canada and the United States, and thus reached a larger if less impressive audience than that of the previous night. My gifted young interviewer, William Strange (whom I described in a letter as "a sort of Canadian Vernon Bartlett, but mostly on books"), suggested that our discussion should move from the particular to the general. We would begin, he said, by referring to my own writings, and thus lead up to a talk on peace and the League of Nations—in which I still hoped, though the hope had faded a little since my eager work for the Non-Partisan Association in 1926. Our carefully prepared conversation gave my *vis-à-vis* the opportunity to describe Canada as a pacifist country:

W. S. "One gathers that your war-time experiences have made you into a confirmed pacifist?"

V. B. "Yes. My pacifist philosophy, such as it is, is largely due to personal experience."

W. S. "And yet there were those who professed to be enjoying the War!"

V. B. "Well, I always want to know just what part those people played in it, and they're not always willing to tell me."

W. S. "I am pursuing this line of discussion for a very good reason. I think that it can be said, without fear of contradiction, that Canada is perhaps the most definitely pacifist country in the world. It is even an open question whether the majority of Canadians would be willing to take up arms on some future occasion without a great deal of pressure being brought to bear on them. We have no army, navy or air force worth speaking about and are less interested in what people call the 'art' of war than the English. It would not be fair to claim any particular credit for this attitude, for I think that most people will admit that we rely—unconsciously perhaps—upon the Old Country to look after matters of this kind. It may be said of Canada— only with far more truth—as was said of England by the little German student in that section of your book entitled "Piping for Peace", 'Oh, you in England don't know what Europe is. How can you? You're so *safe*.' It is because of our remoteness from the complexities of the European diplomatic madhouse that our worries about these things are secondhand worries, dulled by distance and lulled possibly by ignorance."

Canada, I agreed, was fortunate in her geographical position on a war-threatened earth. I might have added that she was doubly fortunate in her immediate neighbour. I knew already that the Rush-Bagot Convention, which brought about disarmament on the Great Lakes and established the undefended frontier in 1818, had been one of the great historic triumphs of rational nineteenth century diplomacy, and the more time I spent on the American

M s

continent, the more clearly I perceived that war between the United States and Canada was as inconceivable as war between England and Scotland.

I came out of the studio to find a young woman waiting for me in the entrance hall of the broadcasting station. Her face was vaguely familiar, and I understood why when she said that she had been a V.A.D. nurse at the 1st London General Hospital in Camberwell, where I was posted at the end of 1915.

"I was ill in bed when you left for Malta," she told me, "and you came up to say good-bye."

She was now married to a minister at Aylmer, Ontario, and learning from the newspapers that I was lecturing in Toronto, had travelled two hundred miles in the hope of seeing me. After trying all day to trace my movements, she had tracked me down at last to the broadcasting station.

I was sorry that our conversation had to be so brief, for I was due in fifteen minutes at the ill-fated dinner party, and had already become conscious of a perplexing lightness in the head and a disturbing uncertainty about the feet. Whatever, I wondered, could have made the long expedition worth her while? I left the broadcasting station feeling humbled and a little ashamed.

In Boston I actually found a measure of the peace for which I now craved with weary desperation. This respite, as I soon realised, was due rather to the stubborn protection given me by my English host, Professor T. N. Whitehead of Harvard, than to any exceptional demonstration of self-restraint on the part of the population.

I had never met North Whitehead or his wife Margaret before; I accepted their invitation to stay with them in Cambridge, Massachusetts, because he had written me one of the two most moving letters that I received among the many hundreds which followed *Testament of Youth*. The other letter, curiously enough, came also from Massachusetts, but its author was an American, R. Minturn Sedgwick, nephew of Ellery Sedgwick, the famous editor of the

Atlantic Monthly. I had already met this immensely tall and disarming young man in Chicago, and before I left New England the Whiteheads and I dined with him and his wife at Dedham, Massachusetts.

As a fellow guest he had tactfully invited one of my kindest reviewers, Edward Weeks of the *Atlantic*, slender, keen-faced and dynamic, who in his turn took me to see the great Ellery Sedgwick himself at the *Atlantic* office in Boston. Mr. Sedgwick, whose lionlike dignity recalled that of an eminent British war-time editor, Clement Shorter of the *Sphere*, catechised me with ironic but unimpeachable courtesy, and then invited me, to my astonished delight, to write him an article about my tour. It appeared under the title "Listeners English and American" the following June.

As my four New England engagements were all accessible from Cambridge I spent five days with the Whiteheads, thankfully finding relaxation in the unostentatious quiet of their apartment and the friendly disorder of books and papers so reminiscent of Oxford and my Chelsea household.

"He is, as I think you know," I wrote to Winifred, "the son of A. N. Whitehead of *Science and the Modern World* (a very great old man with whom I dined two nights ago). It is *queer* being suddenly back in the Oxford (or rather Cambridge, England) atmosphere after the Middle West. T. N. Whitehead is like his letters, one of the most charming, gentle and perceptive people I ever met . . . who appears to have shown the most astonishing courage and had the most extraordinary adventures during the War (through having had an engineer's training when they were short of engineers he actually got out in time for the retreat from Mons, and later volunteered for East Africa and went all through that campaign). From his present appearance and manner . . . you'd never believe it, except that the whole War was incompatible with everything normal."

As soon as I had lectured for the League of Nations Association at the Boston Repertory Theatre—with Professor Manley Hudson as Chairman and a pulverising audience of

Boston *élite* and Harvard intellectuals—North and Margaret Whitehead answered their telephone and guarded their front door with implacable vigilance. Thanks to this generous transference to themselves of the perpetual interruptions which beset a lecturer who is rash enough to spend nearly a week in one city, I was able to shift the piled-up avalanche of my correspondence, and prepare an isolated lecture on Journalism for the Brooklyn Institute of Arts and Sciences.

Occasionally, when each of us could steal half an hour's leisure, North Whitehead took me for brisk walks and talks in the sharp November wind beside the Charles River, its bright serpentlike coils reflecting as in a live mirror the golden maples on its banks. Their yellow leaves, loosened by the frost, fell in vivid showers beneath a clear autumn sky shading from deep sapphire to pale aquamarine.

From Cambridge a young representative of my publishers' Boston office drove me to lectures at Fall River, Wellesley, and Clark University. The last of these followed a cold and windy forty-mile run to Worcester over dark, open moorlands, which was compensated by a friendly welcome from Professor Dodd of Clark University and one of the pleasantest audiences that I met throughout my tour. Fall River gave us a less dramatic and more comfortable ride through a country jewelled with turquoise lakes and topaz-yellow woods. The beautiful, decrepit little dockyard town on a shining inlet of the sea provided visible evidence that many small industries on the eastern seaboard of America are far older than the corresponding larger industries in the black areas of Great Britain. I learnt that it began to fall into decay long before the depression, when new mechanised ships replaced the old sailing vessels once built there.

At Wellesley I spoke to four hundred enchanting girl students from the Dana Hall Schools, who gazed at the platform with bright, limpid eyes, and all but mobbed me after the lecture. Their lovely young enthusiasm enabled me to establish a record, for they presented me with three hundred and ten copies of *Testament of Youth*, purchased in the small college town, to autograph before I addressed them.

No doubt really popular authors, such as A. J. Cronin and Margaret Mitchell, would regard with scorn the selling and signing in one afternoon of a mere three hundred books; nothing short of three thousand would astonish or fatigue them. But to me it represented a day's grand total which I hardly hoped to exceed.

VI

WHENEVER I RECALL the autumn of 1934, two northern cities eclipse the rest in vividness of memory.

The one, Minneapolis, Minnesota, appeared to justify the inexplicable sense of some waiting experience which had haunted me on the Atlantic. The other, Grand Rapids, Michigan, showed me that, almost unconsciously, my attitude towards the United States had changed completely in two eventful months.

The unique exhilaration of Minneapolis and St. Paul, Twin Cities which face one another across the infant Mississippi, probably owed a good deal to the peculiar character of Minnesota. A northern agricultural community separated from the urban states in much the same way as Norway and Sweden are separated from Europe, this state of rolling farm lands, despoiled forests and ten thousand lakes resembles Scandinavia the more because its earliest settlements attracted chiefly the peoples of Northern Europe.

So many Scandinavians came into Minnesota that the state has elected only three Governors whose name did not indicate a Scandinavian ancestry. In 1934 the Governor was Floyd B. Olson, leader of the Farmer Labour Party, who might have been a President of the United States if he had not died during his campaign for the Senatorship in 1936.

"There are now two and a half million people living in Minnesota", runs a recent letter from my gifted Duluth correspondent, Izetta Winter Robb. "They have a certain pioneer sturdiness and integrity. Slightly chastened by adverse economic circumstances of recent years, they are more in character than in those days following the War when prosperity made them awkward Babbitts. Never believe one of our novelists who, ascribing wealth to the

Middle West, described hunt breakfasts attended by fashionably garbed hunters as if we somehow had become middle-aged and entitled to traditions of aristocracy. There may be hunt breakfasts, but the thousands of hunters invading our woods annually are more likely to get to their cabins in trusty Ford V-8's; and at breakfast they themselves swear at coal-oil cookstoves, and no chef hears them. No, we were never rich, only slightly affluent with a tendency to act as if this civilisation which industrially accomplished miracles was all we'd ever known."

Like Scandinavia itself, this community developed a liberal and pacifist philosophy, never destroyed by the incongruous circumstance that war brings great prosperity to the area owing to its rich ore deposits. In 1916, many voters from then Republican Minnesota joined the Democrats in support of President Wilson's campaign slogan: "He kept us out of war", and to the astonishment of the Republican party leaders, the Democratic Presidential candidate lost Minnesota only by the narrow margin of 392 votes. When Wilson's adherents turned against him, Minnesota's geographical detachment preserved her faith in international co-operation. From 1927 onwards, she studied the evidence of numerous masculine war-books, and became more peace-minded than ever. When *Testament of Youth* was published in America in October, 1933, her citizens were amongst its earliest readers. A year later, I was invited to deliver three lectures in Minneapolis.

Those lectures gave me four days of incessant pandemonium. They also brought me two friends of a kind that I had believed, eight years earlier, to be non-existent in the United States. Never, since meeting Ruth Gage Colby and Izetta Winter Robb, have I cherished the illusion that no American wants to talk intimately or be "alone together" with one other person.

In New York, before my tour began, I received a letter from a St. Paul correspondent, Mrs. Woodard Colby, inviting me to stay with her when I visited Minneapolis. Although I had then no idea who she was, and had decided, on the advice of both publisher and manager, to guard my freedom by refusing hospitality from private households, some indefinable quality in the letter suggested that this rule might have more than one exception. I told my manager that in Minneapolis, as well as in Boston, he need not arrange for hotel accommodation.

Later I discovered that the graceful young woman with the fine, pale face who met me at St. Paul was the wife of a child specialist, Dr. Woodard Colby, and was herself a poet, an artist, and the Minneapolis Chairman of the Women's International League for Peace and Freedom. Since each of these rôles appealed to some quality of my own, we could never find enough time to talk between my crowding engagements.

In spite of the emotions aroused by the Twin Cities' disproportionate offering of public acclamation, my clearest recollection of those days is still an evening when Ruth and I escaped at sunset to the banks of the young Mississippi. The woods, with the river deeply dividing them, were so silent that we could imagine ourselves alone in the undiscovered land which only the Indians knew.

"It is strange," she wrote to me afterwards, "that in your memory of being here you hold the same picture first, as I do, the steep sandstone banks, the smooth, swiftly flowing river, and the evening sky as it might have been in the days of the red men, with only you and me out of today".

At her house I met one of my readers, Izetta Winter Robb, a brilliant young woman trained at the University of Minnesota, who has told me nearly everything that I know of her state and a great deal that was new to me about the rest of America. I have already quoted her three times in this story; I shall have reason to quote her again before it is finished. Ruth and Izetta, who is now an administrator of education in the Duluth area, remain two of the best friends that America has brought me.

My first Minneapolis lecture followed a dinner and reception arranged by the College Women's Club at the

Nicollet Hotel, where the behaviour of the audience gave me the same sense of being somebody else as my New York interviews when I read them afterwards. I had not then visited Toronto, and innocently believed that my powers of endurance were taxed to their limit by the evening's programme.

"Before the dinner," I reported to Winifred, "I had to stand for an hour in a reception line and shake hands with hundreds of people, then wait for extra guests to assemble, and then (at nearly 9 p.m.) make the hour's speech. . . . I didn't know how I should do it, and then as I watched the audience coming in I knew I should, for the College Club had expected about 400, and got a scrambling crowd of over 1,000. . . . I was so tired that I was quite blind and couldn't see my notes, so I put them down and talked."

Among the guests who appeared before dinner was an English friend, Mrs. T. F. Tout, the widow of the historian. She had been living in Minneapolis with her son, who belonged to the University faculty, but she was sailing for England by the same boat as myself. Her benevolent delight in American society had done more, I was told, for Anglo-American friendship in the Twin Cities than years of direct propaganda could have achieved. Now, kindly and reassuring, she lent me her moral support through the long ordeal of hand-shaking. Wasn't it dreadfully tiring, she inquired, to meet so many strangers in so many places, and say the right thing to each?

It was, I admitted, and I feared that I said the wrong thing at least as often as the right. Where hundreds had to be greeted, it wasn't always possible to give individuals as much time as they expected. But I might have added that I had known circumstances in which cordiality, though less exhausting, was far more difficult. Remembering the critical reserve of my first year in America, I now realised how easy graciousness becomes when one is the privileged visitor, the guest of honour, the person whom everybody wants to meet.

Whenever I hear tales—and I have heard a good many—about the boorish manners of some British "lion" ("You must not forget," my manager once wrote, "that many of your predecessors did things in this country, outside of speaking, which has made it even more difficult for visiting lecturers"), I can only suppose that the ungrateful celebrity has never known the humiliations of failure or the bitter ranklings of thwarted ambition.

The next afternoon, another large audience was collected for me by the Woman's Club of Minneapolis. On my last morning, the strange excitement which seemed to possess everybody culminated at a grand assembly of the University Convocation.

I knew already that the University of Minnesota was one of the most liberal and pacifist in the United States. Now I learnt that it had abolished compulsory military training; it also ran a unique "International Relations Project."

In the University Post Office, where students came and went throughout the day, hung a six-foot map which was used as a setting for current news from Berlin, Geneva, Tokyo and other political capitals. Electric lights on the map, connected by dark cords to newspaper clippings, marked the "hot spots" of each day's events. Occasionally the map was arranged instead as a "topical display", showing the countries from which the students came, the cities where University graduates were working, or the centres of business relationship between North and South America. A small pamphlet describing this "Project" quoted a recent newspaper editorial: "Once more let it be reiterated, the world of today is one. Its conditions are world conditions, its movements are world movements. However great our responsibility for our own people, we must be world citizens no less than Americans, or we shall not be good Americans." The pamphlet concluded with the words: "'All the world's a stage and we're the actors.' To know our fellow actors and the parts they play is essential to intelligent acting of our parts."

The day before I spoke to Convocation, the Minneapolis Branch of the American Association of University Women

invited me to a luncheon arranged to discuss the purpose of
academic research. Would I come to it and give them my
opinion, as an Oxford graduate, on the value of pursuing
small historic and scientific facts in a world distressed by
urgent political problems?

I had then forgotten the severe letter which I wrote
from New York in 1926, lamenting the destructive influence
of academic society on creative writing. But by 1934 I
no longer felt that so superficial a scholar as myself was
entitled to display anything but humility before the stern,
disinterested and too often unrewarded persistence of
those who spend their lives in dispelling ignorance or
abolishing falsehoods; and I said so.

Two months later, when I was crossing the Atlantic on
my way back to England, I found a long manuscript roll
awaiting me in the Purser's office. The wrappings disclosed
a beautiful pictorial map of the United States, inscribed
to my son and daughter "in memory of their mother's
stirring words in support of the search for truth". The
map now hangs framed above the mantelpiece in the
children's nursery. If they do not already know by heart the
contours, mountains, lakes, rivers, races, animals and
products of the United States, it is neither my fault
nor that of the American Association of University
Women.

Convocation itself, in its terrifying immensity, resembled
a visible broadcast rather than a lecture. As the President
of the University, Lotus D. Coffman, led me to the great
platform of the Northrop Memorial Auditorium, the students
broke with a roar into their college song, "Hail, Minnesota!"

> "Like the stream that bends to sea,
> Like the pine that seeks the blue!
> Minnesota, still for thee
> Thy sons are strong and true.
> From thy woods and waters fair,
> From thy prairies waving far,
> At thy call they throng,
> With their shout and song,
> Hailing thee their Northern Star."

The music died, and I looked apprehensively at the assembled audience of five thousand faculty and students with their eyes turned expectantly to the platform. It seemed quite simply incredible that I, who nine years ago had thought a Foreign Policy Association audience of eight hundred colossal and overwhelming, should have to stand up and address this terrific gathering. As I knew by now, it was no use trying to look old, or important, or impressive, so in desperation I pulled off my hat, threw it on a chair, and talked quite informally. My speech on Women and War, broadcast over Minnesota, was halting and mediocre, but in that extraordinary city its hesitations seemed hardly to matter. The students, I learnt later, followed it up by organising a demonstration against war, and their response at the time made me long to run away.

"Twenty years ago," I confessed to Winifred, "it would have seemed like a wild fantasy. I pictured myself then as writing, but never as the centre of cheering, wildly excited crowds."

I have often meditated since upon those remarkable experiences, which would have seemed, it must be candidly confessed, as wildly fantastic to my friends at home in 1934 as to myself two decades earlier. The acclamation that I received was certainly not the consequence of my moderate platform performances, about which I cherish few illusions; at best I am no orator, but merely the competent interpreter of a point of view.

Throughout those abnormal days in Minneapolis, a sentence ran in my head from the First Epistle of Peter: "Humble yourselves therefore under the mighty hand of God, that he may exalt you in due time." A friend had quoted this passage to me years ago, when as a cocksure ex-schoolgirl in my teens I had imagined myself an excellent pianist, and then, on acquiring a better qualified teacher, had learnt to my utter dismay that my work was inexpert and slovenly, and I must start again from the beginning. The trivial episode came back to me from that distant past just when I needed it, for after each new manifestation

I was terrified of losing my head, of coming to believe that the enthusiasm surging round me was due to anything that I was, or said, or had written.

Today I know, as I suspected then, that it had nothing whatever to do with me. The invincible idealism of Minnesota, and the post-depression psychology of America, alone explained it.

Throughout five years of misery and loss, all that was most intelligent in American life had sought to account for the catastrophe, and had recognised it at last as a distant result of the War, which in a world of mutually dependent nations had smashed the stable economic basis essential to human welfare. The men and women who perceived this succession of cause and effect, realised also that its repetition would destroy not merely the prosperity of America and the peace of Europe, but the whole treasure house of civilisation, annihilating in one mad orgy of terror everything that mankind had placed to its credit through long aeons of conflict and pain. And they wanted to know that the other nations which had suffered felt as they did, and would work with them to prevent humanity from repudiating its own mental and spiritual power. They looked desperately for a message of co-operation and reassurance from any individual representative of those peoples who appeared to speak with authority.

It was the very fact that they had been intimidated and defeated which made these Americans, to my own astonishment, transform what I had thought of as an ordinary commercial lecture tour into a kind of spiritual pilgrimage. In the commonplace remarks that I made, they insisted upon finding something which would never have been there if they had not looked for it. They spoke of my being an inspiration to them, but it was they who had been the inspiration to me, calling forth the strange human capacity for rising, however insignificant the individual, to the expectation of others. The same capacity during the War caused bank-clerks and shop assistants—who habitually thought of themselves as unadventurous cowards—to per-

form astounding acts of courage which afterwards seemed as
incredible in their own eyes as in those of their sceptical
friends. Under such circumstances a person loses his identity,
and merely becomes the temporary embodiment of public
aspirations.

Nevertheless, there is no challenge equal to the exaltation
which springs from these collective hopes, no emotion so
compelling as the sense of dedication to a common purpose
which transcends individual accomplishment. I had known
this emotion in war; I realised now, more keenly than ever,
that it could also arise from the quest for peace.

The memory of that exaltation returned to me a month
later during a twelve-hour visit to Grand Rapids, Michigan.

After a busy Armistice-tide week in New York, I had gone
down south to lecture at a women's college in Greensboro,
North Carolina. From excess of fatigue I could not sleep
on the long night journey, and afterwards remembered that
lovely state as a dim waking dream of rose-red earth and
terra-cotta woods. At Richmond, Virginia, where I spent
the next day on the way to Columbus, Ohio, the air was
so soft that I could walk comfortably in a thin silk dress
without a coat, though the leaves had all fallen from the
trees. Still too dazed by another wakeful night to think
coherently, I found myself repeating the idiotic lettered
advertisement for some brand of shaving soap which I had
seen stretched along the railway embankment outside
Greensboro the previous morning:

> "College—boys—your—courage—muster,
> Take—off—that—mussy—feather—duster."

Throughout the twenty-one hours' journey from Richmond to Columbus I remained almost alone in my Pullman
compartment; the trains which had been so crowded in
1926 were unprofitably empty in 1934. It was a strange,
solitary day, in which I awoke from fitful hours of sleep
vaguely troubled by dreams to see the Blue Mountains
across dark green pine-forests, and watch the sun set in an

ecstasy of crimson and violet above distant sapphire hills. At Columbus a hot, heavy wind like a Mediterranean sirocco blew steadily for three exhausting days. After I had explored the main streets, and crossed the great bridge once or twice over the Scioto River, I began to weary of the large sprawling city, and should have found it tedious but for the American Association of University Women, whose members, with tactful kindness, entertained me sufficiently but never too much.

Now, crossing Michigan from Detroit to Grand Rapids, I returned to winter; the bleak morning was bitterly cold, and a north wind blew steadily over the bare rolling pasture lands. The violent varieties of climate on this huge continent were certainly trying to long-distance travellers, I decided, as I gazed, tired and depressed, out of the carriage window at the cheerless dun-coloured landscape. With its endless undulating downs, its forests of stark brown trees, and the flocks of grey sheep cropping the short dry grass, it reminded me of Derbyshire without the stone walls. The lovely autumn colours which still enriched North Carolina had faded into the boundless neutral desolation of earth and sky.

In the small furniture-manufacturing city of Grand Rapids, a long half-day of typical obligations awaited me. I arrived shortly after noon, and had to leave again for Detroit by the midnight train; between these hours I found myself dated up for luncheon, an afternoon visit to the local bookstore, tea with a group of high-school girls, a dinner party at my lecture organiser's house, the lecture itself, a Press interview, and late supper with a reader who was motoring fifty miles from Kalamazoo to hear me. In addition the hotel mail clerk presented me with twenty-one letters, and a cable from Winifred containing the news that my son, now almost seven, had just lost his first front tooth.

Among the letters I saw also a bulky envelope in her handwriting. I opened it to find enclosed the report of an Armistice-eve broadcast by the British Broadcasting Cor-

poration, *Scrapbook for* 1918. This broadcast was a dramatisa-
tion, in several scenes, of the final year of the War. Just
after sailing for America, I had been invited to read some
relevant extracts from *Testament of Youth* in the scene
describing the great German offensive of March, 1918. As
I was abroad, the extracts were allocated to an anonymous
"Nurse", and the wave-length used had made it impossible
for me even to listen-in from New York on November
10th.

Thirteen days afterwards in the small Michigan hotel,
I read Winifred's report of the broadcast with growing
suspense. The authors of *Scrapbook for* 1918 had obviously
intended their work as a plea for peace; had they, who had
perhaps never crossed the Atlantic, also realised the importance of being fair to America in their story of that year's
events? Did they mistakenly imagine, as I had imagined
in 1925, that everybody in the United States had long
forgotten the War and cared nothing for its consequences?
Or did they know how many Americans there were who
still resented our ungenerous refusal to recognize America's
part in the War, and really cared that we should have
the honesty and the decency to admit that she saved us
from defeat? Had they chosen the passage from *Testament
of Youth* which described the march of American troops
through Étaples and explicitly acknowledged that salvation?

When I wrote those paragraphs I had merely borne
truthful witness to the sense of relief which the men and
women serving in France during that critical spring had
felt at the first sight of the rescuing battalions. I had not
realised the significance that would be attached to them
in America until I was repeatedly asked to read them aloud
at the end of my lectures. In the Woman's Club of Minneapolis, the silence of the listening audience became so
tense that they and I might have been transported back to
Étaples in 1918, to watch together, as I had once watched,
"the United States physically entering the War, so god-like,
so magnificent, so splendidly unimpaired in comparison
with the tired, nerve-racked men of the British army. . . ."

Breathless with memory and anticipation, I turned the pages of the reported *Scrapbook*, and began to read.

> "Dedicated to the memory of those,
>   Who in the splendour of a simple thought,
>   Whether for England or her enemies,
>   Went in the night and in the morning died.

"COMPERE: Between January and March a dreadful menace gathered over us."

March, 1918. . . . Yes, it was all there—the collapse of Russia, outmanœuvred the previous spring at Brest-Litovsk; the massing of 150,000 Germans on the Western Front before the United States could land an effective force in France; Winston Churchill's visit to the 9th Division during the sinister deathly silence of March 20th; the sudden earth-shaking uproar of the guns at dawn; the bludgeoning of shells on the battered trenches and the advance of thirty-seven divisions of German infantry through the fog; the bitter rain of telegrams upon British households waiting in speechless terror for news. . . .

With the pile of unopened letters completely forgotten, I read Sir Philip Gibbs' description of the retreat through Amiens:

"There was nothing more splendid in the War than the way our troops fought every mile back during that great retreat in March, snatching half an hour's sleep in any pause of the fighting, then getting their rifles and machine guns ready for another battle. In a few days the enemy had all the old fields of the Somme in his clutch again. A year before, when the war had seemed to pass from this region, the peasants had crept back to villages behind the line and patched up their shattered homes. Now suddenly they found themselves engulfed again. In the town of Albert I saw refugees leaving their homes, trundling barrows with their poor belongings. Dead horses lay about the ruined streets. When Amiens was threatened there was a panic flight from the shops and streets where young British officers had flirted with pretty girls and enjoyed a

Ns

spell of civilisation before getting back to the line. Amiens became a deserted town into which presently the shells came crashing, and the silence of this abandoned city, which many of us had loved because of its old beauty and cheerful life, was broken only by the whine of high velocities and the tramp of soldiers marching through."

Then came the section which described the new offensive at Armentières and included the testimony of the young nurse from Étaples—the section round which my hopes and fears had gathered with so odd a vehemence of anxiety. At the moment, for some reason which I could not explain, it seemed a matter of life and death that justice should have been done to America in this particular broadcast. I read on:

"1st Narrator: April the 9th! Ludendorff strikes again. The British lose Armentières. In a day 24 miles of front are engulfed.

"2nd Narrator: British troops are hurriedly shipped to France from Italy, Salonika, Palestine; new armies hasten from England. . . . In the House of Commons: Prime Minister Lloyd George . . .

"Lloyd George Voice (echo): We have had some very anxious moments, and those who knew the most were the most anxious. The losses were considerable, and had they not been immediately made up the second German blow might very well have overwhelmed the British Army. In a fortnight 286,000 men were thrown across the Channel.

"Compere: A young nurse in a hospital at Étaples wrote down her impressions of that time. The nurse was Miss Vera Brittain, and this is from her *Testament of Youth*:

"Nurse: Motor lorries and ammunition waggons crashed endlessly along the road; trains with reinforcements thundered all day up the line, or lumbered down more slowly with their heavy freight of wounded. The wards were never tidied and the work was never finished; each convoy after staying its few hours was immediately replaced by another, and the business of dressing wounds began all over again. England, panic-stricken, was frantically raising

the military age to fifty and agreeing to the appointment of
Foch as Commander-in-Chief, but to us with our blistered
feet, our swollen hands, our wakeful, reddened eyes, victory
and defeat began to seem—as indeed they were afterwards
to prove—very much the same thing. On April 11th, after a
dizzying rush of wounded from the new German offensive,
I stumbled up to the Sisters' quarters for lunch with the
certainty that I could not go on—and saw, pinned up on
the notice board in the Mess, Sir Douglas Haig's 'Special
Order of the Day'. (*Fade in faint background of side drum.*)

"HAIG VOICE: Many amongst us now are tired. To those
I would say that Victory will belong to the side which holds
out the longest. . . . There is no course open to us but
to fight it out. Every position must be held to the last
man: there must be no retirement. With our backs to the
wall and believing in the justice of our cause each one of
us must fight on to the end. The safety of our homes and
the Freedom of mankind alike depend upon the conduct
of each one of us at this critical moment.—D. HAIG, F.M.
(*Drums up and with them the brisk marching of troops. Superimpose :*)

"NURSE: Only a day or two afterwards, I had to wait to
let a large contingent of troops march past me along the
main road that ran through our camp. . . . An unusual
quality of bold vigour in their swift stride caused me to
stare at them with puzzled interest.

"(*At this point men start singing 'Over There' as a background
to the rhythm of marching feet :*)

> "Over there! Over there!
> Send the word, send the word over there,
> That the Yanks are coming, the Yanks are coming,
> The drums rum-tumming ev'rywhere.
> So prepare, say a pray'r,
> Send the word, send the word to beware,
> We'll be over, we're coming over.
> And we won't come back till it's over, over there!

"NURSE (*continues from above point without pause*): Then
I heard an excited exclamation from a group of Sisters
behind me. 'Look! Look! Here are the Americans!' (*Pause.*)

In the fearless swagger of their proud strength they looked
a formidable bulwark against the peril looming from Amiens.
Somehow the necessity of packing up in a hurry, the
ignominious flight to the coast so long imagined, seemed
to move further away. . . .

"(*During this speech change singing to 'Marching Through
Georgia' :*)

"Bring the good old bugle, boys! we'll start another song—
Sing it with a spirit that will start the world along—
Sing it as we used to sing it, fifty thousand strong,
While we were marching through Georgia.
Hurrah! Hurrah! We bring the Jubilee!
Hurrah! Hurrah! the flag that makes you free!
So we sang the chorus from Atlanta to the sea,
While we were marching through Georgia!

"*Now fade up singing and marching. After a few moments
the singing dissolves as though the party in song has passed beyond
earshot. The marching continues at full strength, then it also
dissolves away to silence.*

"COMPERE: The tide was stemmed. The crisis passed.
And so that blood-stained page in the War's accounts is
closed. And this was the price: Of all the British troops
in France on March 21st, one quarter had been lost a
month later.

"1ST WOMAN: Killed, wounded, and missing, 303,000
British men.

"2ND WOMAN: Killed, wounded, and missing, 349,000
German men."

The script looked blurred as I put it down with a sense
of relief beyond expression. So it *had* all been in; the
story of our own most critical days had ended with the sound
of American feet tramping into the War, of American
voices singing "Over There!" Grudging, critical, self-
righteous though we were, we had learnt something in the
past sixteen years—or was it only in the past six? Were
we, perhaps, more ready to admit America's services,
America's value, now that she too had suffered. . . .

I did not then realise how effectively I should be able, in my remaining lectures, to use this broadcast passage. I only knew that I did not want at that moment to meet people, or answer their questions, or lecture on the morals of modern youth; I wanted to be alone, to think, to take something in . . . and there was no time. . . .

After the luncheon and the visit to the local bookstore, I found that I had, after all, half an hour to spare before the high-school tea-party. Hurrying out of the hotel lest the telephone or a caller should interrupt me, I walked quickly up a steep hill which seemed to lead out of the town.

I understood now what had happened to me; I realised that, gradually and only half consciously, my feelings towards the United States had undergone a complete revolution during the past few weeks. By their kindly generosity, their considerate organisation of my work and time, my friendly American publishers had begun the process as soon as I landed; the changed, gentler manners of a people who knew adversity had continued it; and it had been completed by the three astonishing days in Minneapolis. The critical antagonism of nine years ago had all vanished away; I loved and admired this nation which I had once left so thankfully; perhaps, even, I was beginning to understand it a little. . . . If only, I thought, this understanding could become universal! How much, if we knew each other better, the Americans and ourselves could accomplish together towards the redemption of an irrational, passion-torn world!

At that moment, halfway up the hill, I noticed a double cenotaph on a raised platform overlooking the city. Going up to it, I found that it was the Grand Rapids War Memorial, "dedicated November 11th, 1926, to the memory of the men and women of Grand Rapids who made the supreme sacrifice in the service of their country in the World War". Some of the Armistice Day wreaths still lay on the steps of the platform, and a bouquet of flame-pink carnations and silver leaves had recently been left there.

The bitter afternoon had turned colder than ever. With the wind blowing tiny snow-flurries across the cenotaph, I read some of the names inscribed on the stone—Baranowskas, Kulhawik, Kadecki, Romanowski, Sandusky—and realised that half these Michigan soldiers who had died for America, and therefore for England, were Polish or Slavonic in origin. Their fathers, perhaps, had come from the alleys of Riga and the ghettos of Warsaw, but time and the civilising process of co-operation with a great community had turned them into good Americans, ready to lay down their lives in a War which would conclude, they were told, for ever the tragic misunderstandings of hostile nations. . . .

Standing there in the icy wind, still thinking of the *Scrapbook* and the newly awakened consciousness which it had brought me, I uttered an inarticulate prayer that even the minor enterprises of travelling writers might help to cement the growing friendship between two great peoples.

VII

T HE DETROIT VISIT which followed Grand Rapids
was actually not an anticlimax. In my lecture next day to
the English Club there, I used for the first time the *Scrapbook*
broadcast, spoke with some trepidation of Anglo-American
relations, and discussed our closer understanding since
the depression because we had both been through much
tribulation.

A month earlier, on the way to Minnesota, I had spent
the inside of a day in the mushroom city with its tall skyscrapers and lakeside harbour, in order to address twelve
hundred members of the Women's Club in the great
oblong ballroom of the Book-Cadillac Hotel. As the sky was
still light when this afternoon function concluded, my
intelligent chairman—a fierce radical who told me that she
voted Labour in elections—offered to take me out in her
car.

"There's plenty of time before dinner," she said. "I can
run you anywhere you'd like to go."

To her surprise, for she had never troubled to visit them,
I told her I wanted to see Henry Ford's works in the suburb
of Dearborn. Not one of her alternative proposals about
metropolitan museums or woodland roads round Lake St.
Clair could tempt me away from the territory of "The
Flivver King", whose dramatic labour contest with the
United Automobile Workers of America still belonged to
the future.

"I shan't be able to show you any of the beauties of
Detroit," my hostess commented regretfully. She was right.
For mile upon tedious mile we drove out of the city down
a wide, straight, semi-suburban avenue, indescribable in its
unvaried dreariness. At last we crossed a railway bridge
and came suddenly upon the huge plant, with its acres

of parked cars, and its tall white chimneys looming like bland ghosts against the dull red of the October sunset.

"It reminded me," I wrote home afterwards, "of seeing Krupp's works exactly ten years ago, spread out beneath the rainy sky of an October evening at Essen."

Back in my room on the twenty-fourth floor of the Book-Cadillac, I looked down through a well of darkness upon the skyscraper lights and the twinkling eyes of boats on the distant lake. My reaction to heights was now very different from the alarmed uncertainty of 1925, but not all Europeans become thus acclimatized. One Englishman visiting the country told me that the loftiness of the hotels combined with the shallowness of the bedroom window-sills drove him almost insane.

During the War, he said, he had been buried in his dug-out by a shell, which later made him walk in his sleep and try to climb through windows. At home he slept on the ground floor, and the high hotels so terrified him that whenever a room on a low storey was unobtainable, he piled all the bedroom furniture against the window-sill and went to bed in misery. I have never understood why these sills in front of windows which look over a five-hundred-foot precipice of sheer unbroken brick cannot be made a few inches higher. As they stand, they are permanent temptations to would-be suicides and certain death for any somnambulist.

Back on the twentieth floor a month later, I went down in the lift to the long, narrow ballroom where the English Club luncheon was also held. From the crowded tables a pencilled slip of paper was passed up to me: "Please tell the young people who write asking with what organisation they may unite in this country to work for peace, to join the National Council for Prevention of War, 532, Seventeenth Street N.W., Washington, D.C."

My chairman, a tall young teacher of English, combined his introduction of myself with an appeal to the members of the club to contribute generously to its funds.

"I want," he concluded, "to have enough in hand to get some really good speakers for next year."

The instant roar of delighted laughter meant confusion for him but an easy lecture for me. I have heard several variants of this story from fellow speakers, and can only conclude that numerous chairmen must temporarily assume the function of treasurer with embarrassing results. The *faux pas* in question might even be recommended as a deliberate expedient to those who preside at meetings, for it immediately puts the audience in sympathy with the lecturer. So many more serious errors are made by introducers, that I recently drew up a private list of "Rules for Chairmen" which I should like to see distributed to its engaging organisations by every lecture bureau:

(1) It is not the chairman's job to make a long speech on the subject of the evening, but to put the speaker in touch with the audience. I have had chairmen who have given enthusiastic addresses on international relations, modern literature, the League of Nations and the women's movement, but have entirely failed to acquaint the listeners with such qualifications as I possess for lecturing on these topics.

(2) The chairman who is too brief is even more disconcerting. I have been "introduced" by chairmen who have dashed on to the platform with me, uttered a brief and inaudible sentence ending with my name, and rushed away before I have had time to look round the hall or gauge the size of the audience. Chairmen should remember that the speaker (especially in the United States, where long-distance trains are apt to arrive late) may have had to hurry at top speed from station platform to lecture platform, and be in urgent need of getting his breath. He also requires time to remove his coat (and if the lecturer is a woman, rather more time than a man in order to dispose of coat, fur and gloves), get out his notes, take stock of the auditorium and audience, and discover how desk, light and microphone (if any) are arranged.

Five minutes is the ideal time for a chairman. If the speaker has hurried to the platform, he can take ten with advantage. A longer address than ten minutes makes the audience impatient and the lecturer nervous through over-prolonged anticipation.

(3) The chairman should never tell anecdotes which put the speaker in a ludicrous light, and above all should never indulge in pleasantries about the speaker's name.

Most names, perhaps, are not susceptible to jokes or puns, but any one who knows enough Latin to translate my first name will realise that I am not among the fortunate majority, and have already suffered as many facetious imputations of national patriotism as my endurance can stand. I am almost as bored by hearing myself introduced as a "True Briton", as Mr. J. B. Priestley by being described as a "Good Companion". In any case, the repetition of a quip heard many times before fills the lecturer with a sense of *ennui* which may easily communicate itself to the audience and spoil the whole evening.

(4) The chairman's address should always include a brief summary of the speaker's history and attainments. However well-known a lecturer may be, it is never safe to assume that every member of the audience is familiar with these details. Most listeners know only those celebrities who are at the top of their own particular tree.

(5) The chairman should never imply that a meeting is foredoomed to failure by emphasising or apologising for the small size of the audience. A poor attendance is not, in any case, the fault of those who are there, and the implication that the lecturer may be responsible does not help him to be interesting or confident. Special care should be taken to avoid this error of tact when the lecturer originally engaged has been replaced by a deputy.

(6) When the speaker is a substitute, the chairman should not underline the disappointment felt by himself and the audience in the non-appearance of the original lecturer. He hardly helps the situation by beginning with the words (which a rueful fellow-speaker once told me were actually used about herself): "I much regret to have to tell you that as Mr. X. has influenza, Miss Y. has been sent by headquarters to take his place." The chairman should

stress those qualities in the substitute which make the audience fortunate to obtain him.

(7) Long interruptions, such as local announcements or the taking of a collection, should not come between the lecture and the question period, as they destroy both the eagerness of the audience and the wrought-up vitality of the speaker. Notices are better remembered if distributed on typewritten slips, and collecting boxes at the door are less of an anti-climax than a plate passed round in the middle of a meeting.

(8) At question time the chairman should not harangue those cranks and pests who make speeches instead of asking questions, but should appeal to their sense of fair play before the questions begin.

(9) If the chairman has not agreed with the lecturer, he should not rebuke him before the audience at the conclusion of the meeting. Concluding remarks in any case are to be regretted, as they diminish the final impression left by the speaker on the audience.

Return visits to Pittsburgh and Cleveland followed Detroit; then came a three days' break for Thanksgiving which I had promised to spend with G.

Friends had suggested that I should meet him, and lecture, in the small University city where we had lived for the first six months of our marriage, but though I should have returned in circumstances so different, I hesitated to face them. Those months had been memorable for their private happiness, but they had also meant retrogression and failure, and I was still too new to recognition to recall with equanimity the long period of frustration. G. too was still on the University faculty—it was the last year of his part-time Professorship—and I felt that my reappearance on that early scene after so many years might cause him embarrassment rather than pleasure.

So we met once or twice in New York instead, and spent Thanksgiving together in Washington. There we arranged a final week-end at Buffalo, where I was to give the evening service address at the First Presbyterian Church on the second Sunday in December.

I reached Washington at breakfast-time by the night train from Pittsburgh, with a day to pass alone until G. arrived in the evening. I do not know whether I was discouraged by the long wait for him, or exhausted by emotions which had seemed as overwhelming as all emotions experienced in solitude, or merely depressed by sitting in a dismal hotel bedroom, with a dark outlook into a well, which the management were reluctant to change; but whatever the reason I suddenly began, as at Toronto, to cry like a baby. This time, however, I cried and cried; I could not have told anyone why I was crying, but I was quite unable to check myself.

I had just reached the stage when my nose was swollen double its normal size, and my eyes had become too red and inflamed to see across the room, when the telephone bell rang with the effect of a bomb bursting in a desert. Hoping for a short respite from publicity, I had asked for my letters to be forwarded to Washington in G.'s name; no one, so far as I knew, was aware of my presence in the city, and the shattering ring so startled me that I stopped crying at once. Violently blowing my nose and mopping my eyes, I scrambled across the room and picked up the receiver.

"Is that Miss Vera Brittain? This is the Washington Pictorial News Service speaking. We understand you have just arrived in the city, and would like to have the privilege of taking your picture. . . . When? Well, the studio is empty right now, Miss Brittain. Could you come straight away? . . . Oh, no, that's not necessary. Come right along just as you are."

It would certainly be a privilege to take me just as I am, I thought, regarding the red-nosed, swollen-eyed apparition in the mirror.

"An original portrait of Miss Vera Brittain, the English author, taken at the conclusion of a fit of crying."

Why on earth had I said yes? . . . Well, just because it was even more tiring to say no. But let me hear anybody,

ever again, complaining that they want more publicity . . .
Oh, come along, you fool, pull yourself together!

I washed my face, tidied my hair, powdered my nose,
and went to the News Service studio with a fatuous smile
on my lips and rage in my heart.

When G. arrived late that evening in a colleague's car,
I felt better at once; the familiar comfort of his presence
restored me to normality after the abnormal life of the
past few weeks. But our three days together were less of a
holiday than I had expected, for the News Service telephone
call had been followed by a telegram from my publisher,
reporting that the League of Nations' Association had
arranged for me to broadcast a farewell message over "a
nation-wide hook-up" at the end of my tour. As Thanksgiving was my last free period, much of the time had to go
on the preparation of a two-thousand-word manuscript.

The weather too was unkind, for it rained incessantly.
On the few occasions that we could get out, the city which
I had last seen radiant with April blossom dripped and
panted in the atmosphere of a Turkish bath. As ambitious
walks were impossible, we struggled round under umbrellas like a couple of tourists, visiting monuments and
reading memorial inscriptions.

Why, I wondered, had I ever imagined that America
was all geography and no history? It had almost as much
history as ourselves, and quite as much rain, I decided,
taking charge of both umbrellas in order that G., whose
passion for inscriptions is insatiable, might copy the words
of Abraham Lincoln from the walls of the stately colonnaded
temple which enshrines his statue:

"It may seem strange that any men should dare to ask
a just God's assistance in wringing their bread from the
sweat of other men's faces. But let us judge not that we be
not judged. . . . Fondly do we hope, fervently do we
pray, that this mighty scourge of war may speedily pass
away. Yet, if God wills that it continue until all the wealth
piled up by the bondman's two hundred and fifty years
of unrequited toil shall be sunk, and until every drop of

blood drawn with the lash shall be paid by another drawn with the sword, as was said three thousand years ago, so still it must be said, that 'the judgments of the Lord are true and righteous altogether'."

That afternoon we went out to the National Cemetery at Arlington and copied more damp inscriptions from the Unknown Soldier's tomb. "Here rests in honoured glory an American soldier known but to God." "We here highly resolve that these dead shall not have died in vain"—and, more characteristically, "When we assumed the soldier we did not lay aside the citizen". These words still recall to me the splash of rain upon trees and monuments, and the blurred Romanesque silhouette of Washington, stretched across the Potomac like a soft etching upon a colourless background of rain-washed sky.

We parted at night on the station, G. taking one train to his University city and I another to Cincinnati, the first stage of a second south-to-north journey which resembled transportation from a wet tropical jungle to the North Pole. At Cincinnati I stopped to give a luncheon address to the local League of Women Voters, an intelligent group whose responsive eagerness obliterated from my mind the scorn aroused by a small-town branch in 1925.

They allowed me an hour to myself before the lecture, and though snow-flurries like tiny feathers whirled in the air before a fierce northerly gale, I ran across the monster suspension bridge spanning the Ohio River into Covington, Kentucky, in order to add another state to my growing collection. The bridge divided a typical Midwestern city of stone buildings and giant skyscrapers from a more primitive southern community, huddled untidily at the foot of Kentucky's wooded hills.

"Groups of little wooden shanties amid bare brown trees and no building looking as if it would stand a hurricane," I wrote home of Covington—a comment which the great floods of 1937 rendered only too prophetic.

Next day I left Chicago, where the Hauptmann trial now monopolised the newspaper placards, for Winona,

Minnesota. From the Pullman car travelling swiftly along
the Milwaukee Road I could see the bare flat fields of
Illinois spread round me like a brown empty map, but in
forest-clad lake-diamonded Wisconsin the snow began to
fall, gradually concealing beneath its white shroud the ice-
floes on the rivers and the tall grasses growing like brown
feathers from the frozen earth. As the sun set, casting its
sanguine reflection over the ice-covered lakes and the piling
snow, a frightening loneliness descended upon the uninhabited monotony of prairies and hills.

The long journey filled the day, but I had come to welcome
the comfortable trains which gave me my only hours
of freedom from questions and crowds. I was now so
accustomed to travelling that no place, even on the American
continent, seemed really far from any other. Settling down
contentedly at the writing desk in the lounge car, I began
a long letter to Winifred:

"By the time I arrive at Winona this evening I shall
have been 1,000 miles from south to north within forty-
eight hours. My map gives the exact distance from Washington to Minneapolis (a little further north than I am
going today) as 1,191 miles. . . . I have been altogether
in seventeen states—New York, New Jersey, Connecticut,
Massachusetts, Pennsylvania, Virginia, West Virginia,
North Carolina, Kentucky, Ohio, Indiana, Illinois, Missouri,
Iowa, Michigan, Wisconsin, Minnesota—so I know a
little more about America than I did in 1927! I may make
Kansas from Kansas City, Missouri, by crossing the Missouri
as I did the Ohio River the other day. . . .

"And now it's all nearly over. In a week I shall all but
have finished travelling from north to south and east to
west; in a fortnight I should be on the Atlantic; in three
weeks taking the children to tea with Mother as though
all this had never been. . . . It will come back to me afterwards, I think, chiefly as a series of pictures: the sky line
of New York as the *Berengaria* sailed up the Hudson; a
warm dark evening in a boat, with the lights of Long
Island Sound twinkling in the distance; the train at

Pennsylvania Station leaving for West Virginia; the Ohio River with huge suspension bridges like the Danube at Budapest. A blue bird fluttering in the park at St. Louis; the whitish-grey steel chimneys of Ford's works at Detroit standing like ghosts against a sullen red sky; Archie Macdonell and I walking along the shores of Lake Michigan with a crimson sun setting over Chicago and turning to blood the crests of the waves; an evening with Ruth Colby on the banks of the young Mississippi at Minneapolis; the Lake at Toronto, very formal and complacent. New York again, and a marvellous early morning crossing of the Hudson from New Jersey, with the skyscrapers gleaming in the sun and the *Berengaria* with her three red funnels lying placidly in the Cunard-White Star dock as the ferry went by; the warm half-waking dream of North Carolina with its red earth and chestnut-brown woods; dirty grey bridges across the dreary Scioto River at Columbus; the scattered lights on hills and valleys of Pittsburgh at night; Washington spreading in a damp grey mist across the Potomac at the feet of the Unknown Warrior, and rain falling in a steady splash through the brown Arlington woods; the towers of Cincinnati looking across the Ohio River at shabby, beautiful, wooded Kentucky. What more shall I have to remember before it finally comes to an end? What further pictures, what other moments?"

By the time that I reached Winona—a small town with twenty thousand inhabitants, a shack of a station and no porters—the grey daylight had long departed and the snow was lying fifteen inches deep. Descending from the train on to an uncovered platform which appeared to rise from the middle of a snow-field, I eventually discovered a solitary taxi in the dimly lit darkness. Throughout that night and all the next morning, a blizzard—the worst, they said, for five years—swept over the town. As I sat in the window of the small country hotel, which provided the usual excellent meal and unlimited hot water, and watched the heavy snowflakes obliterating the outlines of a church across the road, the prospect of being snowed up too long to get

back to three engagements in Chicago and Milwaukee
threatened to spoil a record so far unbroken.

I had calculated without America's resourcefulness,
acquired through centuries of conflict with nature at her
worst. In the late afternoon the snow ceased falling; an
hour or two afterwards, a snowfall which would have
disorganised any English railway system for days on end was
already half cleared from the tracks. When the hour of
my lecture arrived, cars were slithering along roads twenty
inches deep in snow, and I had quite a good audience. By
midnight, when I left for Chicago, the trains were running
on time.

Three days later, I found Kansas City bright, beautiful
and bitterly cold. A spotless shining blanket obscured all
distinctive colours and contours; even the slender flower-
like column of the famous War Memorial was draped in
snow. Nevertheless, an intrepid lecture organiser motored
me across the frozen Missouri into the state of Kansas, and
I changed "seventeen" to "eighteen" on my list of states.

After another thousand miles of travel, I met G. on
Buffalo station at midnight. It was our last week-end
together, but in two months' time he would join me in
England. I should say good-bye to him now with envy as
well as regret, for I had only four days left in America,
and already felt reluctant to leave the country.

Before the Sunday afternoon service at the First Presbyterian Church we had time for a joint expedition to Niagara,
its black and white columns of thundering water crashing
between titanic pillars of ice. To my surprise G. came
back with me to the church, for he usually avoided my
public appearances as carefully as, in the early days of
our marriage, he had expected me to avoid his. Although
we had now been married for over nine years, this address
would be the first full-length lecture that he had heard
me deliver.

"It went well," he told me afterwards, and because his
standards were exacting, I believed that it had. The subject

Os

chosen, "Youth and War", was the lecture prepared for the Boston League of Nations' Association. I had often been asked to repeat it, for it attempted to answer, in the form of a story, the four questions most frequently put to me during that autumn:

"What are the chances of another War in Europe?"

"Is the Fascist movement getting stronger in England?"

"Has English youth the same interest in peace as young people here?"

"What do you think of the desire for peace among the youth of America?"

The story that I told linked three memories of three decades—the eve of August 4th, 1914; a return journey from the despairing Germany of 1924; the nineteenth anniversary of the War which found me on Thiepval Ridge in the golden mockery of harvest sunshine, reading the 73,000 names on the great Memorial to the Missing of the Somme. These word-pictures concluded with a passage from Dr. Harry Emerson Fosdick's famous Apology to the Unknown Soldier, given as a sermon at the Riverside Church, New York, on November 12th, 1933, which ranks for me with the great indictments of War produced by the sublime rage of human compassion:

"Do I not have an account to settle between my soul and him? They sent men like me into the camps to awaken his idealism, to touch those secret, holy springs within him so that with devotion, fidelity, loyalty and self-sacrifice he might go out to War. O War, I hate you most of all for this, that you do lay your hands on the noblest elements in human character, with which we might make a heaven on earth, and you use them to make a hell on earth instead. You take even our science, the fruit of our dedicated intelligence, by means of which we might build here the City of God, and using it, you fill the earth instead with new ways of slaughtering men. You take our loyalty, our unselfishness, with which we might make the earth beautiful, and using these our finest qualities you make death fall from the sky and burst up from the sea and hurtle from unseen ambuscades sixty miles away; you blast fathers in the trenches with gas while you are starving their children at home with blockades; and you so bedevil the world that fifteen years after the Armistice we cannot be sure who won the War, so sunk in the same disaster are victors and vanquished alike. If wars were fought simply with evil things, like hate, it would be bad enough, but when one sees the deeds of war done with the loveliest faculties of the human spirit, he looks into the very pit of hell."

VIII

DECEMBER 10TH, 1934. New York again, sunny, windy, cold. The Macmillan windows which had been scarlet and black with copies of *Testament of Youth* when I arrived in September were now blue and white with the latest printing of Mary Ellen Chase's novel, *Mary Peters*.

Its exquisite cover design, so appropriate to the blue and gold exhilaration of the early winter morning, showed a beautiful Maine sailing ship with its wings widely spread. I wanted to sit down and read the book at once, but my final four-day programme permitted no such luxury.

"Three lectures, two of them outside New York," it said. "Luncheon talk. Broadcast. Buy Christmas presents. Finish dictating letters. Give farewell interviews to Press. Pack."

My one engagement in the city was a morning lecture at Town Hall—which is not, as English readers might suppose, the main centre of municipal activity, but America's most distinguished lecturing club. The Town Hall movement in the United States links America's past to her future; it is an adaptation of her first forum, the early town meeting. Many cities outside New York run Town Hall clubs or a Town Hall lecture series, but the New York Town Hall, which organises daily morning or evening lectures, is the leader and prototype of them all. Its direct ancestor, the League for Political Education, was founded in 1894 by six leaders of the American woman suffrage movement, who actually believed that would-be women voters should educate themselves for their responsibilities. In 1921 the League acquired a building of its own in West Forty-third Street, and in 1937, changed its name to The Town Hall, Inc. Mr. George V. Denny, Jr., its president, has now developed his organisation to a point where it periodically makes use of radio to become a Town Meeting of the Air.

I have never known more urbane and accomplished chairmen than the introducers of my Town Hall lectures in 1934 and 1937, nor an audience that asked keener and more searching questions. As both these engagements were in the morning I had exclusively middle-class listeners; 11.00 a.m. is an hour when only the leisured, or the creative organisers of their own time, can attend lectures even in America. The evening meetings attract groups of workers who add colour and vitality to the gracious intelligence of the morning atmosphere.

Already, during November, I had spent ten days in New York for a series of Armistice-tide lectures round the city. It was after a school lecture at Ogontz, Pennsylvania, that I took the ferry across the Hudson on a morning of crystal water and opal skies. At dinner that night before my address at the Columbia University Institute of Arts and Sciences, my host was the doctor—now connected with Columbia faculty—who had attended G. during his attack of measles in 1926. He had read and liked *Testament of Youth* when it first appeared, and had just heard from our mutual friends the Bruce Blivens that the author of the book, and the "little wife" of the young scholar who caught measles, were one and the same person.

This Columbia series of lectures was organised by Dr. Russell Potter, whose adverse comments on women lecturers were destined to receive widespread Press publicity in November, 1937. The *New York Times*, amongst other newspapers, reported him at length:

"American audiences as a rule do not like women on the lecture platform, it was declared yesterday by Dr. Russell Potter, director of the Columbia University Institute of Arts and Sciences. Of course Dr. Potter made exceptions of Mrs. Franklin D. Roosevelt, Dorothy Thompson, Ruth Bryan Owen, and a score of women lecturers who appear on the Institute's programme. The trouble with the women lecturers, according to Dr. Potter, is largely in their costumes and the high pitch of their voices. Dr. Potter, speaking from his experience as director of Columbia University's public lecture and entertainment course, said the 'frou-frou' of a silk gown is a distraction in the ears of any chronic lecture-goer, and a gown with a train is the despair of every platform chairman. . . . Oh, there are exceptions, of course."

Dr. Potter's list of American exceptions, in addition to the three especially mentioned, included Mary Ellen Chase, Margaret Ayer Barnes, and Sarah Wambaugh, the plebiscite expert. I was relieved to find myself, together with Mary Agnes Hamilton, Lady Drummond-Hay and the Countess of Listowel, among the four English exceptions. This Press interview appeared during the 1937 Thanksgiving period, which I was spending with Mary Ellen Chase, and the fortunate inclusion of our two names saved us both, we agreed, from what might have been an awkward social situation. Dr. Potter's comments concluded with an anecdote calculated to reassure any woman lecturer who fears that diffidence in pushing her claims may cause her manager to overlook them:

"Here is a modest little English lady who wrote recently as follows to a leading New York lecture manager: 'Will you extend your courtesy in stating if you are interested in a course of lectures in America? I have just returned from a most successful lecturing and advisory tour at the invitation of a foreign Government . . . . and our Ambassador, also Foreign Office, confirm that my honours were unprecedented. I am the woman on whom one of our most noble professions conferred the Hon. Mem., the only woman in the world on whom such distinction has been conferred. My book (it is being published in America) is a huge success. Our Queen wrote to tell me she is reading it with very great interest, and no woman has received such world distinction. I was presented at Court last year and am one of the best known and honoured women. I am the sole Rep. of Britain chosen by the foreign Gov. and held a conference with other experts, chosen from various

European centres, to create its new capital, and so I have made English history, and can say with truth that I am almost the most distinguished woman in the world'. The manager wisely replied, on a postcard: 'I am sorry I cannot encourage you.' And that was that."

On Armistice Eve—a Saturday—G. had joined me in New York. Together we delivered "a message from England" at the Women's Overseas Service League dinner, where I sat next to John Erskine—vaguely reminiscent of John Drinkwater—whose *Private Life of Helen of Troy* had once provided a welcome contrast to the lugubrious tragedies of *The Perennial Bachelor*.

My publisher, George Brett—who shared my memories of war-time France and had been gassed in the Argonne—took us on to his box at the "Victory Ball" which followed immediately afterwards. Like most of his contemporaries he wore resplendent full dress uniform—navy blue adorned with gold braid and a pale-blue lined navy cloak—which transformed them all from practical New York business men into figures of Gilbert and Sullivan fantasy, who no more suggested the mud-spattered veterans of the battle-field than the ornate flag-decorated ballroom at the Waldorf-Astoria resembled the Western front.

I described the scene afterwards in a letter to Winifred:

"The show began. . . . Crowds of people in and out of the box all the time and the usual constant round of drinks. . . . Below in the huge ballroom followed the trooping of the colours—banners and pennons of all kinds, stars and stripes, the American Legion, Daughters of the American Revolution, War of Independence, Napoleonic War, Civil War, Spanish American War. It was all very colourful and magnificent, and a series of national anthems were sung while everyone stood to attention. In my mind all the time two distinct points were hammering:

"(1) This is what the peace movement is up against.

"(2) This has nothing *whatever* to do with modern war as it is waged today.

"If only you could convince the peace movement of (1) and the readers of jingo newspapers of (2), you would have got somewhere; this, I feel, is something for us to concentrate on here and now. . . . Later George Brett sat with me in the front of the box, and as we looked down upon the dancers (many of whom were now getting rather tight), he talked seriously about bayonet fighting—how wildly patriotic he was when America went into the War, how eagerly he learnt bayonet fighting and instructed other people, and then the mixture of disgust and sheer insanity which seized him when he was face to face with the real thing—also his theory that the best way to stop the next war is to announce beforehand that you will conscript *everyone*, both men and women, up to the age of ninety."

Next day G. and I watched the Armistice Day parade in Fifth Avenue—a multi-coloured forest of banners, pennons and spears moving slowly into St. Thomas's Church. Eighteen months afterwards, in my novel *Honourable Estate*, I tried to recapture the strange, elusive impression made upon me by this ceremony, though with a novelist's license I attributed it to the wrong year, and fitted it into an imaginary church and a fictitious story.

Although I knew no one among the marchers except my publisher and a few of his guests from the previous night, the pageant gradually became for me a procession of familiar ghosts, translated from Arras, the Somme, Asiago, Gallipoli, to walk through the streets of New York. It gave me the sense—customary, I believe, amongst the very old, but exceptional for those in their thirties and forties unless they belong to my generation—of having lived interminable years, and numbering more friends on the other side of the grave than on this. . . .

At the same hour Winifred was writing to me in London: "We have just come in from the usual Sunday walk. At 11.0 we stood on the steps of the little paper shop and listened, through their loud speaker, to the sounds at the Cenotaph, Big Ben, the silence, the sharp words of command, the trumpets, the clatter of shifted rifles, the stir again as the silence ended. John and Shirley stood very still, each clasping my hand and being very solemn. Only once Shirley spoke. She lifted her little face and said in a worried voice, 'I *can't* think of the dead soldiers'. Afterwards we crossed the river to the Park. A grey haze dimmed the outlines of the Embankment, roofs and ships. The air was very still and grey and cold. It was like so many Armistice days on the Bridge that we have spent together."

Inside the church, G. and I sat in the gallery and looked beneath the vivid pennons at the greying heads and developing paunches; the khaki uniforms that still fitted were in the minority now. Seeing the scarlet, blue and orange of the standards, a brilliant gently-moving rainbow against the austere grey walls of the church, I felt sick at heart once more, for I realised how ineffective the peace movement must always be until it can create its rival pageantry.

The service arranged for that military demonstration came the more as a surprise. It began with the hymn "O valiant hearts", but the prayers, collects and lesson united to emphasise America's desire for peace. Finally, in his address, ex-Governor Whitman, the war-time Governor of New York State, reminded the assembled veterans that he had reviewed troops bound for war bearing some of the colours gathered in that church, and recalled the fact that wars are never initiated by those who have to fight them:

"The history of these groups is the history of New York, the most wonderful place to live in that the sun shines on today. These boys were going out to end war for ever—that was the only true justification for their act. The peoples of the world are now united in sorrow and mourning—united in protest against the waste and horror of war. Wars are fought by soldiers but they are not made by soldiers. Here today the banners of peace are joined with the banners of war. They are gathered in solemn observance of Armistice Day, the day that marked the end of the most fearful conflict the world has ever known.

"The decision as to whether that day shall mark the

end of war and bloodshed rests with the people, not with their kings or rulers. In these times of strife, a nation that forgets its heroic dead is not a nation that can expect heroic achievement. First and foremost we are interested in manufacturing an established peace. . . . Pray God that he will make the nations of the world his kingdom. Is it too much to hope that from gatherings like this in our land and in every land today shall go forth a spirit of universal brotherhood?"

We did not realise, even in 1934, how much too much it was to hope for the immediate future. Still in the devotional mood left by the ceremony, G. and I saw our host and hostess off to Connecticut for the Armistice holiday, and dined together on the sixty-fifth floor of Rockefeller Centre, *alias* Radio City. From here, as I wrote home later, "we looked over the night lights of New York as from an aeroplane; a crescent moon winked above the still higher Empire State Building, and far in the distance we could see the twinkling scarlet lights of lighthouses out to sea, and a liner like a toy moving slowly down the river. When we were half through dinner, who should come to the next table but Beverley Nichols—plump, pink, chubby, with two male companions."

It seemed a strange transition from the religious atmosphere of the church to these incursions of the world at Radio City.

Radio City had other moments, however. When next I entered that great rocklike building, it was to broadcast my farewell talk for the League of Nations Association from WJZ on the day before I sailed. Why, I wondered, did the flat stark immensity of the huge skyscraper suggest a phenomenon of Nature rather than the achievement of man? It brought into my mind four favourite lines from Goldsmith's *Deserted Village* :

"As some tall cliff, that lifts its awful form,
     Swells from the vale, and midway leaves the storm,
     Though round its breast the rolling clouds are spread,
     Eternal sunshine settles on its head."

Eternal sunshine? Surely that was possible for America, and perhaps, even yet, for Europe? In the talk which I had prepared in Washington with memories of Minneapolis and the Grand Rapids cenotaph still vivid in my mind, I had tried to embody the hopes and aspirations shared with me, as I now realised, by so many American friends. At least two members of the Macmillan Company were listening in, I knew; and there would be Ruth Gage Colby and Izetta Robb at St. Paul . . . and perhaps some of the hundreds of young men and women whom I had met at Wellesley and Columbus and Buffalo. And last yet first among my listeners would be G. at his University—not an American, but so rich in experience of the United States that he had learnt to identify himself with American aims and beliefs and desires. He at least would understand how closely linked with the remembered Armistice Day service in St. Thomas's Church were the words that I had now to broadcast:

"This talk that I'm giving you on behalf of the League of Nations Association takes me back to a spring afternoon nearly nineteen years ago, when a young Red Cross nurse from a London military hospital spent half a day's leave in revisiting the Oxford College that she'd left the previous summer in order to do war work.

"Two of her friends gave a tea-party for her that day, and afterwards the young nurse and the group of students sat over the fire and talked about the War. In those early months of 1916 we'd at last begun to realise that the War would be a long one. The Germans were already hammering at Verdun, which was later to become so well known to the American army, and our British Tommies were characteristically remarking that the first seven years would be the worst.

"All the same, we hadn't yet quite lost the patriotic idealism which sent the youth of England so swiftly into war in 1914. People have often asked me since just what were the motives that moved us most in those early days, and I still find it rather difficult to explain.

"We who were growing up when war broke out belonged to an unsophisticated generation which was, I suppose, both more idealistic, and less aware of its political and international background, than any young generation will ever be again. Before 1914 most of us had never heard of the Treaty of 1839 which guaranteed Belgian neutrality, so newspaper excitement about 'heroic little Belgium' left us quite cold. We may have been influenced to some extent by stories of German atrocities, but I don't think we ever accepted them with quite the same bloodthirsty satisfaction as our elders who sat out the War in armchairs.

"On the whole our reactions were mainly emotional, as I imagine yours were here. Partly, of course, we were influenced by the wish to be 'in it' with our friends, and partly by a secret terror of being branded as cowards by that militant crowd of noncombatants, with their battery of sneers and innuendoes and white feathers, who went about trying to induce other people to die for them. But chiefly, I think, we were moved by the naïve idealism which the war-propagandist in a non-conscription country found it all too easy to exploit. We'd been brought up on such books as Charles Kingsley's *Heroes*, with its stirring reference to those who are slain 'in the flower of youth on the chance of winning a noble name', and we went to the War to justify to ourselves our secret worship of 'heroism in the abstract'. For this noble but completely nebulous ideal, the youth of 1914, in the words of Rupert Brooke who so thoroughly typified their spirit,

'. . . gave up the years to be
Of work and joy, and that unhoped serene,
That men call age; and those who would have been,
Their sons, they gave, their immortality.'

"In 1916 we were still clinging passionately to that tarnished and tottering faith. When patriotism wore threadbare, when suspicion and doubt began to creep in, the more ardent and frequent was the periodic rededication of ourselves, the more deliberate the self-induced conviction that our efforts were disinterested and our cause was just.

"Today it seems almost incredible that I was myself that young Red Cross nurse who sat with her fellow-students over the glowing college fire. Once I believed that I knew her intimately, but today she seems a stranger who walks like a ghost in the dim ranks of old recollections. But even less credible than my identity with her is the memory of that conversation in which we talked of the honour and glory of War, and put into halting words our pathetic faith that a nation which laid down the best of its youth would somehow achieve for them life everlasting. It seems strange that we really made ourselves believe, all those years ago, that their dust would be more valuable to their countries, twenty years after, than their living presence in our homes and our schools and our churches and our political councils.

"For what, in fact, has happened to the nations which bore the heaviest burden of the War? I often think how odd it is that so many people today seem to have forgotten that, within their own lifetime, the flower of a masculine generation disappeared into the ground or under the sea. Looking uncomfortably around, they wonder why the Church is so lethargic, why so few great 'names' have lately emerged in music and literature and art, why our politics seem an ineffectual chaos, and the League of Nations has so often been abused and mishandled by elderly cynics whose minds were hard set before the War. They complain that there seem to be so few 'younger men' to receive the torch from those chilly, cautious hands, and ignore the fact that the men who should now be taking their places as leaders in every department of national life are buried beneath the fields of France, or the sands of Gallipoli, or the pine-forests of Italy, or the mud of Mesopotamia.

"Sometimes, except by the individuals who lost them, those young men seem to have vanished from memory almost as completely as the Spanish sailors who went down in the Armada, or the obscure Greek soldiers who battered the walls of Troy. 'And some there be', wrote the author of Ecclesiasticus, 'which have no memorial; who are perished, as though they had never been; and are become as though they had never been born; and their children after them.'

"The Unknown Warrior sleeps in his honoured grave at Arlington or in Westminster Abbey; but on every battle-field of the world lie unknown warriors who were never found or never identified; whose bones are scattered and whose names, in a few short years, will be clean forgotten.

"It was partly as a memorial to the generation of young men who were once my contemporaries that I wrote *Testament of Youth*, that book which has been so generously received in this country. But I meant it to be much more than just a memorial to the betrayed and exploited dead, for it represents a vehement protest against the vain-glory of war and a passionate plea for peace—a plea not so much to the heart as to the head. I've been told that my book makes some people weep, but I care much more that it should make them think, for I don't believe that anyone now living will ever understand so clearly as my generation, whose lives have been darkened by the universal breakdown of reason in 1914, how completely the future of civilised man depends upon our present halting attempts to control our political and social passions, and to substitute for our destructive impulses the vital authority of con-structive thought.

"In effect *Testament of Youth* says to the reader: 'This wastage of life and youth and joy actually happened. From it has resulted the world that we know today—the world of unemployment and chaos and depression, in which every activity of life is hampered by lack of the first-class men who fell in the War. Do you think that anything which has happened since has made that wastage worth while? Do you want such ruin to happen again? If not, what are you going to do about it? for if you don't do something this tragedy is bound to recur. Surely the rescue of mankind from those primitive passions which lead to war could be a more exultant fight than war itself—a fight capable of enlarging the souls of men and women with the same heightened consciousness of living, and uniting them in one dedicated community whose common purpose would be greater than the individual? Only the purpose itself would be different, for its achievement would mean, not death, but life.'

"Quite often, though, both here and in England, people have said to me: 'It's all very well to appeal to your contemporaries; they'll listen because they know what war means. But it's just a waste of time talking to the boys and girls of the present day about peace and the use of their reason. They're just as much moved by emotion and passion as youth ever was. If another war broke out tomorrow, they'd fling themselves into it as ardently and senselessly as the youth of 1914.'

"Would they? I wonder. That's not quite the impression one gets from the fine support given by the young people from many student organisations to the League of Nations Association signature campaign. And it isn't the impression I've had in this lecture tour of the United States which ends when I sail for England tomorrow afternoon. It's true that I haven't been able in nine weeks to get in touch with as many groups of young men and women at schools and universities as I personally could have wished—but the ones I've met have been scattered rather widely over the East and South and Middle West of this great country, and they seem to me to be fairly representative of American opinion as a whole. I shall never forget the morning that I spoke to 5,000 students and faculty at the Convocation of the University of Minnesota, nor the groups of girl students at Wellesley and at the Woman's College of the University of North Carolina, nor the young men and women who came to my lectures at Columbus, Ohio; at the Ogontz School, Pennsylvania; at Mason City, Iowa; and at Western Reserve University, Cleveland. At the last of these cities I was asked a very interesting question after the lecture, and the question was this: 'What can your generation do to help the present generation of boys and girls to prevent another war?'

"And I am glad to say that I felt justified in answering: 'I don't think they need our help except in so far as we can leave them records of those terrible four years which they can't remember. They're far better equipped than we were in our own youth to face problems and make decisions. They have opinions based on knowledge, and they're not afraid to stand by what they believe. They realise, as we never realised, that in this shrinking, interconnected world, the private lives of men and women must be for ever linked with what George Eliot has called 'the larger destinies of mankind', and that never again will any man or woman be able to live in disregarding isolation from the problems which beset our civilisation'.

"I don't believe that the thoughtful and instructed section of modern youth wants war, and I'm sure that the youth of my own generation would not have accepted it so readily in 1914 had the keen, intelligent awareness of current problems which now prevails at schools and universities been substituted for the naïve, uninformed generosities and enthusiasms which made such easy victims of the boys and girls of twenty years ago.

"With modern youth, at any rate, will be the choice between death and life. The older generation is already passing; the war generation, shattered and bankrupt, recklessly poured away its sweet wine of youth and talent, and has left only a few individuals to set their faces against that spirit of defeatism, never permitted in war, which lies like a blight upon the work of reconstruction.

"What is happening today—in Europe especially, but elsewhere as well—is a race between the war elements, as represented by Fascist movements all over the world, and the peace groups which grow more slowly because reason is a flower that takes longer to mature than passion, but which every year, in every country, are becoming stronger and more widespread, especially among those under thirty.

"If only we can avoid war for ten years or even five, if only we can keep the peace machinery in being for that length of time, I believe that from modern youth will come the constructive personalities who will fill the gap left by the lost generation; who are capable of imagining the warless world visualised by the Kellogg Pact, and who won't be afraid of using the revolutionary machinery of the League of Nations. Some day, perhaps, within the framework of the League, American and English youth will join hands in the task of building that new order which both desire.

"Nearly two thousand years ago, a Jewish community was told that it was expedient that one man should die for the people. Maybe, as part of that inscrutable design which according to our beliefs we call the logic of history or the dispensation of Providence, it was expedient that one generation should die for the people in order to demonstrate, once and for all, the waste and futility of war. Through the loss of them the world today is bankrupt and shattered, but if the courage which my contemporaries once gave to war can be used by their successors on behalf of peace, the martyrdom of man may still lead at last to his redemption. If modern youth has realised, as I believe it has, that to live for one's country is a finer type of patriotism than to die for it, then the youth of my generation will not, after all, have laid down the best of its life in vain."

.   .   .   .   .

It was nearly over now, my second experience of America. Six hours hence, my boat—again the *Majestic*—would again sail at midnight. My clothes were packed, my last Christmas presents purchased; only three months' accumulation of books and papers remained to be put away. In my room at the Bretts' town house—so hospitably open to me whenever my lecture programme had brought me to New York—I glanced hurriedly through the heap of press-cuttings which had pursued me from city to city. There had never been time to read them properly, but a swift inspection revived the memory of one or two typical comments:

"The customer with the very delicate face and the very British accent" (*Bridgeport Post*).

"Looks rather un-English, slender and dark-haired and dark-eyed and pale" (*New York Herald-Tribune*).

"Miss Brittain appeared in blue chiffon just the colour of her eyes" (*Detroit News*).

"One could not be sure of the colour of her eyes. One minute they appeared to be brown and the next grey" (*St. Paul Dispatch*).

"Amiable but not talkative" (*Chicago Tribune*).

"She speaks with an accent, decided, but easily understood" (*St. Louis Star and Times*).

How often, I wondered, as I filed the clippings, had that small word "accent" (containing as it does the exasperating implication that the speaker is half educated) been the cause of unintentional ill-will when used by the Americans about the English and, far oftener, by the English about the Americans? To use the term "accent" in saying that an Englishman or an American speaks the language habitual to his country, makes about as much sense as stating that a Frenchman speaks French with a French accent. If we must draw constant attention to the obvious fact that England and America use different versions of the Anglo-Saxon tongue, it would be more diplomatic to discuss "intonation" or "pronunciation".

These small absurd things did matter, I thought, because they were now perpetual hindrances to mutual affection between the two peoples. The larger obstacles of ten years ago—American complacency, English envy, and the antagonisms which grew out of both—had diminished with the new American capacity for self-criticism. Three months on the American continent had only strengthened my first impression that the brash boastfulness of 1926 had given way to a deeper confidence, born of the knowledge that a country could endure adversity and still survive.

"We know we can take it," my friend Izetta Robb was to write me afterwards of the depression. Could any sentence express a profounder and better justified national pride?

It was this new spirit, I concluded, which explained the revival of American interest in Europe and especially in England. The remoter communities of the Middle West had not yet shown that interest, but throughout New England, the East and the North, its eagerness had been manifest. How had England solved *her* economic dilemmas —or how was she trying to solve them? At last America, and especially American youth, wanted to know.

I had expected, at first, to find this youth quite different from the youth of Great Britain, and instead I had met with the same interests, the same idealism. There was greater vitality, perhaps, and more sardonic humour; in 1935, when the jesting debunkers of war at Princeton enrolled a great army from two hundred colleges as "The Veterans of Future Wars", I doubted whether the serious-minded English "war-babies" of 1914 could have conceived so grotesque an invention. It was a courageous crusade to ridicule war out of existence, and it sprang from the same fierce desire to extinguish the passionate follies which destroy humanity as my lectures had uncovered amongst other student groups.

Apart from their wider knowledge and keener awareness, these young men and women seemed closer in spirit to the ardent, adventurous youth of 1914—so early exploited, so swiftly perished—than the devitalised generations of the disillusioned nineteen-twenties. In 1934 I too was nearer to the emotions of the war years, and the resolutions to which they had led, than I had been in 1925, when the effort of assessment that *Testament of Youth* represented had not yet been made. For this reason, though I had neither planned nor at first even realised it, the younger generation in many cities had regarded my visit to America as a reminder of the War, and a summons to them to apply its lessons in the making of peace. And their enthusiasm had been, in turn, a challenge to myself to work on, to refuse to lose faith in the future, from a country which had never accepted defeat.

Late that night, when my friends had left me on the *Majestic* and the great ship's engines started to throb, I could hardly have been aware of a greater contrast between this homeward voyage through December storms which was just beginning, and the first midsummer journey down the Hudson more than eight years ago.

There was no threat to privacy now in the small, comfortable cabin, and I knelt on my bed amid letters and cables and boxes of flowers, and looked out of the porthole as the boat began to move down the dark river beneath the starless winter sky. I stayed there watching, with an indescribable fathomless regret, the black silhouettes of the skyscrapers growing smaller and dimmer, until the liner had passed beneath the uplifted torch in the hand of the Statue of Liberty and the lights of New York had disappeared.

How long, I wondered, before I should see them again? Brave, gay, beloved city, I can never leave you unvisited so long as before. I'll write another book, I'll arrange another lecture tour, I'll work as hard as ever I can, and soon come back!

III.

(1937)

"It is time, I think, that someone said a few harsh words on behalf of Anglo-American relations. Many of us believe that with the state of the world what it is today, it is highly desirable that Great Britain and the United States should understand each other. . . . We are both anxious for peace, and for the restoration of decent international relationships. And there is no basis for conflict between the two nations."

Dorothy Thompson, *New York Herald-Tribune*,
December 17th, 1937.

"O remember
That in the general doom of nations, there
Is but one certain immorality,
          . . . and that is not the thrust
Of courage against the world, nor the beating down
Of all the barriers of a continent
However bravely—but the searching out
Of the new way that a new country makes,
From all the blind impulses of its life,
A vision of the universal heart
That recreates the living form of man
In the unique and individual way
That is the shape and spirit of that land."

Paul Engle, *America Remembers*.

I

Yᴇᴛ ᴀɴᴏᴛʜᴇʀ ᴛʜʀᴇᴇ years went by before I returned to America.

This time I had not meant the interval to be so long, but again the events of those years had claimed, shattered and absorbed me. In the midst of them I had planned, written and published a long novel, *Honourable Estate*, which reflected too mournfully the aftermath of loss for which no future success or happiness could bring compensation.

In America I should no longer receive Winifred Holtby's vital, stimulating, consoling letters, for Winifred was dead. But the youngest member of my family had now grown old enough to write, just before my second lecture tour concluded: "Dear Mummy, I am looking forward to your coming home! We have bought all our presents except one. I feel so exited about Xmas. It is better to give than recieve."

When I left Waterloo for Southampton this little girl of seven, hurrying after me to the platform, had fallen suddenly on the slippery floor of the Booking Office and bruised her nose and forehead. My last impression, as the train left the station, was the picture of her small tearstained face trying to smile. This pathetic memory haunted me so persistently that more than once on that crossing in the *Georgic*—which seemed quiet and slow after the six-day liners of the previous voyage—I lay dismally prostrate in my cabin, too wretched with homesickness and anxiety for my children to make any effort to go up on deck. This time I travelled alone, leaving my household and family in G.'s charge while I carried out another tour for the same efficient lecture agent who had managed my last.

It was a warm, unaggressive September: half the passengers lounged on deck chairs in summer frocks, reading *The*

Citadel, And So—Victoria, Northwest Passage and *American Dream*. On September 22nd our *Ocean Times*, reporting the progress of the new Japanese invasion in China, announced that Great Britain would discuss with the United States the possible withdrawal of the British Ambassador from Tokyo. This proposal seemed hardly a favourable augury for the maintenance of that troubled semi-peace which I constantly feared might not even endure for the thirteen weeks of my absence from Europe. On our last day at sea, a terrific swell from the tail of a Florida hurricane caused our boat to roll like a drunken leviathan, though the sky was cloudless and the ocean a placid ultramarine. Mentally perturbed and physically uncomfortable, I cursed with the old awareness of irreconcilable conflict the lure of adventure and experience which had again summoned me from home.

But when the *Georgic* drew nearer to America, sailing like the *Berengaria* three years before into the orange afterglow of a dramatic sunset, my troubled longing for my family was eclipsed by an upward surge of excited anticipation. My feelings towards the land beyond the western horizon were now very different from both the prejudiced antagonism of 1925 and the uneasy apprehensions of 1934. I was travelling to a country which I knew and loved, to carry out work with which I was familiar, and to meet once more some of the best friends that I possessed.

As we moved up the Bay in the evening darkness to the lively music of a ship's concert, and anchored off Quarantine for the night while a young baritone sang the German lyric "*Ich liebe dich*", I went out on deck to see all around us the lights of Staten Island and the Brooklyn shore. At once the affection for America and her vivacious people swept over me that I had felt when we crept down the river in the opposite direction during the small hours of a December morning. The friendly golden eyes seemed to guarantee the same benevolent welcome, the same kindly vigilance, as I had experienced throughout an unforgettable autumn.

I could hardly wait for the hot, oppressive night to pass and allow me to get off the boat. Although I had seen it so often before, I hurried to the window with the other "aliens" waiting for the immigration officials in the lounge when the titanic green figure of the Statue of Liberty suddenly loomed through the pale swirling fog. An English critic of the New Deal satirically apostrophised his American fellow-passenger: "Well! Still raising statues to your dead?"

My confident expectation of an agreeable welcome was more than justified. A representative from my publishers met me on the docks and took me to the Brevoort for breakfast; two other members of the firm had converted my hotel bedroom into a flower-garden of pale pink lilies, mauve gladioli, and monster dahlias with huge coral-tipped petals, such as we see only at flower-shows in England. In the evening an alert, sophisticated Macmillan editor picked me up in her car and carried me off to a cocktail party and dinner.

I spent the sweltering interval dizzily repacking six trunks and suitcases in preparation for my tour and the two country visits arranged to precede it. Like most New York hotel bedrooms, my room overlooking a side-street close to Washington Square was so planned as to admit the minimum of air and light. Though I flung up the windows and fastened back the voluminous layers of curtain and net, the dim, hot room seemed to roll like the *Georgic* on its last day at sea, and at intervals I was forced to leave my disordered possessions and lie panting on the bed till the unsteady floor recovered its equilibrium.

I had landed on a Sunday, and New York was quiet; but through the open windows came a restless, continuous murmur which I speedily recognised. One of the many changes that I have observed during my visits to America is the development of an anonymous voice, urbane, experienced, persistent, carrying on from some unknown studio an endless, unintelligible commentary on the universe with a ubiquitousness not yet achieved across the Atlantic. Sometimes the voice appears to be describing a football game, a political gathering, or a Presidential reception; at others it merely discourses, interminably and at large.

When I first came to the United States, this audible ghost announced its presence only in occasional restaurants and hotel lounges. By 1934, it had become a recognised feature of entertainment houses, and was beginning to penetrate into trains and taxicabs. Today it is everywhere. If I walk through the peaceful streets of some small, isolated city in Iowa, Oklahoma, Georgia or Maine, it addresses me, subdued but relentless, through the doors and windows of innumerable dwellings. If I travel from Chicago to New Orleans, it greets me from club cars and yellow cabs at every stage of the journey. If I ask for a quiet back room in a New York hotel, it echoes until long past midnight from wall to wall of the canyonlike courtyard.

I have a feeling that even if, like the psalmist, I took the wings of the morning and flew to the uttermost parts of the sea, even there its determined accents would pursue me, and its sibilant undertones give me insistent news of the latest baseball sensation.

By the next morning I had recovered sufficiently for a cheerful breakfast with my publisher, George Brett, and a visit to my lecture manager's office, where I listened with comparative equanimity to the long tale of engagements and itineraries. That evening my publisher drove me out of the city for four days in Connecticut. His New York house was closed, I gathered, until the end of November; the growing burden of State and Federal taxes was driving many New Yorkers to live in the country for more than half the year. He had already begun to build a new home for his family on a wooded hillside in the wild virgin country near Easton, Connecticut, seven miles from Fairfield.

This change, I soon noticed, was not the only one that three years had brought. We ran out of New York past the clean, lofty span of the George Washington Bridge, which had existed only as a project in 1934, and the new green car travelled beside the Hudson along a recently opened orna-

mental parkway, branching into the country between
beautifully landscaped banks and gardens. It was a gentle,
windless evening, and we drove under the usual superb
American sunset, like the gates of heaven opening with
approval upon this aspiring city eternally renewed.

I had already learnt that the Connecticut family were not
alone in spending all their available time in the country.
Since I was last in New York my friend Harold Latham had
bought a property, pleasantly named "Content", at
Onteora in the Catskills, where he had invited me for a long
week-end. On the same Friday, I was driven back from
Connecticut into New York and out again along the hundred
and-thirty-mile road through the Hudson valley to Onteora.
The two drives totalled less than two hundred miles—a mere
bagatelle of a journey to hardened Americans, who in one
day can cover six hundred miles of level Midwestern high-
way without any apparent effect upon head, hands, backbone, eyesight or hearing.

But though I have almost completely adapted myself to
American train travel, I suspect that my obstinate Staffordshire organism will never achieve accommodation to the
speed standards of an automobile-minded nation. Thanks
to the long rapid drive, and the sudden ascent after dark
from river level to the three-thousand-feet altitude of the
Catskills, I spent my first night at Onteora dreaming that I
was fastened to an overturning boat in the company of Mr.
Justice Black, whose recent appointment to the Supreme
Court put sound and fury into every political conversation.
Three weeks after President Roosevelt's second inaugural
address to Congress, the American people had been presented with his proposals for reforming the Court, which
had become a barrier to his social plans. The result was a
political struggle of first-class proportions.

On the evening of our late arrival at Onteora, I listened
with Harold Latham, his mother, and the rest of their
house-party to the former Senator from Alabama defending
over the radio his vehemently critisized early association
with the Ku-Klux Klan. His explanation sounded irate, and

reminded me of the familiar French proverb, *Qui s'excuse, s'accuse*. It would have served its purpose better, I thought, if instead of angrily minimising his youthful allegiance, he had described, with the frankness which fallible humanity always finds disarming, a change of political faith not peculiar to himself.

We awoke next day to rain and damp, drifting mist, which obscured the august pageantry of the Catskills; the season was late for the Onteora community, and Harold Latham had kept his house open longer than usual on my account. In that rarefied, vigorous air, which challenged my fatigue with the scintillating sharpness of strong smelling salts, I was tempted to spend the morning lazily before the enormous fireplace, where half a tree-trunk could burn at a time, in the large, comfortable living room with its baronial semi-gallery and rich abundance of Persian rugs, Indian mats and soft thick carpets. But a seasick dizziness persisted, and I knew that my powers of recuperation would serve me better if I plunged courageously into the rain and wind of the wild mountain woods.

One or two intrepid fellow guests plunged with me, and for two hours we walked rapidly up and down the hillside along paths of saturated grass beneath dripping trees. Occasional frame houses, now closed, nestled cosily within the forest, and at a junction of two mountain paths we passed an old log-cabin labelled with the immortal name of Mark Twain. Though the thick white mist still hung like a drop-curtain beyond the woods, I had a persistent consciousness of vast spaces and dominant altitudes on its further side. Once or twice a corner of the curtain unrolled, and we caught, as in a mirage, intermittent glimpses of distant cloud-raked peaks, or isolated grey roofs appearing amid the subdued brilliance of tree-tops in the rain-soaked valley far below.

By the afternoon, my dizziness and the mist had alike disappeared. Standing with Harold Latham on the great verandah which opened out of the living room, I realised that his house was built on the steep side of an ascending slope. Its balcony and lower bedroom windows looked directly down upon the brushlike boughs of a young fir plantation, where wild cyclamen grew in pale magenta patches between the slim red-brown trunks.

"I've been looking forward for weeks to showing you this," he said, and I understood his fear that the mist might not disperse and uncover the glory which their hanging veils had concealed.

As though from the high gallery of a theatre, I gazed over the mountain side upon the most incredible miles of unimpaired forest that I had ever beheld. Incalculable in their climbing myriads, oaks and maples, beeches and firs, silver birches, scarlet sumac and mountain laurel filled the huge open cup of the valley with a transcendent pandemonium of orange and gold, purple and vermilion, amber and chestnut and peacock-green. Opposite our verandah, surrounding this spectacular arboreal tumult on every side, range upon range of still higher Catskills piled themselves arrogantly against the distant pale horizon.

Unable to tear myself away from the sight of this rich unimagined paradise, I was made to lie idly in a lounge chair while the rest of the household prepared a tea-party for eighty guests who had been invited to meet me. These guests represented the hardy surviving remnant of the Onteora community which had not yet returned to the city for the winter. As soon as I saw the first-comers, I realised that here was a type of American society which I had not yet encountered, and was unlikely to meet anywhere else throughout the United States except in a few historic cities of New England. With their keen intellectual faces, reserved demeanour and austere, practical clothes, these Catskill dwellers might have come from an English Cathedral city or one of the older English universities.

I enjoyed that tea-party, with its unexpectedly British atmosphere and familiar conversation. But long after I have forgotten the names and faces of the kindly, cultured men and women whom I met there, I shall remember lying on the wide verandah with the early October sunshine caressing my face, still dazzled by the prodigal beauty of a primeval world which stretched beyond sight of mortal eyes to the shining illimitable highlands of eternity.

Early the following week in New York, working in the same Board Room, dictating letters to the same accomplished secretary, being interviewed by the representatives of similar newspapers who asked me many of the same questions, I felt at first as though the interval since my previous visit had blown away on the winds of Manhattan. But soon I became aware of a sense of stability, both in my own existence and in America's, which had not been there in 1934.

Like every erstwhile "arrival" on the literary scene, I had settled down. Editors, interviewers, photographers and agents were now part of life's normal routine; they did not intimidate, excite and bewilder me in the perturbing fashion of three years ago. I had ceased to be a "new sensation" and had become an "established author"—which means that the persons concerned no longer radiate with enthusiasm if your latest book sells in thousands; they merely show annoyance if it doesn't.

With one completed American tour and a dozen years of English platforms behind me, I could also perhaps claim to be an "established" lecturer. At any rate, I knew that I should accept the rough with the smooth, adapt myself to huge auditoriums and exacting audiences, take ecstatic appreciation as much for granted as hostile criticism, and remain reasonably undisturbed by the less pleasant incidentals of American travel, such as porterless junctions, midnight crossings of unknown cities, and the catching of abominable trains at dawn.

America too had achieved a balanced self-possession, which resembled the nervous apprehensions of the depression as little as the boastful confidence of prosperity. The country which had lost its terrors for me now appeared to have few for itself; bitter as the years of chaos had been, they had not brought those humiliations which create a national inferiority complex. Whatever disasters the Americans had suffered, they had gone on believing in themselves; they remained gaily and gloriously free from the pessimistic apathy which had descended upon the Old World in the nineteen-twenties, and continued to corrode the vital energy of English life.

In the conversations that I shared and the plans which I heard discussed, I felt the same sense of eagerness, the identical consciousness of unlimited constructive possibilities, which had impressed me between 1925 and 1927, and even in 1934. The business "recession" that began soon after my arrival was accepted with a new philosophical calm, though there was far more criticism of the Roosevelt administration, and a great deal of talk about the new taxes. But when I attempted to discover its causes, I found myself stultified, as always in America, by the conflicting facts and figures brought forward by political opponents to prove their contentions.

Perhaps the greatest difficulty encountered by truth-seeking visitors to the United States lies in these incompatible statements, made with apparently equal sincerity by the friends and the enemies of some particular policy, action or legislation. Such statements are usually delivered with far more passion, and far less ability to see anything whatever in an opponent's point of view, than is customary even amongst English party politicians. The reasons alleged for the business recession tended, I found, to differ fundamentally according to the political colour of the person discussing them and the part of the country in which they were discussed.

I was not surprised to find Dorothy Thompson, in her famous column, "On the Record", syndicated by the Republican *New York Herald Tribune*, attributing the 20 per cent drop in industrial production, and the half-million increase in industrial unemployment, to "the accumulations of bad regulation, defective planning and ill-advised taxation". Nor was I astonished when our equally conservative *Times*, in its Report of the Year 1937 which

I read after I returned to England, added the high cost of labour and the twenty-five hundred industrial strikes of the previous twelve months to Miss Thompson's list of causes.

"In several particulars," contributed the more impartial weekly newsmagazine *Time*, "the Recession is more remarkable than the Depression. It is remarkable because the 35 per cent plummet from last summer's high is the swiftest decline in the history of U.S. business and finance. It is remarkable because the big, obvious factors which are usually held responsible for economic retrograde—swollen credit, top-heavy inventories, unmanageable surpluses—are not in existence. . . . In large measure the principal cause of the Recession appears to be purely psychological, the result of Capital's mass pessimism about the future and a consequent reluctance to make future commitments."

Two facts alone appeared certain to a puzzled British observer. Reaction, though it had caused dismay, was this time stopping a long way short of panic; and it was mainly due, not to lack of credit, but to the failure of economic confidence. According to my Democratic friends in Minnesota, the contemptuous slang phrases of this apprehensive period—"Oh, yeah?" and "So what?"—were themselves by-products of the great Depression which had blasted certainty to smithereens.

As I went about my business up and down Fifth Avenue in the warm, heavy dullness of that early October, I discovered a conspicuous omission from the front windows of its numerous offices. The symbolic posters of 1934, with their alert, rapacious blue eagles, no longer hung there; the National Industrial Recovery Act, having failed to create the New Jerusalem, had been thrown on the political scrapheap. It was now fashionable, I found, to despise that well-intentioned but too ambitious experiment.

"In this country, more certainly than any other country," confessed Izetta Winter Robb, "'nothing succeeds like success', and nothing, nothing, is so thoroughly damned as failure. . . . We all believed that the N.R.A. was the way to get round the Corner. Our disappointment bred bitterness. . . . A more perfect instrument must be devised for the regulation of our economic life. I am bound to confess that for me the National Industrial Recovery Act is prophetic of the will of the people to create a commonwealth that is not supported economically by the exploitation and enslavement of a majority of its citizens."

So the N.R.A., born June 16th, 1933, was officially killed on January 1st, 1936. One delighted critic, learning of the legal end of the Blue Eagle, wired his firm, "N.R.A. dead—go ahead", though the persistent bird had risen again like a phoenix in the Wagner Labour Act, which guaranteed to Labour the right to organise for collective bargaining.

But why, I inquired, had the original measure failed so disastrously?

Because it was too difficult to administer, answered the Democrats in chorus. Because its programme was as large as America. Because it had been ruined by the profit-making expedients of "chisellers". But the Republicans, it seemed, had other views, and the Truth About the New Deal proved as elusive a quarry as the Truth About the Business Recession. To the Republicans the colour of the Roosevelt administration was a ruinous red; to the Socialists and Communists it was an ineffective blue; and bewildered foreigners were not alone in their baffled endeavours to find a *via media* of fact between the two poles of tendentious animosity.

One eminent American who understood and regretted these conflicting prejudices was George V. Denny, Jr., President of The Town Hall, Inc., that "clearing house for ideas" where the autumn's list of non-American lecturers included Norman Angell, Count de Sales, Philip Guedalla, Count Keyserling, S. K. Ratcliffe, Salvador de Madariaga, Mary Agnes Hamilton, and myself. In a speech delivered at Harvard University on July 26th, Mr. Denny had already discussed the gathering crescendo of regional dogmatism:

Qs

"A distinguished professor of my university used to say: 'We are largely what we are because we are where we are.' How easy it is to pass on the curbstone opinions of the group or class with whom we live! Last year at this time I could take you to different sections of New York and its environs, and predict with 95 per cent accuracy precisely what opinions you would hear expressed.

"On almost any train leaving Grand Central Station at five o'clock for Westchester County or Connecticut, you would hear Mr. Roosevelt and the New Deal condemned with an intolerance and bitterness that would astonish any reasonable-minded man. If you took a bus to Jersey at the same hour, you would hear fanatical loyalty to the present administration and a blind acceptance of practically all that Mr. Roosevelt was doing. Or if you took a trip to Union Square about the same time, you would hear unbridled condemnation of capitalism by socialist and communist speakers bitterly vying with each other for the attention of available listeners. Would you have expected to hear the New Deal praised in Vermont or condemned in Mississippi? I am reminded of the story of the Scotch minister who prayed: 'Grant, O Lord, that we may always be right, for Thou knowest we will never change our minds.'"

Mr. Denny followed these strictures by quoting Walter Lippmann, who had described in a recent commencement address at Drake University the change in humanity's temper since the year of his graduation, 1910.

"Men," he had stated, "have become increasingly irreconcilable. More and more men divide into groups which totally distrust one another, are unable and unwilling to talk with one another, no longer use the same words to mean the same things, and really believe that unless they conquer their opponents they will be conquered by them."

Alien though I was, I could endorse Mr. Denny's experience, for more than once during that autumn, on trains to Connecticut or in the clubs and hotels of Chicago, I heard some of the "economic royalists" who opposed the New Deal discussing the Roosevelt administration with implacable ferocity. Their criticisms, if challenged, usually gathered slowly but surely round the universal subject of taxation.

The Federal income-tax rate, I learnt, was now a normal of 4 per cent, with a surtax on all net incomes of over $4000 (£800) up to an indefinite figure, the rates ranging from 4 per cent to 75 per cent. The exemption was only $1000 (£200) for single persons, and $2500 (£500) for the married. Then, of course, my acquaintance explained, there were State taxes too, running, for instance, in New York State, from 2 per cent to 7 per cent on net incomes. An emergency tax of 1 per cent on net incomes was also demanded, but I gathered that there was no State surtax, and the same exemptions as in the Federal tax return applied.

These lamenting Republican taxpayers listened with a pained lack of enthusiasm when I pointed out that we in England had endured, with little complaint, similar taxation ever since the War. The astronomical incomes of our few millionaires were burdened, perhaps, no more severely than theirs, but the great bulk of our people above the lowest levels of poverty—our clerks and skilled artisans, our middle, professional and moderately wealthy business classes—paid far heavier taxes than their counterparts in the United States.

Apart from a one-fifth relief on earned incomes, and allowances for marriage, children, working wives, dependents, housekeepers, and old age, designed especially to help moderately endowed families, British subjects had been paying an income tax of 5 shillings in the pound (i.e. 25 per cent) since 1931, and would probably have to pay 5s. 6d. after the next Budget. Exemption, I affirmed, occurred at levels still lower than their own—£125 a year for single persons and £225 for the childless married, with rising exemptions at the rate of £75 a year for each child. Surtax, on the other hand, began at £2,000 a year on a sliding scale. A charge of 1 shilling per pound plus 10 per cent was made on the first £500, 1s. 3d. plus 10 per cent on the next £500, 2 shillings plus 10 per cent on the next thousand, and so on until individuals with incomes ranging between £10,000 and £15,000 paid more than half of it away in taxes (i.e. a surtax of 5s. 6d. plus 10 per cent, in addition to ordinary income tax at 5 shillings or 5s. 6d. in the pound). The few incomes of £50,000 upwards paid a surtax of 7s. 6d. in the pound plus 10 per cent.

These taxes, I emphasised, were paid promptly and with few evasions by rich and poor alike, since the average much-enduring Englishman took the view that government demands, being in the interest of everybody, were just and legitimate. When protests arose, they were usually made on grounds of principle by pacifists like myself, who objected to contributing a proportion of their incomes to military expenditure. It seemed, to put it mildly, an incongruous irony that part of the taxes paid on the royalties from *Testament of Youth* and *Honourable Estate* should go towards financing the rearmament policy of Conservative governments which had been in power since 1931. But, like most middle-class persons with similar incomes, I should not dream of evading the payments demanded for rebuilding schools, constructing roads, improving the national health services or raising the school-leaving age. By making provision for those citizens known to America as "the underprivileged" and collecting my contribution, the State spared me the time and thought which I should be obliged to give to social responsibilities if everything was left to voluntary effort.

Perhaps I presented these facts with a touch of national self-righteousness, though I never rose to the lyric level of the London *Evening Standard* leader for April 12th, 1938. In explaining how small was the minority of tax-dodgers in Great Britain, the *Standard* declared:

"The ordinary British taxpayer is the wonder of the world. The patience with which he bears, and the honesty with which he pays, heavy direct impositions laid upon him by the State astonish foreign nations. For there are countries where the evasion of taxes is a recognised sport and a form of thrift which no prudent citizen would neglect."

My comparisons, at any rate, were accepted with indifference or incredulity; the description of our civic integrity left my listeners unmoved by any emotion but surprised scorn for the incorrigible submissiveness of the British people. Their opposition to the "red" measures of the New Deal remained so caustic that at times I felt tempted to inquire whether, when they refused to listen to the President on the wireless and turned on only those speakers with whom they already agreed, they were not undermining the liberal foundations of their own democracy. I longed to quote to them another comment from George V. Denny's Harvard lecture: "Why, the way we're going now, we're following in the footsteps of the judge who said he never listened to more than one side of a case because it confused him to hear the other."

But when, as Mr. Denny's speech had warned me, I turned to the commentators on the Left, I found truth and impartiality no easier to capture. One trained economic observer from the British Labour Party, visiting America that same autumn, despairingly summed up the Roosevelt policy as a conglomeration of compromises and experiments in which it was difficult to discern any unifying link.

"Practically everything," she wrote, "that has been tried in either of the President's two terms of office is consistent with the attempt to establish a sort of discreetly tempered social-service quasi-democratic capitalism. This is true both of experiments which failed, like the N.R.A., and of those (like the new Social Insurance Laws) which are still operative."

In some of the great American cities, I came across Socialists and Communists whose spoken and published vituperations made milk and water of this circumspect English judgment. The New Deal wasn't really new in any way, they told me. It was a very Old Deal—positively antiquated, in fact. The President had initiated nothing but a crusade of compromise, a claque of Brain Trusters, a hocus-pocus of "intellectual make-believes and administrative monkeyshines", who wanted "the big bad bankers and the good little workers to play together in peace".

In a typical Left-wing condemnation, I read that these inept exponents of "the peculiarly naïve intellectual make-shifts of our liberal mind" had allowed Big Business to manipulate the New Deal to suit itself, and to turn the national policy into a spectacular but fundamentally inglorious attempt to bolster up the tottering capitalist system. Instead of nationalising the banks, the Roosevelt administration had salvaged private banking. Instead of nationalising the railroads, it continued to bolster them up by loans. Its plan for saving the farmers and small home-owners from foreclosure had merely rehabilitated the great insurance companies by relieving them of the burden of shaky mortgages. In attempting to safeguard the property interests of the middle and working classes, it had reintrenched Big Industry and Big Finance. It left virtually undisturbed the power of Big Ownership, which was still able to profit at the expense of everyone else.

But in the South, the Southwest and the progressive Northern States, the loyal Democrats did not agree. Up to the time that I left America and after, they were still prepared to defend the New Deal with their pens and voices. Soon after I returned to England, Izetta Winter Robb sent me the copy of a fighting speech which she had made in the 1936 Presidential campaign. It expressed views that she still endorsed.

"Great agencies," she had said, "were set up by the Government in the gigantic war on depression. The most thrilling drama in history was staged as the Government came to the rescue of its citizens. . . . Under the work programmes and increased private industry, five and one-half million people went to work, and a great consuming public started spending. . . . Work is the way out. The dole means moral stagnation and eventual degradation. . . . The work programme dollar is spent for American agriculture, industries and trades. All this gain is added to the great and lasting monuments of the work programme: the Triborough Bridge in New York, the San Francisco Bridges, the Shenandoah Valley National Park, completion of Boulder Dam, highways, needed federal buildings, stadiums, irrigation projects, soil conservation units, rural schools, low cost housing in large cities, clothing and food for the needy, libraries, technical surveys, and increased medical services. The dollars spent in this fight against the depression have been worthily used."

In the covering note which enclosed her speech, she included a final warning and vindication.

"One more word about the New Deal. It is an attempt to bring some sense into a mad world. We no longer talk of the work programme as an emergency measure; we are facing a long task. After five years of the New Deal, some say we should be nearer the solution of grave economic problems, but to say that is to fail to recognise the magnitude of human need and frailty. We are trying to find out how to regain economic balance after a world-wide depression. We cannot afford not to provide a work programme. . . . We cannot afford to leave the national problem of poverty to the jurisdiction of each state. We must make life better for people, richer than it ever has been. Life in a third-floor-back is easily sacrificed in war or revolution."

From this welter of conflicting testimonies and opinions, one conclusion alone seemed clearly to emerge. The New Deal, in view of its concrete achievements, was at least better than the policy of the previous administration, which had been no Deal at all. Even if it were true that Big Business was the most ardently salvaged victim of the Depression and the chief beneficiary of the Roosevelt experiment, the whole gigantic earthquake had wrought a salutary, profound and lasting change in the national psychology of America.

Never again could her profiteers return to the grandiose untrammelled piracy of the great boom era. Never would she lose the new courage and the quieter endurance which sorrow had added to the adventurous valour of her travellers and explorers. Through nearly a decade of stern experience she had learnt to set her teeth and go forward without the stimulus of success and self-satisfaction. For the first time in history her citizens could say, with Winifred Holtby in *South Riding:* "Quite a few of us have to get through life without too good an opinion of ourselves, and yet we manage."

II

Early in october, before setting out for the Middle West as a preliminary stage of my journey to the Southwest and the Deep South, I had more than a week to spend upon peaceful preparation.

"These eight preliminary days in New York really are delightful," I wrote to G. "I have enough to do to keep me pleasantly occupied, but not the same sense of rush as three years ago, when I had only three days in New York, and everything to be crushed into them."

It was a sombre week of rain and thunderclouds, with sultry nights; whatever I opened or turned off, my hotel bedroom temperature refused to fall below eighty degrees. Despite a feeling of tension due to the exhausting weather, I soon remarked that the atmosphere of stringency and strain which still overwhelmed the city in 1934 had given way to a consciousness of sufficiency without ostentation. There was even time to make rational experiments—which had never seemed possible during the bewildered scramble of my previous visit—in economical living. The cost of personal services, I discovered, appeared to be half-way back to the 1925 level, but I was able to report to G. that I had found a small restaurant in West Eighth Street where I could get an excellent lunch and dinner for forty cents and fifty-five cents respectively.

"I find I can't stand up either financially or physically to more than one per day of the slap-up major meals they provide at these big hotels. . . . Once you get off the rich hotel track, food in this country now seems definitely better and cheaper than at home; there is a sense of plenty and prosperity here quite different from 1934—and again quite different from the cock-a-hoop, self-conscious extravagance of 1925. It is service . . . for which one pays so highly. I can't get a shampoo, wave, manicure and eyebrow trim in any place where cleanliness is guaranteed for less than $5 total." (The complete charge for these four "beauty" items by a high-class London hairdresser is usually about 12s. 6d.—i.e. $3.)

Notwithstanding this preliminary visit to a beauty parlour and a day's intensive study of notes already prepared, my first lecture, on October 5th, was again a failure. I regretted that this ineptitude should be visited upon so eminent an engaging organisation as Bryn Mawr College, but I knew that, as on my last tour, I should soon adjust my English standards to the level of American expectations.

"I felt it hard going all the time, heavy and dull," I admitted to G. "I could make many excuses for myself —the chief being that after a day of incredible heat and heaviness which gave me a cracking headache and made me feel I was going to be suffocated, a terrific thunderstorm followed by torrential rain broke just before my lecture. Everything was hot and steaming like a tropical jungle, but in spite of this they had *heated* the lecture hall; the audience—as various members admitted to me afterwards —squirmed and wriggled with heat. Their discomfort, however, was nothing to mine! My head cracked till I could hardly see my notes, and I was bathed in perspiration from head to foot."

That same afternoon, in Chicago, President Roosevelt was diplomatically delivering his famous "Quarantine" speech on the World Political Situation.

"The peace-loving nations," I read next morning beneath a three-column heading in the *New York Times*, "must make a concerted effort in opposition to those violations of treaties and those ignorings of humane instincts which today are creating a state of international anarchy and instability from which there is no escape through mere isolation or neutrality. . . .

"There is a solidarity and interdependence about the modern world, both technically and morally, which makes it impossible for any nation completely to isolate itself from economic and political upheavals in the rest of the world, especially when such upheavals appear to be spreading and not declining. . . .

"When an epidemic of physical disease starts to spread, the community approves and joins in a quarantine of the patients in order to protect the health of the community against the spread of the disease. . . . We are determined to keep out of war, yet we cannot insure ourselves against the disastrous effects of war and the dangers of involvement. We are adopting such measures as will minimize our risk of involvement, but we cannot have complete protection in a world of disorder in which confidence and security have broken down. . . . "

What did it all mean? I asked myself, my thoughts switching instantaneously to my children as I tried to deduce the President's real intentions from his suave yet challenging phrases. At that moment my publisher came into the Macmillan Board Room, and I held out the *New York Times* in questioning agitation.

"Have you seen the President's speech? Is he making a gesture of support to the collective system? Could war possibly break out while I'm over here?"

"Don't you believe it!" said my publisher cheerfully. "Mr. Roosevelt doesn't want war. All he wants is to get Justice Black off the front page of the newspapers!"

At six A.M. on October 12th, I was literally thrown off my sleeper at Athens, Ohio, where I was to lecture at midday to the Ohio University Convocation of two thousand students. In the disconcerting fashion of American trains when there is no special reason for speed, we had arrived some minutes before time, and in spite of the conductor's assurances, the warm damp mist which shrouded the tracks and the platform made me sleepily uncertain whether I had been deposited at the right destination.

Half an hour later, I stood at my hotel window and watched the crimson sun rising over the attractive little university city, cupped in a brilliant semicircle of wooded hills. After a seven A.M. breakfast, I took an early-morning walk round the town. In that southern section of Ohio only twenty-odd miles from Kentucky, the air still held a soft summer warmth; scarlet bushes, "afire with God", were everywhere, and golden leaves fell gently from the trees in the peaceful sunshine.

In 1934, I remembered, these preliminary perambulations had often taught me more about a city than the lectures themselves. One of the places that I had always sought out when time permitted was the municipal cemetery, since more local history could sometimes be learned from the dead than from the articulate but preoccupied living. That morning, close to a pleasant country road leading from the single main street to the characteristic semi-rural border-land of small American towns, I found in less than half an hour the tranquil acres where the former citizens of Athens were gathered together.

At the cemetery gate a bronze "In Memoriam" tablet had been erected, and I stopped to read it. "Civil War," ran the first heading, and below the words I counted forty-three names. At the foot of the tablet, as though by an afterthought, came a second heading, "World War," but the names beneath this portentous title numbered only two.

All at once, as I stood there alone in the early-morning sunshine, I perceived one explanation of America's comparative indifference to the sufferings of postwar Europe which I had resented so bitterly in 1925. To the citizens of a Union bought by disaster, their "Great War"—the war that decimated families and shattered households—was not the European War at all, but the Civil War. The descendants of the men who fought for the North or the South were still too intensely conscious of that national tragedy to feel any comparable interest in a struggle which took only a tiny percentage of their people to unfamiliar battlefields thousands of miles away.

At that very moment, Margaret Mitchell's *Gone with the Wind* still headed the fiction best-seller list with record

sales which less than a year after publication had reached
the astounding total of a million. Her epic of the South had
brought wealth to our mutual American publishers and made
a fortune for its author—though, like myself on a humbler
scale, she suffered egregiously from income-tax authorities
who remained unmoved by the fact that a book which earned
the bulk of its royalties in twelve months had required
several years of hard unremunerated work for its writing.
No war book of the Great War, in America or elsewhere,
had ever come within sight of such fabulous success as
this novel which embodied the preoccupations of every
American family two generations ago.

Gazing contemplatively at a stone angel inscribed "To
the sacred memory of the Unknown Dead who rest here,
1806–1924", I vaguely recalled a letter from a Michigan
correspondent who had made the same comparison between
America's war and our own. It was to be emphasised for me
during the next few weeks by the little field graveyards
scattered through the South, so pathetically similar to the
war cemeteries on the Western Front.

When I returned to England, I looked up my correspondent's observations in the files which house the letters written
me by readers of *Testament of Youth*.

"Many in this country," I read, "were scarred and racked
after our Civil War, much as you in England are now. My
own father's father was killed in battle on a June 16th when
only thirty-one, leaving a young widow in her early twenties.
All my father's life was coloured by this early grief. . . .
My mother's older brother entered the War at the age of
eighteen, coming back to die only a year later of t.b. from
the exposure endured. He was a cultured boy, engaged to a
beautiful girl, and his diary and letters are most touching.
. . . I tell you these personal facts that you may know that
others in other parts of the world have a like urge to actually do something to influence people to protest vigorously
against a recurrence of such wicked destruction of the
world's choicest spirits."

Travelling next day on to Indianapolis, the meat-packing capital of Indiana, which the State librarians had chosen for their annual convention, I mentally pigeonholed for use at future lectures the estimate of present-day American youth given me on an afternoon drive round Athens by the Dean of Women at Ohio University.

She found her girl students, she told me, more poised and balanced than the students of the nineteen-twenties. To-day, though no more tolerant of parental restrictions and ecclesiastical injunctions than they had been since the War, they were moved by an idealism which led them to seek some voluntary basis of self-discipline for their personal conduct. Her most perplexing dilemmas now, she said, seldom originated from the young women themselves, and never from those whose mothers regarded them as friends and equals. The worst troubles arose in households where girls were coerced and repressed, treated as children, blamed for their youthful inexperience. . . . I was just reflecting how often problem children were the creations of problem parents, when we reached Cincinnati, where I had to change.

Some months earlier, the catastrophic January floods in the Ohio basin had raised the river almost to the level of the great suspension bridge between Cincinnati and Covington, Kentucky, which I had crossed in 1934. The little Kentucky shacks and homesteads which then appeared to me so unsubstantial had been submerged beneath a turgid inland sea or swept away upon a swirling pitiless tide. Hundreds of lives had been lost, and over a million people made temporarily homeless. The damage to trade through the destruction or abandonment of industrial equipment had been estimated at $400,000,000, and the cost of relief was frequently given as one reason for the business recession.

Now, in mid-October, the Ohio valley was at work again, congratulating itself upon the invincible American efficiency which, whatever their cost, took the cruellest "acts of God" in its stride. Nature, as a rule, has little mercy upon the dowerless denizens of an unjust world. She smites the poorest and most populous countries with earthquakes; she pours the lava of destructive volcanoes over lands which foreign gold alone can reclaim; in cyclones she sinks the miniature fleets of small struggling powers; in mine disasters she hurls to death the breadwinners of the largest and most helpless families. Only in the United States, that unconquerable country of hurricanes, tornadoes, droughts and floods, are national resources commensurate with national disaster.

Nevertheless, the story of tragedy and loss was still written on the scarred brown face of the great valley. In Cincinnati and the country beyond, scattered heaps of rotting planks and rusting iron brought back to my mind the devastated towns in the French war-zone which I had seen half reconstructed in 1921. On both the Ohio and Kentucky banks of the river outside the city, every other house appeared to have been deserted by its inhabitants. These derelict homes with broken windows and fallen doors had been left to rot where they stood, mouldering forlornly between others in which a brave attempt had been made to repaint and rebuild.

As I journeyed, during those second and third weeks of October, round the familiar territories of Ohio, Indiana, Iowa and Illinois, I perceived that even the short interval of three years had brought transformations to the Middle West. A congested four hours' run from Indianapolis to Fort Wayne in a so-called "interurban"—half train, half bus, and wholly an invention of the devil—recalled the five hours' purgatory which had landed me at Mason City in 1934; but the development of air-conditioning had increased beyond comparison the comfort of the long-distance trains. The perpetual headaches from which I had suffered on my first tour now returned so infrequently that I recognised them to have been due not to overwork, which so seldom hurts any of us, but to the constant succession of airless, overheated railway coaches and public rooms.

When I looked out of the Pullman windows, I noticed fewer animals than in 1934; except in the Texas ranch country a fortnight later, I saw no cattle on the interminable undulating plains. But everywhere now these great tracts of country were bisected by magnificent highways, enormous clean-cut spears of concrete clearly marked with road signs and white-painted centre divisions. Along the broadest highways leading from one State capital to another, a central ribbon of grass planted with shrubs separated the contrary lines of traffic. The road signs, I observed, were moral and persuasive as well as practical.

"Death never takes a holiday," ran one. "Be careful. Drive safely."

Like the highways themselves, these impartial civic messages made the vast empty landscape more human and less lonely; the void between widely separated cities ached less for their companionable exhortations. The roads were attracting settlers, automobiles and travellers; at frequent intervals appeared the cheerful scarlet or canary-yellow of petrol pumps, side by side with little shacks selling "hot dogs" or chocolate milk-shakes beneath illuminated signs. Even the perpetual coloured advertisements for "Texaco" or "Coca-Cola" gave these interconnecting highways a life of their own. Each new stretch of placarded concrete represented one more victory by man over the mute hostility of Nature.

Before my tour was over I was again to become familiar to the limit of fatigue with this Middle-Western territory— the flat, monotonous stretch of railway line between Chicago and Buffalo, the grey roofs and high shining water-towers of Toledo, where I once alighted from the train at the same moment as a smartly dressed mother with white hair and a young face who was bringing home her three-weeks-old baby from a Chicago hospital. On the station platform a slim six-year-old child, her short plaits swinging, broke from her father's hand and rushed to greet the little sister.

"Oh, honey! Oh, honey!" she cried, jumping excitedly up and down. I recalled, with a pang of homesickness, a ridiculous conversation between my small fair-haired daughter and myself the previous spring.

"Oh, Mummy, I wish it was July!"

"Whatever do you want it to be July for, darling?"

"Well, 'cos July's my birthday and I'm going to have two rabbits, and people say they have a baby nearly every day. Only a lady and gentleman rabbit, of course. Not two ladies, or two gentlemen."

Despite the uniformity of the prairie landscapes, these long-distance trains with their small human incidents, their helpful American ticket-collectors and their friendly negro porters, offered me the same relief and refuge as in 1934. The railway employees seemed even more co-operative and efficient, more illustrative of the fact that though America has her classes, she is infinitely less class-conscious and class-divided than ourselves. I remember the patience with which a well-to-do "drunk" who refused to recognise his home station was quietly escorted from the parlour car to the platform at Evanston, Illinois, and the kindly interest displayed by the ticket-collector who tucked me up on an expanding Pullman seat during a cold midnight journey from Elkhart, Indiana, to Chicago.

"You the lady that was givin' a lecture in our town? Elkhart's my home, and when you got on the train I said to myself, 'I bet that's the lady that was lecturin' there tonight.'"

Next morning, on the stream-lined Zephyr to St. Paul, another ticket-collector, with the same dignified and courteous mien, explained to the negro conductor how his son at "the University" had helped two fellow-students to write a twelve-hundred-word thesis.

"Twelve hundred words—that's a lot, you know. Yes, sir-r! There they were last Sunday, up at our place, and my boy was dictatin' to those two lads. Um, they figure it all out right from the beginning nowadays, do these young people!"

Late one October night, at Davenport on the Mississippi, the Iowa librarians welcomed me like a long absent friend. When the midday lecture was over, their secretary, his wife and another convention speaker, escorted me across the

Rs

river to lunch at Rock Island, Illinois. Because Illinois had abandoned Prohibition, whereas Iowa was still virtually "dry", I found myself for the first time on the expansive bosom of the Mississippi. Unlike the Danube, which cuts the Hungarian plain with the straight sweep of a bright metal sword, the Mississippi divides the United States as a wriggling titanic serpent stretched from top to bottom might divide a huge and variegated meadow. Its basin, I was told, is larger than the whole of Europe apart from Norway, Sweden and Russia.

We crossed on one of the ancient paddle-steamers, known as "stern-wheelers", which still clumsily navigate the river like huge top-heavy water tortoises. At Rock Island, my host selected an eating-house called "Harper's", famous for its "sea-food" and the newspaper-decorated bar where we gratefully drank our Manhattan cocktails. Piles of old newspapers, I learnt, had been discovered in a cellar when the place was refurnished, and a politically minded proprietor had used their front pages as an original form of wall-paper. Most of the selected sheets contained big headlines announcing important events—"ROOSEVELT ELECTED", "DEATH OF PRESIDENT HARDING", and, stretching conspicuously across the centre wall, "THE END OF THE WAR".

On our return crossing to Davenport I watched for the first time the American gambling game called Bingo, played on the steamer by a gregarious crowd of frowzily dressed women with over-painted faces, who alternately chewed their peanuts and used them as counters. This peculiar choice of location for their afternoon game was explained, said my companions, by the laws which prohibited gambling in both Iowa and Illinois. Unable to gratify their passion in either State, the fanatical ladies took to the Federal waters, where each crossing of the Mississippi cost them five cents apiece. The intense concentration that they brought to Bingo was sufficient to create a new and workable disarmament programme for a world of war-threatened states.

That evening, with the assurance of another lecturing invitation the next time I came to America, I said goodbye to my Iowa friends and returned to Chicago for engagements in Columbus, Ohio, and Madison, Wisconsin.

"So far, in spite of late nights ", I had written to G. the previous day, "I don't feel as worn down as I did last time —perhaps because I know the ropes, perhaps because I worry less about the lectures. I have discovered that the audiences really seem to like it better if I more or less abandon my notes and talk informally about whatever comes into my head. . . . The Indiana librarians decided, when I got to the lecture with the notes on the subject they had chosen, that they really preferred one of the other topics, so I talked for eighty minutes with no notes at all."

Already I realised that the questions asked by the audiences of 1937 would differ considerably from the typical inquiries of 1934. They tended to divide into two mutually exclusive series, the one turning upon the abdication and marriage of Edward VIII, which had filled so much space in the American newspapers, the other centring round England's rearmament programme.

After nine months of vehement controversy, it was still impossible to escape from America's obsession with our monarchical crisis. I had only to utter the words "Edward", "Mrs. Simpson", and "Duke of Windsor", and a crowd would materialise from nowhere exactly as it does when a street accident occurs. I was thankful that I already possessed reasonably strong minority views on the subject, for if I had not had them I should have been obliged to invent them. On every occasion I urged my questioners to read the recently published *Magic of Monarchy*, by Kingsley Martin, editor of our weekly journal *The New Statesman*; it would explain to them, I felt, their own fascination with the topic, as well as the peculiar manifestations of British snobbery and hypocrisy.

I preferred the second group of inquiries, which were linked with problems of wider importance, though their discussion meant heavy work and much altercation. No longer, now, could I proclaim myself an eager advocate of the League of Nations or an ardent sympathiser with its supporting societies; the two Japanese invasions of China, the annexation of Abyssinia and the Civil War in Spain had exposed not only the unworkableness of sanctions, but the latent militarism of those who cried for wars of vengeance in the name of peace.

For nearly twenty years, peace organisations in Great Britain and elsewhere had protested their belief in negotiation rather than war. Presumably they had meant only easy negotiation with an agreeable adversary who offered his opponents no temptation to fight, for since the emergence of resolute and unattractive aggressors, the erstwhile peace-lovers had begun to talk in terms of the battlefield rather than the council table. I could not advertise the League of Nations as the supreme instrument of peace when its supporters appeared more likely to use it as a convenient moral camouflage for the old type of "punitive" war.

Nor could I forget, moving as I did amongst American groups genuinely anxious for peace to be maintained or restored, that if only the United States had been a member of the League from the beginning, the expedient devised to cure the mortal sickness of international politics might never have degenerated into the dangerous half-League of 1937. I could not forgive the opponents of President Wilson for sacrificing world recovery to party triumph, nor wholly acquit them for the failure of the greatest peace-making machinery ever created by the mind of man.

For myself, I told my questioners, I had reached the point where halfway houses to the peace ideal no longer offered me a spiritual home. I knew as well as anyone else that this ideal was unlikely to be fully realised in the lifetime of my generation, but if it was not upheld through the dark hours when men and women lost faith in their own noblest qualities, it would never be realised at all. Thank God, I was not a politician, wedded to the ignoble expediences of the hour; I did not have to begin advocating peace by agreeing to compromise with war. As a Sponsor of the

Peace Pledge Union, founded in 1936 by Canon H. R. L. Sheppard and George Lansbury, I had pledged myself— together with the hundred thousand members of that young but rapidly growing organisation—to renounce war, and never again to support or sanction another.

I had known that we were a minority in England, despised, like the conscientious objectors of 1914 to 1918, by the robustly patriotic lip-servers of peace, but I was not aware until almost the end of my tour that some of these lip- servers, as lecturers on the European situation, were making full use of their opportunities in America. Late that autumn, when I was about to leave one large city for a Sunday engagement in another, an anxious missive arrived from my lecture manager's office:

"We are in receipt of a letter from our representative, contents of which concern you and your lecture engage- ment in X. The gist of it is as follows:

"It seems that the Program Chairman has engaged, including yourself, three English lecturers, all-in-a-row, and you will be the third. The first one introduced the thought that if peace cannot be maintained, then England expects the U.S.A. to back her to the man. The second lecturer continued much along the same vein, and they feel that if you followed suit, it would be just too much.

"Of course, she doesn't want you to feel that they are restricting you from speaking your own mind but, on the other hand, they don't want their pulpit used for war propa- ganda and would appreciate it if you would talk 'Peace'."

Fortunately, it was easy to send my perturbed corres- pondent a reassuring reply.

By the time that I reached that final stage, the United States, even in the Middle West, was concentrating more attention upon the grave complications of international relationships than I had found apparent earlier in the autumn.

"I have been interested," I wrote to G. on October 15th, "in the anti-Roosevelt reactions of the Cleveland and Chicago newspapers since the 'Quarantine' speech—so different from the warm endorsements of the East. The Middle West doesn't care if Japan mops up the whole of China. And after all, why should it?"

Reading the newspapers on many long railway journeys, I realised that in America the year 1937 had been one continuous struggle for power between conflicting groups. The legislative battle over the Supreme Court had its economic counterpart in the fight for the domination of organised socialism between the old-fashioned craft unions of the American Federation of Labour under William Green, and the aggressive industrial unions of the Committee for Industrial Organisation led by John L. Lewis.

This bitter contest appeared to be only one expression of a general revolt against wealth which had now become widespread throughout the United States, and was responsible for much adverse criticism of the New Deal on the ground that it allowed the privileged to escape too lightly. Already I had seen evidences of this mood in the pickets who, throughout my three months in America, constantly paraded Fifth Avenue between Fourteenth Street and Washington Square. Most of them carried placards or sandwich boards declaring that the workers of some particular trade, firm or restaurant were on strike, and urging the public to refrain from supporting employers who were hostile to organised labour.

American Socialism, it seemed, had three obstacles to overcome before it could hope for serious political influence. It must heal the breach in its own ranks—at present a remote probability; it must win the widely distributed farm vote, and must overcome the fierce hostility of an unprogressive middle class inclined—as I had perceived for myself —to ferocious hysteria. At present the future of Labour appeared to lie with the C.I.O., despite the fact that its adherent unions—some of them the best-run in the United States—were being busily excommunicated by the A. F. of L. The C.I.O. had already begun to organise the backward agricultural workers of the South and Southwest, and its membership numbered three and three-quarter million as against the three and a quarter million of the older craft organisation.

From a British Labour economist who had made close contact with the C.I.O., I learnt that an atmosphere of urgent excitement electrified its ranks. Workers of all kinds —automobile factory operatives, paper-bag makers, confectionery employees, lumbermen and even teachers—were crowding into trade unions, or creating them, where they did not exist, almost overnight. In addition to the struggle within the movement itself, Labour was fighting Capital for recognition, establishing the right of unions to exist and to compel employers to recognise and deal with them.

The attitude of the Administration appeared to be dubious. Mr. Roosevelt, declared some commentators, was Labour's most adaptable ally; his fate and that of John L. Lewis were bound up together, and his Government had watched with great anxiety the vigorously debated Wagner Act slip past the vigilant "Nine Old Men" of the Supreme Court. Big Business certainly suffered a series of electric shocks that autumn from the La Follette "Civil Liberties" Committee of the Senate. As a vice-president of the unofficial Council of Civil Liberties in Great Britain, I tracked the progressive La Follette Committee down to its source.

The idea originated, I discovered, in February, 1936, at the Cosmos Club in Washington, where a group of fifteen radicals—amongst whom were John L. Lewis, Gardner Jackson of the American Civil Liberties Union, and Dorothy Detzer of the Women's International League for Peace and Freedom—discussed with Senator Robert La Follette the possibility of a Senatorial investigation into violations of civil liberty.

An active subcommittee resulted. It was instructed to examine alleged infringements of the rights of free speech and assembly, and to investigate interferences, such as strike-breaking and industrial espionage, with the freedom of labour to organise and bargain collectively. By February, 1937, sums amounting to $55,000 had been appropriated to the use of this Committee. Its first reports, issued on

February 8th and July 22nd, made the unofficial testimonies of the British Civil Liberties Council appear mild and unalarming. Evidences had been discovered of violent intimidation, and some conflicts had even resulted in death, such as the seventeen deaths which occurred during the savage struggle between the non-combine steel employers and the Steel Workers' Union.

One of the organisations "investigated" by the La Follette Committee during my visit to America was the New York State Economic Council, a group which—like many "patriotic" conservative bodies in Great Britain—saw the red hand of Communism in such innocuously roseate societies as the Woman's International League. A heart-rending appeal on behalf of Private Enterprise, issued by the Council after representatives of the Senate Committee had begun to examine its records, happened to fall into my hands and seems worth reproducing as a social curiosity:

"To ALL AMERICANS

"The next six months may decide the fate of free America.

"If the radical forces win, your property may presently cease to be worth anything. Your income may completely stop. Private Enterprise will languish. There will be misery among the people that government alone may not be able to relieve. Government by trying to own, or to run, or to control, everything, will have completely stalled American Private Enterprise.

"These radicals recognise the fight the New York State Economic Council is making for Private Enterprise—for do they not apparently seek Senate aid to destroy us?

"If Council Letter 51 strikes a chord in your sense of Patriotism, then please reach for your pen and send us the largest check you can write."

From every political and social angle, that autumn of 1937 was a confused period of fermenting opinions and new alignments in which unchallengeable facts were all but impossible for a stranger to collect.

America herself seemed unable, for instance, to estimate the exact figures of her own unemployed. The Committee on Economic Security had reckoned that by February, 1938, the total number of the workless would exceed nine million, but the only known figure was that of the five million, with their fifteen million dependents, who had been on the relief rolls in January, 1935. The famous November Census, of which I read many reports during my tour, cast only a flicker of light into dark confusion. Since the inquiry was voluntary, many of the question cards issued to the unemployed were answered incorrectly or not answered at all, while the rate at which men were losing their jobs was calculated to put any census out of date within two months. In the general atmosphere of half-informed uneasiness, constant rumours were circulating of a new "Third Party"— which was to emerge in the spring of 1938 as the National Progressive Party whose allegiances, according to the preliminary announcements of Governor Philip La Follette, would probably be somewhere to the left of the Democrats.

Before the end of 1937, these domestic agitations and perplexities were overshadowed by the successive international crises which developed in the Far East. Startled and affronted by the sinking of the gunboat *Panay*, the American nation was compelled to turn its eyes upon the bleak world beyond its frontiers, and to take cognizance of that new invasion which—whatever might have been the coincident claims of Mr. Justice Black—had provoked the President's "Quarantine" speech. The situation presented American diplomacy with a typical dilemma of modern international politics, since the war, like all recent "wars", had never been declared.

"It is a remarkable tribute to the strength of new ideals current in the world, that even the militarists are willing to wage war in the field, but not on paper," wrote John Gunther in a *Saturday Evening Post* article, "This Peace Is a Cheat" which I read on a long journey from Springfield,

Massachusetts, to Rockford, Illinois. "The word 'war' is ugly these days to normal ears. Before 1914, war was perfectly 'respectable'; nowadays it is not. But it is even more remarkable that so many people are willing to swallow a war which is not a war, painlessly, while a war overtly declared gives a moral headache."

No war, he emphasised, had been declared in Europe or Asia since the Kellogg Pact was signed in 1928, for no one knew just what the United States might do in the event of its formal violation. "The inference is that no power quite dares to ignore it. They wage only undeclared wars— and at least the piece of parchment is inviolate."

Thus the Roosevelt administration found itself confronted by an international "incident" of the first magnitude, in which the *Panay*, unofficially present, was irregularly sunk by unauthorised Japanese bombs.

The tense uneasiness of that restless autumn seemed to influence even the climate, which never rivalled in the East and Middle West the rich Indian summer of 1934.

"How cold it is this year!" I wrote to G. just before leaving Chicago for Oklahoma in the last week of October. "Everyone says the weather is a month ahead. . . . Cold, cold, bright weather at Madison, with vivid trees. At Columbus the gale took handfuls of orange leaves and flung them in the air, almost as high as the skyscrapers themselves."

By mid-October snow had already fallen lightly between Gary, Indiana, and Chicago—and remembering the sultry days of my previous visit, I had deliberately left my fur coat a thousand miles away in New York. It was as well, perhaps, that the bitter wind made lakeside wanderings unattractive, for I found the Lake shore of Chicago, where Archie Macdonell and I had walked three years ago, in the throes of reconstruction at the hands of the Works Progress Administration.

My elegant lakeside hotel allotted me an excellent bedroom, with an unusually large and luxurious bathroom, for the modest sum of four dollars a day, owing to my acceptance of a disadvantage which, I gathered, gave most American travellers the jitters. When I arrived there, late at night, from Davenport, the room clerk explained that owing to the presence of the inevitable convention, there was only one room on the quiet side of the hotel at a reasonable figure.

"And that, I'm afraid," he said sadly, "you wouldn't take at any price."

"Why not?" I inquired.

"Well, you see, it's got a fire-escape outside the window. We find guests don't like these rooms, and we can't get ladies to sleep in them at all."

I calculated that, so far as I knew, I had no enemies in America, very little money to attract Chicago gangsters, and no jewellery with me except for the large peacock-shaded opal ring—G.'s gift—which I always wear. The only alternative was a noisy little closet of a bedroom on the main street.

"I'll take the room with the fire-escape," I said—and did not lose one hour of sleep for the presence of the iron staircase outside my window.

I had come to Chicago to lecture on "Literature and World Peace" at the Arts Club, where my chairman was Fanny Butcher, the brilliant, vivacious literary editor of the *Chicago Tribune*. I had been disappointed by her absence from Chicago three years before, for she had given *Testament of Youth* one of its finest reviews; but this time I had the good fortune to see her on several occasions, visit her office, speak later under her auspices to the Chicago P.E.N. Club, and meet her tall, attractive husband, Richard Drummond Bokum, at dinner in their pleasant apartment.

She told me that Harold Latham—whom I was expecting to see in Chicago, since business again brought him there at the same time as myself—had already arrived at his customary hotel.

"But I doubt if you'll get hold of him," she added. "When I called him, he seemed to be just about inundated with authors."

I rang up the Macmillan office to discover from Harold himself that this information was only too true. The preliminary announcement by a Chicago newspaper that he was coming to the city to look for another *Gone with the Wind* had brought such an army of would-be best-sellers to his hotel with their manuscripts, that he was obliged to escape to the office and conceal himself behind a barrier of secretaries.

"Even now," he said, "I'm seeing authors at the rate of one every seven and a half minutes. Never in all my life have I had such an experience!"

I was obliged to leave Chicago without meeting him. At the Union Station, a tall young porter with a keen face made a half-amused, half-rueful gesture at my pile of luggage.

"Don't you want to check these big bags through?"

"No," I said, "I can't. I'm on a lecture tour, and they contain all my platform clothes. I must have them with me."

He dropped the barrow and turned to me eagerly.

"Say, I wonder if you could just give me a few hints about public speaking. I'm taking a course on it at the University."

"You don't mean to do this work always, then?"

"Sure, no! I'm going to be a ventriloquist."

"I'll tell you what I can," I said, and gave him a résumé of fifteen years' experience while we waited for the St. Louis express.

III

THE COUNTRY BETWEEN Chicago and St. Louis looked bleak and cheerless on that Sunday afternoon. Since nothing was to be seen from my parlour-car window but acres upon acres of flat maize fields turning from gold to silver in the withering autumn wind, I settled down comfortably in my chair and opened my copy of the *Chicago Sunday Tribune*.

Perhaps as a comment on the President's "Quarantine" speech, this isolationist Republican newspaper had published a remarkable anti-war cartoon. It showed a blandly smirking armaments manufacturer pointing out to three young recruits a number of pictures illustrating the most brutal ways of inflicting death in war, and asking them to decide which they preferred. The caption beneath the cartoon amiably inquired: "WHY DOESN'T HE ASK MOTHER WHICH IS THE GENTLEST METHOD OF DYING?"

I was just about to cut out the drawing and send it to the Peace Pledge Union for reproduction in their magazine, *Peace News*, when my eye was attracted by a short paragraph at the foot of a column. I read it with intense excitement, hardly believing what I saw.

"PACIFIST BEATS CHURCHILL IN GLASGOW U. ELECTION

"Glasgow, Oct. 23 (AP).—Canon Hugh Richard Sheppard tonight was elected lord rector of Glasgow university, defeating three other candidates, including Winston Churchill. Election of Canon Sheppard, a prominent pacifist, who has criticized other churchmen's views on armaments and war, was interpreted as a condemnation of the government's defence policy. Sheppard polled 538 votes and the conservative Churchill got 281."

From the moment that I landed in the United States that autumn, one of the first questions asked me by reporters everywhere had been: "Why does no one in England oppose your rearmament programme?"

I had replied promptly: "But there *is* opposition! We have a vigorous pacifist movement, but you never hear of it because the Press is hostile and won't report its meetings."

I had found so much interest in this reply, and had been pressed for so many details, that from the beginning the history of the young Peace Pledge Union had found a place in my lectures. And now, it seemed, a leading British university had emphatically underlined my answer to the reporters. Not only had I a crusade to describe, but a climax, a triumph, to add to my story. I had known that Canon Sheppard was offering himself as pacifist candidate for the Lord Rectorship of Glasgow University (the Scottish equivalent of an English Vice-Chancellorship); it would be a useful bit of peace propaganda, he had said, with his customary cheerful readiness to submit himself to misinterpretation and hostile Press criticism. But never had I, nor any, I believe, of his other friends and supporters, imagined that in the sad, apprehensive year 1937 his policy of faith and courage could be victorious even amongst young men and women whose lives were darkened, like the lives of their predecessors, by heavy thunderclouds of threatening war.

Having no one to whom I could communicate the radiant satisfaction which turned the grey autumn landscape back again to summer, I expressed it, then and there, in a letter to "Dick" himself. In the same envelope I enclosed the cartoon from the *Chicago Tribune*, knowing how delighted he would be by the coincidence of that vigorous anti-war protest occurring in the same edition of an American newspaper as the announcement of his election.

"It didn't seem even possible," I wrote later to G. on the same journey, "that he could defeat Churchill and J. B. S. Haldane, let alone by such a substantial majority, and in the University where Lord Birkenhead, as Rector, once made his notorious speech about 'glittering prizes'. As I have just written to Sheppard, it shows that there are times when the

powers of self-interest and materialism can be defeated by
the spiritual forces of this world. As soon as we get to St.
Louis I am going to cable him."

A fortnight later, in Nashville, Tennessee, I received
Dick's characteristically amused acknowledgment of my
cable—the last of several similar little notes written to me in
the brief year that I had known him.

"DEAR VERA BRITTAIN,

"I think it was lovely of you, in the midst of your turmoil, to send me a cable.

"I never thought I had an earthly chance at Glasgow,
but I got there through the magnificent efforts of people
like Morris, Joad, Murry and Rose Macaulay. And as my
constituents hadn't seen or heard me I romped home!

"Bless you. Come back soon. I think it was specially
delightful of your husband to send me a congratulatory
wire.

"Yours,
"DICK S."

When I read this letter he was already dead, but I did
not know it. The newspapers in the South carry little
English news, and such space as they devoted to it was then
clamorously occupied by speculations about the proposed
visit of our ex-sovereign and his bride to the United States.
They made no mention of the fact that a fifty-six-year-old
Canon of St. Paul's, famous for his peculiar belief that
professing Christians should live in accordance with the
teaching of Christ, had died in his study chair, with a half-
finished letter before him, on the morning of All Saints'
Eve.

Two weeks afterwards the New York papers carried long
obituaries of Ramsay MacDonald, but I gathered that even
they had barely referred to Dick's departure. Yet the one
had outlived his usefulness by seven years, and the other,
had he survived for another decade, might have changed
the course of history as individual leaders and idealists have

changed it in the past, however hopelessly ahead of their
times their message appeared when they first delivered it.

It was not until my itinerary took me back to New York
on November 9th and I opened a packet of letters from
home, that I learnt that Dick had left his associates for
whatever greater glory may await men and women of his
calibre beyond the recognised confines of earthly experience.
My reply to G. that day is quoted here only because it
illustrates the impression created, even upon those who had
known him for a very short time, by that extraordinary
showman-saint, so skilfully histrionic yet so transcendently
sincere, so deeply absorbed in human beings yet so implac-
ably dedicated to one of those simple, all-powerful ideals
for which men have died and will die for ever.

"I got through my business letters and then opened
yours. I looked first at the one containing the cutting and
only mentioning his death at the end. It was as though the
bottom had dropped out of the world—a cloud had eclipsed
the bright New York sun. All day I have wanted to go away
and weep—which of course has been impossible; thirty-five
letters altogether by the three posts today. . . . I can't take it
in—nor begin even to try to estimate what a blow it will be
to the pacifist movement just when the tremendous advance
it was making had been symbolised by the victory at Glasgow
University. God certainly seems to have retired from
the scene at the moment, and left the Devil to do his worst
with the big battalions. . . . His life in itself represented
England's challenge to war—to death, the impulse of death
in society. Who will, or even can, take his place? . . .

"I can't write any more about it. I meant to take a day in
bed as soon as I'd given my business letters to Miss Z.—but
I just couldn't. It seems so absurd to make a fuss about being
a little tired when he, like Winifred, fought infinite pain
and did twice as much as everybody else in spite of it."

For a week the foundations of life seemed to have crumbled
into dust, for I could not imagine how the genuine advocates
of a peaceful civilisation could so recreate their movement
that it would function without him. Constantly through my

mind ran Maurice Baring's war-time lines "In Memoriam:
A. H.":

> "We shall be there, alas!
> But not with you. When spring shall wake the earth,
> And quicken the scarred fields to the new birth,
> Our grief shall grow. For what can spring renew
> More fiercely for us than the need of you?"

Then came more letters from home, cuttings from
various newspapers describing the memorial services and the
final ceremony at Canterbury, G.'s account of the Thames
boatmen standing bareheaded on their barges as the funeral
procession passed along the Embankment—and with these,
and the note of renewed resolve struck in the obituary
articles by his friends, came the rebirth of determination.
From that time onward the story of the Peace Pledge Union
included an account of Dick's life and death. It became a
tale of tragedy and glory to which American audiences
listened with growing interest and respect.

Halfway through the night of October 24th, I woke up as
the Texas express into which I had changed at St. Louis ran
through southern Missouri. Lifting the blind of my sleeper
window, I gazed out at the rugged upland of ancient rock
known as the Ozark Plateau. Stark and enormous in the
brilliant moonlight, its forests standing like black phantoms
above the strange irregular outline of its hills, it gave an
extraordinary effect of terrifying desolation. Towards the
southwest corner of the huge empty state, a friendly congregation of lights close to the railway line brought comfort,
and I had fallen asleep again by the time that the train
entered Oklahoma.

The prospect of visiting the Southwest had given me the
thrill of excitement which comes to every travel-lover who
is able at last to see for himself distant places hitherto
realised only as names on a map. Already I knew that
Oklahoma was a newly-rich State, adding to the moderate
resources already derived from its wheat, peaches, zinc and

cotton the fabulous profits from recently developed oil-wells. During the previous five years, I learnt, the United States had produced about seventy per cent of the world's total output of oil, and had annually exported nearly half a billion dollars' worth to other countries.

"Until the oil boom began, these people had no money," I was told of the inhabitants of Oklahoma. "Now they have so much that they don't know what to do with it. A good deal goes into stadiums and racing tracks because they can't think what else to spend it on."

In the endeavour to teach them another way of spending it, public lectures, for which the Southern States had hitherto been too poor to pay, were now being organised in the Southwest as a kind of subsidiary pioneer industry, following humbly in the wake of Big Business. "Names" were selected and advertised without any special regard for congruity.

"Such an odd collection of English lecturers going to Tulsa this season," I reported to G. "Lord Marley, Priestley, Ellen Wilkinson, besides myself."

Never having been to an oil-producing region before, I had pictured an industrial area of Pennsylvania-like blackness, and was quite unprepared for the warm, clean, luxurious loveliness of a spreading rural city. Oklahoma, I discovered, was not flat like the Middle West; I awoke to see rolling country with long low ranges of wooded hills, where the trees now glowed with the same vehement shades of orange and crimson as they had worn a month earlier at Onteora.

"This Southwestern country is perfectly enchanting," my letter to G. continued. "Leaving Chicago to go to Tulsa was just like leaving London and going to Monte Carlo. It took about the same time and I imagine is about the same distance. At 12.0 on Sunday midday, when I left Chicago, the temperature was 33 degrees. On Monday in Tulsa, at the same time, it was 84 degrees. One went straight from winter into summer. Tulsa is a most attractive place, a new city built in among trees, so that from a distance, except for

the collection of little skyscrapers in the main street, it
looks like a pleasant wood covering many square miles and
interspersed with small white houses."

Although uneasy recollections of Upton Sinclair's novel
Oil lingered at the back of my mind, from the vantage point
outside the city where I was taken to "get" the view, there
was nothing to indicate the existence of poverty or slums in
Tulsa. But Lord Marley, who went there later and was able
to stay longer, told me that this agreeable impression was
quite illusory; Tulsa possessed slums as disreputable as any
he had seen in an American city. He was partly responsible, he said, for starting a social service council to tackle
the problem.

That night, from my lofty hotel bedroom, I watched the
most remarkable sunset of my recollection even in that
dramatic continent of superlative evening skies. My window,
which had as magnificent a view as any in that part of
America, looked due west over the Arkansas River to a
group of oil refineries at the foot of a low hill known locally
as Turkey Mountain. Covering the entire western firmament
in a gigantic circular sweep from north to south, brilliant
flamingo-shaded fissures of light glowed fiercely incandescent
between deep furrows of heavy purple cloud. Not a whisper
of wind stirred the living colours of the flaming sky; the pale
cylinders of the oil plant across the river turned to pearly
roseate jewels, gleaming faintly through the twilight which
gathered round the lower slopes of the darkening ridge.
It seemed unbelievable that ugliness, cruelty and exploitation could thrive in the midst of so much beauty.

I was obliged to leave Tulsa early next morning after an
evening lecture to the local Classroom Teachers' Association
—an unusually intelligent group which kept me for a further
hour discussing politics, autographing books, and answering
the inevitable questions about the Abdication. A friendly
newspaper woman drove me, in the hospitable American
fashion, over the sixty miles from Tulsa to Muskogee on the
Missouri-Kansas-Texas Railroad (known as "Katy" for

short), where I had to pick up a main-line train from Kansas City to Dallas, Texas. Our drive carried us through an undulating landscape vivid with multi-coloured woods. Occasionally, between the changing trees, we could see the winding curves of the Arkansas River—"a fraud of a river," I recorded, "as in summer the bed silts up until all you can see is miles and miles of clean brown sand with narrow rivulets running between. If it weren't for quicksands in the middle you could walk across it—about a quarter-mile—in most places now."

My escort, who was obliged to return to her job, left me at Muskogee with an afternoon to spend in the shabby, somnolent old town—once an Indian settlement—before my train was due. For an hour I meandered up and down its placid sunny streets, feeling as unambitious and sleepy as the place itself. Oddly enough, as I wrote home, it recalled memories of a Cornish summer holiday which G. and I had recently spent together.

"If you can imagine anything so incongruous you might call it the Bodmin of America, but a very lost Bodmin indeed. There is no oil there; its interests are purely agricultural as far as they exist. Even there, however, there was a Woolworth's, and a shop full of very fashionable-looking hats, price one dollar, with small veils and gold ornaments. Everywhere scarlet cannas were in bloom, with big sulphur-hued butterflies hovering over them in clouds. Trees and bushes sang with tree-frogs; the grass was alive with grasshoppers and crickets in various colours, and even in the main street of Muskogee large beetles like cockchafers crawled . . . about the pavements."

When the train came in, I climbed through the observation car to the outdoor seats behind, and rode for two hours in the open air without hat or coat. Beside me sat a fellow traveller from Minnesota who two days earlier had quit snow and ice just as I had left wind and frost in Chicago. As we travelled due south we both revelled in the beneficent glow from the evening sun, suffusing the verandah at the tail of the train with a soft luminous warmth.

"I feel a different creature," continued my letter, "as soon as I can get outdoors into the sun and the trains aren't over-heated. The air seemed to be full of bright-coloured butterflies and dragon-flies and flying stalks of maize or fluff from cotton as we went along. Everywhere were cotton-fields, ready for picking, some filled with stooping darkies, others quite empty still. The little towns at which we stopped (and we stopped at them all; it was one of those slow, heavy, comfortable trains) had such fascinating Indian names as Checotah, Eufaula, Atoka. They weren't so romantic in appearance, looking rather dilapidated and neglected."

Soon we should enter Texas, the Lone Star State larger than Germany, with its rice-growing coastal plains and southern citrus plantations, its northern wheat-fields and rich supplies of oil, sulphur and potash. To the west lay its enormous cattle ranges, and now, in the northeast, we were running through the western fringe of the Cotton Belt.

Before me, from the eastern borders of Texas to the Deep South of Louisiana, Mississippi, Alabama and Georgia, stretched the land which Erskine Caldwell, the author of *Tobacco Road*, had described as "a worn-out agricultural empire." Today its ten million subjects lacked even the minimum necessities of decent living. Degenerate, frustrated, retarded, penniless, they were kept alive on Federal subsidies, amounting to $537,000,000 distributed to cotton farmers under the Agricultural Adjustment Administration in the past four years.

The South, I knew, presented not one enigma but a whole series, which defied solution by the Roosevelt administration or any other. At the beginning of the production control era established under the New Deal, cotton had been ploughed out and trampled down; this year the fields, allowed to grow again, had produced a bumper crop of over eighteen million bales, which would increase economic dilemmas instead of solving them. Half a decade of experiment with "cotton programmes" had cast a dubious light on the government's ability to plan or execute a sane agricultural policy. "During the past five years," wrote one critic, "the Cotton Belt has travelled in a circle, and is back in the ditch from which it started."

Meanwhile families that had worked industriously for a lifetime had fallen into the poor-white class and never emerged; the share-croppers' children went barefoot, half-starved and underclad; the hopeless misery of millions without a future showed itself in crumbling walls and emaciated human features. Successively victims of climate, slavery, the Civil War, the boll-weevil, soil erosion, the share-cropping system, the Great War, the depression and the agrarian experiments of the New Deal, the population of that lovely, glowing land nourished its youth on ignorance and prejudice, imposed isolation on itself, and maintained hostility towards its neighbours. Cotton, though cradled in beauty, had now become, like other deposed sovereigns, a monarch minus a crown, the out-at-elbows ruler of retrograde subjects living without hope or self-respect upon derelict acres of depleted soil.

My first Texas lecture was scheduled for the next afternoon at the Hockaday School in Dallas. Throughout the week I had dreaded this engagement to address two or three hundred schoolgirls and their seniors at the adjoining Junior College; the critical, half-informed candour of girls in their early teens alarms me, and my lecture manager had persuaded me to break my hotel rule and stay with the headmistress. I foresaw regulations, starchiness and discipline, and my heart sank a little as the train slowed down in the late evening darkness to stop at the small suburban station.

My apprehensions proved to be completely unfounded. The school so enchanted me that within twenty-four hours I was discussing with Miss Hockaday the possibility of leaving my little daughter in her charge for a term or two on some future tour. The rich colourfulness of the Southwest, I felt, would warm my child's Anglo-Saxon blood, and she would perhaps acquire a measure of young America's chic maturity with which to combat the hoydenish dowdiness of typical English schoolgirls. I had already seen many schools in different areas of the United States, but never one that I liked so well as this little college unexpectedly uphold-ing the finest educational standards in a State regarded by most Europeans as utterly raw and barbarous. Its raw and barbarous acres are still many, for Texas has only twelve cities with a population larger than 25,000, but Dallas, for all the pioneer strenuousness of its half-million inhabitants, can claim to be a civilised community. In the ambitious battle of the Southwest against primitive crudeness, the Hockaday School and its slim, brisk Principal have taken no negligible share.

"It is as lovely a place, and she as wide-awake and pro-gressive a person, as you would find anywhere in this country," I admitted to G. "Everywhere they say here that she combines Eastern standards of culture with the liberal pioneering spirit of the Southwest. When I arrived they placed at my disposal a little ground-floor suite—bedroom, sitting-room, and bathroom—exquisitely furnished and equipped with everything imaginable; books, magazines, face and bath powder, a toilet set, a vase of adorable Talis-man roses. Everything that I had heard about Southern hospitality came true. The bed was perfectly equipped with embroidered linen; outside the window the cicadas sang in the trees, and in the morning a real gem of a coloured maid brought me breakfast in bed and pressed all the clothes I needed for the day."

I learnt from Miss Hockaday that it was her custom to entertain the few foreign lecturers who visited Texas; she enjoyed getting to know them, she said. One of my recent predecessors was Gertrude Stein, who had stayed at the school for several days with her secretary, Alice B. Toklas. The friendly staff described her eccentricities with zestful appreciation. She sounded, I thought, a somewhat brusque and exacting guest, but to them she was a "character" in whom normal standards of adaptability would have been disappointing.

"These Southerners are quite unbelievable," I commented in a later letter. "They seem touched beyond words if one is ordinarily decent to them, astonished beyond expression if one utters a word of criticism of one's own country."

In the morning some of the older students escorted me round the loveliest little campus that I had seen in America. They showed me their charmingly furnished bedrooms, spacious common-room and green-shadowed swimming pool, and took me into an excellent library enriched by gifts from the Carnegie Endowment Fund. The ages at the school ranged from seven to sixteen, at the Junior College from sixteen to nineteen. Though it was evident that these girls came from well-endowed families, they appeared to possess political consciousness rather than the acute wealth consciousness of the same class in the East. For an hour at midday I sat amongst them in the common-room and answered their eager, intelligent questions.

A luncheon followed with the school staff and their friends, of whom one was Mrs. Clifford Weaver, the "doll lady of Texas" well-known to the Southwest. Since the publication of *Testament of Youth* I had received occasional letters from this Texas missionary's wife, whose original collections of international cotton dolls were designed to promote friendship between the children of different nations. Before I left America she generously presented me with her last set, a dress-box filled with tiny fair-haired, dark-skinned, green-skirted and velvet-jacketed figures. My son and daughter could have them first, she said, and then perhaps some English museum visited by thousands of children would give them a home.

When luncheon was over the school photographer followed us up and down Miss Hockaday's private garden, where flaming scented roses climbed a rustic wooden trellis and cast their delicate shadows over a shallow flight of sunlit stone steps. After she had taken several successful "snaps" the party considerately vanished, leaving me to rest in the garden before my lecture or wander at will round the golden lawns of the radiant campus.

For an hour, intoxicated with warmth and beauty, I strolled from garden to campus and back again in the

sparkling sunshine, pursuing unfamiliar birds and butterflies, or examining the luxuriant leaves of strange semi-
tropical trees. A member of the school staff who joined
me for a moment identified a few; one, I learnt, was known
by the attractive name of *bois d'arc*, and others had borrowed
the musical titles of *piñon* and *madroña* from the Spanish.
Little jade-green cypresses, their compact vaselike forms
tapering to slim feathery tufts, stood out darkly against
less easily recognisable trees and shrubs—pecans, redbuds,
chinquapins, white hickories, and Spanish bayonets like
arborescent lilies with rough-lined, peacock-blue leaves.

In the garden a cardinal bird plunged suddenly through
the bushes, a flash of crimson as he darted with prominent
crest and stiff black-tipped tail past the green-shuttered,
white-painted walls of Miss Hockaday's cottage, uttering his
loud clear whistle. From the campus came a glimpse of
vivid blue, and the shrill screech, "Jay! Jay!" which I had
first heard at St. Louis. Immediately a mocking bird
answered, his widely spread wings a moving grey and white
patch upon the bright, crisp grass where tiny beetles
gleamed in the sun like coloured jewels, and little emerald
grass-hoppers jumped as though galvanised by invisible
wires.

Poised above purple asters and petunia velvet-petalled
zinnias, the same semi-tropical, lemon-hued butterflies as
I had seen at Muskogee quivered in gaudy sociable clusters.
Officially, I was told, they were named Large Brimstones
or Cloudless Sulphurs, but many Americans called them
"Redhorns" because of their scarlet antennae. Close to the
flower garden, a lily pond half covered by cool olive leaves
palpitated with glistening monster goldfish, their feathery
pale yellow tails and fins resembling those of tropical fish
in the London Zoo.

Before I left the school for the Adolphus Hotel in Dallas
and a lecture at Fort Worth, a socially minded teacher took
me to see some artisan housing estates on the indeterminate
suburban boundaries of the city. Painted white and standing in oblong patches of new unfenced grass, the neat little

dwellings looked clean and attractive if somewhat un-substantial. I cannot now recall the rent demanded, but it struck me at the time as a reasonable enough charge for a pleasant living room, two small bedrooms, and a compact bathroom-kitchen. The design reminded me of London's cramped "luxury flats"; the artisan and his wife could hardly have occupied their home in comfort unless they had severely limited both their family and their possessions.

It seemed strange to find such carefully planned economy of space on the edge of vast undeveloped miles of virgin land crying for cultivation. No contrast could have been greater than the negro quarter of the city, where I asked Miss Hockaday's coloured chauffeur to drive us before we returned. But these large, ramshackle wooden dwellings, with their derelict verandahs and scrubby attempts at flower-gardens, were far from the dreariest coloured habitations that I saw in the South.

Already, in St. Louis, I had spent an hour between trains at twilight rashly wandering round the negro quarter near the great railway junction, and from Dallas onwards, when-ever my crowded schedule permitted, I saw what I could of the coloured sections in various Southern cities. More than once—though not in Dallas—I was urged to refrain from judging the circumstances of the Southern negro by my own standards of cleanliness and comfort. Negroes, I gathered, were cheerful, good-tempered and accommodating; they weren't used to other conditions and wouldn't appreciate them if they had them; they *liked* living in rotting shacks with broken windows and malodorous back yards. . . .

We of the British Empire, into whose annals the Recording Angel will write the sorry tale of our treatment of native populations in Kenya, in South Africa, in Irak and on the Northwest Frontier, are hardly entitled to criticise America for her refusal to assimilate an alien race. Every great power seduced by the barbarous game of imperialism has wrought an abomination of desolation in the lives of its subject peoples, though there are American districts, such as Harlem, where the negro inhabitants have achieved a higher degree of civilisation than anywhere else in the world. When, therefore, I am assured by kindly and courteous Americans that the Southern negro is content and desires no better standard of living, I can only listen, say nothing, and make my own deductions from the few facts that I have gathered for myself. I am ready enough to admit that a mere fortnight in the South teaches an alien next to nothing about the colour problems of its great cities, with their ambitious main streets and surrounding areas of sprawling dilapidation.

I am even willing—though with less abstinence from argument—to acquiesce when my Republican friends insist that, however familiar I may be with British Labour problems, I am completely ignorant about the American brand of Socialism, which is quite, quite different. My friends are undoubtedly correct in assuming that an intelligent European can spend two years in the United States and still suffer from benighted perplexity with regard to negroes in the South, industrial conflicts in the North, and the working conditions of immigrant labourers in mines and textiles. Economically, America is huge, chaotic and diverse, a land of bewildering elusive facts which defy her own experts, and American labour—outnumbered, semi-organised and not yet fully conscious—has reached only the same stage of confused political development as British labour in the Victorian era.

But there are some conclusions which even a stranger, by the mere use of eyes, ears, nose and brains, can draw without knowing anything at all.

On the morning that the assiduously protective manager of my publisher's Southwestern Office drove me from the Hockaday School to the centre of Dallas, the thermometer had soared from the eighties into the nineties. Blasts of furnacelike heat rose from the burning pavements between the skyscrapers in the business section of the city, and though I kept the electric fan running day and night, the air in my hotel bedroom was saturated with odours of petrol and cooking.

After the cold of Chicago the rising temperature reduced my depleted energy to its nadir, but seemed not in the least to interfere with the driving activity of everybody else. My arrival plunged me into an epidemic of telephone rings, hotel callers and would-be interviewers, from which the dauntless magnanimity of Macmillan's manager, Jack Phillips, alone protected me.

"I have been constantly on the go," I wrote to G. just before leaving, "and for the last three nights have not been able to get to bed till 2.15, 2.30 and 1.30 a.m. . . . Thank God the Macmillan office here let me dictate all my letters."

Comparative peace descended only when my lecture manager's Southern representative, who was living in the same hotel and feared my complete annihilation by Southwestern zeal, altered my programme and hurried me to New Orleans two days before time.

Soon after I arrived in Dallas, she drove me for thirty monotonous miles to my Fort Worth lecture at Texas Christian University—where the vigorous uncompromising students, I was told, just walked out in platoons if they didn't like a lecturer. Hot suffocating breezes blew in through the windows of the small car from the baking prairies; the sun beating on the roof made my head throb till my sight all but vanished, and the soles of my shoes resting on the floor seemed to burn through my stockings into my feet. All through my lecture—where floor and galleries were overpoweringly crammed with two thousand students, faculty and townspeople—I melted and panted, but thankfully observed that none of the students walked out.

My fellow passenger in the car—Blanche Yurka, the American actress—was impressively unmoved by the pulverising temperature. She had first made her name as Madame Defarge in *A Tale of Two Cities*, and was now touring the country under the same lecture bureau as myself. A striking fair-haired woman dressed in black, her exotic white gloves trimmed with enormous cuffs of monkey fur, she appeared inexhaustibly amused by my diminutive stature and my undisguised affection for America. Throughout the

blasting journey to Fort Worth, she and our escort teased
me with good-natured persistence for naïvely supposing
that one small Englishwoman could hope to atone for the
numerous errors of behaviour made by British visitors with
less experience of the United States.

The next day, when two new acquaintances called immediately after breakfast to show me the Southern Methodist
University on the outskirts of Dallas, the dry windless air
seemed hotter than ever. Looking from a window of the
University administration block over a beautifully planned
Italian garden, where tiny cypresses like marching sentinels
guarded the wide white paths intersecting the dormitories,
schools, halls and auditoriums of the still unfinished campus,
I was astonished to learn that three leading members of
the Faculty had postponed their lectures in order to receive
me. From this exceptional courtesy, and their subsequent
conversation which I found strangely disarming, I gathered
that my Oxford degree and the ancient, proud culture which
it symbolised had filled them all with a yearning inferiority
complex.

"You see," one middle-aged Professor explained humbly,
"we're only twenty-one years old. Everything here must
seem so raw to you—so new and experimental. We're still
so young. . . ."

"Be thankful that you are," I told him. "I've spent most
of my adult life fighting old, bad traditions, and it seems so
queer to hear people in this country apologising because
they haven't got them to fight. In Europe, years of effort go
on struggling to free ourselves from the past, whereas you
can start straight away to build for the future. Don't envy
me, or Oxford, or England; it's we who should be envying
you."

Some day, I suggested, a writer would surely arise who
would produce a great fiction-epic of the Southwest. The
fighting tale of its pioneers still remained to be told, though
such a novel, if it were faithfully to embody the spirit of
that land, would have to concentrate on to-morrow instead
of dwelling, like *Gone with the Wind*, upon yesterday.

A dark young lecturer smiled, a little self-consciously.

"Perhaps," he said, drawing me aside, "some of us are trying to write that story now. . . ."

From the University I was driven, with characteristic Texan indifference to mere barriers of space, across another sixty miles of parching prairie to lunch with the Douglas Chandors at Weatherford, beyond Fort Worth. At a dinner party on my last evening at the Hockaday School, I had met this tall, thin, *déraciné* English artist with the dreamy blue eyes and super-Oxford voice, who now amassed annual fortunes by painting the portraits of American celebrities. He showed me some of these pictures at Weatherford, a rural townlet on the edge of the ranch country where he and his eager, golden-haired Texan wife owned a large house and studio. As we drove there I saw at last the anticipated herds of shaggy, large-horned cattle, roaming over limitless prairies now dull yellow with rankly spreading ragwort.

We found Douglas Chandor making an English garden on virgin ground adjoining his estate—a formidable experiment in that region of sharp-edged vistas and harsh, waterless soil. His guests at luncheon included young Mrs. Elliott Roosevelt, the daughter-in-law of the President, a pretty, dark-eyed, unassuming girl in an attractive red frock. She had to leave early because her baby son was ill, she told me, and throughout the meal we discoursed sympathetically on the habitual untimely emergence of domestic problems. This unexpected friendly contact with a member of the President's family would have surprised me more had I not already been offered the chance of another.

On the evening of my first meeting with the Chandors, Miss Hockaday's guests had also included John William Rogers, a successful Dallas journalist to whom I expressed my astonishment at finding the name of Mrs. Franklin D. Roosevelt on my lecture manager's list.

"I can't think how she finds time," I said. "She must have the most amazing energy. I'd like to meet her."

"And she'd like to meet you," he responded unexpectedly.

"I'll tell my friend Mrs. Percy V. Pennybacker at Austin. She's an old friend of Mrs. Roosevelt's, and I know she'd love to arrange it."

"Oh—thank you!" I managed to exclaim ineptly, feeling quite overwhelmed by the promptness with which a rhetorical aspiration had been transformed into a practical probability. This, I thought, is what it means to be a genuine democracy; nobody—not even the first man or woman in the land—is completely inaccessible to anybody else. Already I had noticed with some amusement the inability of American reporters to understand the social exclusiveness of British royalty.

"Do you know Edward?" they asked me with simple directness. And when I replied that the Royal family were not book-readers and I was hardly of the social type from which their friends were chosen, I caught the puzzled, suspicious glances of questioning ingenuous eyes. What's wrong with her? they mutely inquired. Does she drink, or take drugs? Is she living in sin? There must be *some* reason why he doesn't know her.

I left Dallas when the sinking sun poured over the western plains, its brick-red glow luridly emphasising the hard, vivid colours of that dry illimitable land. The train to New Orleans was again no rapid modern express—as my manager's representative had warned me, "it just keeps milling along" —but in the air-conditioned Pullman car I felt cool for the first time in three unutterably exhausting days.

As the passionate aftermath of the sunset turned swiftly to dark-blue twilight, I sank into my corner with a sigh of relief and began to write down for G. a few recent conclusions:

"This past week's experiences since leaving Chicago have taught me—or rather impressed upon me—the character of this country more than ever before. Fancy being able to travel, as it were, from Oslo to Tunis under the same administration, the same language, the same civilisation. What we in Europe might learn from these people, who have welded together the inhabitants of so many races, nations and climates into a comparatively harmonious whole which lives in security and at peace with its neighbours!

"They still think they are poor, victims of the depression and of the recent stock-market crash, but when I think, for instance, of the way A.'s parents live on bread and margarine, the prosperity here seems to me incredible. Every time I eat a meal I marvel at the way they 'throw in' foodstuffs that we should have to pay for individually at quite a high price—bread, butter, biscuits, vegetables, olives, radishes, salad, tea and coffee. . . .

"Jack Phillips of Macmillan has written to three bookstore owners in New Orleans, asking them to show me everything of interest and introduce me to New Orleans authors, who seem as numerous as the literary inhabitants of Rye."

But when I reached New Orleans the next morning, my first communication was a telegram from Dallas. It ran as follows:

"Great Brittain will please keep reminding herself she is just an isle. She is not to assume responsibility for the whole blooming Empire. Remember.
"BLANCHE YURKA."

IV

I FOUND THAT the Roosevelt Hotel ("Pride of the South"), where I stayed in New Orleans, was owned and directed by Seymour Weiss, friend and political associate of Huey P. Long, the former dictator of Louisiana. The late Senator's assassination the previous year had now entered the realms of historic legend, though its real facts were still the subject of secret controversial speculation.

If G. were with me, I thought, we should spend our time here investigating the hidden, baleful origins of Fascism in the South. But as I am alone and without the co-operation of his expert political mind, I shall use my three days in seeing, like any wide-eyed European tourist, all that I can of this fragrant, bizarre, colourful potpourri of two centuries and three civilisations. Perhaps I shall learn enough to perceive why the French and Spanish settlements, so appropriate to the South and potentially so dominant, have counted for so little compared with the vigorous compelling standards of Anglo-Saxon America.

"It's such a relief to be here," I told G. after a half-hour morning stroll down Canal Street to the Mississippi, where dark-skinned cotton loaders and banana packers were placidly at work on the docks; "to escape from the dry, baking heat of the Texas prairies into this moist, heavy, somnolent atmosphere of an old city built between the river and the swamps. The weather may be as hot as it was in Dallas, but it doesn't feel like it. The air is like that of Devon in a warm mid-August. Poinsettias and gardenias grow out of doors here, and gigantic chrysanthemums like giant O-Cedar-mops, which you can buy outside Woolworth's (fancy Woolworth's even in New Orleans!) for thirty-five cents apiece. . . .

"The meals here are marvellous. One sits in a coffee-room with frescoes painted on whitewashed walls and an orchestra

Ts

playing. . . . Show the children on the map where New Orleans is, and tell them I have bought them each a little darkie doll as a souvenir. Tell Poppy (the self-selected nickname of my daughter Shirley, who inherits the family dislike of insects, and lies awake on summer nights anxiously inventing them if they do not exist) that large yellow-green locusts fly about here just like daddy-long-legs at home, making one thankful of the wire-netted windows. Perhaps she wouldn't mind them any more than I do if their large flopping presence were safely excluded."

I had already discovered that Canal Street, a few yards from my hotel, was the chief thoroughfare of New Orleans, dividing a business section of skyscrapers, offices, department stores and cafeterias. Except for its scented luxury of flowering shrubs and the glamorous advertisements of "Ramos Gin-Fizz" outside the restaurants, it seemed no different from many less romantic American cities. But only a few squares away from this noisy modern activity, the deposed main thoroughfare of Royal Street led narrowly between jewellers' shops, heterogeneously displaying a few genuine and many pseudo "antiques", into the ancient, decaying New Orleans of the original Vieux Carré.

Here the praline-sellers, their smooth dark heads covered with bright coloured scarves, still offered their cardboard packets of pecan candy to strolling inquisitive tourists. Here a few old families, refusing to move with the *nouveaux-riches* to the azalea-bordered mansions of "uptown" New Orleans, still lived behind mouldering plaster walls and listened to the melancholy tinkle of iron fountains in flagstone courtyards, coolly shadowed by tall green palms and flowering white oleander. In Jackson Square, once the Place d'Armes, where the surviving French civilisation bravely defies change and time, the high flat windows and iron lacework balconies overhanging the banquettes would have recalled the similar façade of my own eighteenth century house beside the Thames in Chelsea, but for the lavender-blue plumbago and scarlet hibiscus foaming between the slender twisted bars.

Never, even in Southern Europe, had I seen such a city of flowers. Oleanders bloomed in the Cathedral square, and azaleas, pink and cerise, adorned the municipal flower-beds between the tramways, though neither flower was in season. Beds of cannas and fuchsias glowed like sunset embers round hibiscus bushes with their large candid blossoms, mauve, vermilion and saffron-yellow. Tall poinsettias, winter flowers in New Orleans, showed long tightly sheathed scarlet buds, and delicate creamy-white tips were appearing amid the golden-green foliage of sweet olives and the stiff lacquerlike leaves of camellias. Later I found the bayous—narrow inland waterways penetrating like spears into the outlying regions of the city from the Mississippi or Lake Pontchartrain—thickly covered with a mauve orchid-shaped water-lily which natives of Louisiana treated as ruthlessly as a weed.

It was not surprising to find this sublime corner of the earth's surface commercially conscious of its beauty, and over-impressed with its age—a melancholy attribute, all too common in tired, shabby Europe, for which virile young America has so strange an admiration. In Canal Street, for the first time in my New World experience, charabanc drivers and taxicab owners, detecting with practised eyes some betraying English quality in my face or carriage, solicitously pursued me with offers of expeditions. As I walked through the crowded lounge of my hotel between glass-fronted stalls showing scarlet carnations, sweet-scented carmine rosebuds and pale gold or silver-white giant-headed chrysanthemums, neatly uniformed couriers handed me coloured leaflets self-consciously describing automobile tours of the city. One orange-hued pamphlet judiciously advertised an adventurous inspection of New Orleans "night life".

"To satisfy all types of people and in response to urgent demand," ran the announcement, "we offer a safe, conducted tour for ladies and gentlemen (no children) manned by gentlemanly guides and lecturers. . . . See the popular 'hot spots' in widely separated and outlying sections. . . .

Rub shoulders with every stratum of society. . . . And end this great five-hour night life tour in the traditional New Orleans way—with coffee and doughnuts at a quaint 'stand' in that famous old French Market, after which passengers are returned to their respective hotels."

I did not patronise the "gentlemanly guides" nor learn how one rubbed shoulders with a stratum, so the particular form of night life which the tour displayed still remains unknown to me. But I gathered from the chapter on "Voodoo" in Lyle Saxon's *Fabulous New Orleans* that the midnight city has its sinister murky excitements, only too likely to reduce unsophisticated tourists to a condition requiring their involuntary "return" to their places of residence.

In spite of this omission I found New Orleans, as I told G., more delightful than Dallas "because the air is heavier and the inhabitants less furiously energetic." The life that it offered me, though merely day life, was certainly active enough. My lecture organisers from Newcomb College, close to Tulane University, were courteously ready to act as guides; I was also taken charge of by the three bookstore owners to whom Jack Phillips of Macmillan had introduced me, Maurice Hansell, Tess Crager and Dorothy Oechsner. I already knew Miss Oechsner's brother, I discovered; he had been generous with information eighteen months earlier at the United Press Association office in Berlin, when I was travelling through Germany writing up the Rhineland election for the *Sunday Chronicle*.

My escorts assumed with eager kindness the obligation of showing me the "sights"—the more readily, perhaps, because J. B. Priestley, who had recently spent a week in the city to write an article for *Harper's Magazine*, had avoided invitations to parties or left them early. I did not blame him, for parties were many and Southern authors plentiful; the one whom I recall most clearly is Lyle Saxon himself, with his huge, impressive stature, genial countenance and twinkling, humorous eyes. For the moment, having three days in New Orleans and only one lecture, I was in a mood to enjoy both authors and parties—though as usual my desire for experience and my muscular intolerance of long automobile rides proved sadly incompatible.

"Yesterday afternoon," I wrote home, "I was driven round and round New Orleans for three solid hours!—and now I am glad of it, for I shall remember what I have seen long after I have forgotten my stiff knees and aching back. I really think humanity must have to be conditioned almost from birth to life in high-speed cars alternating with life in noisy crowds. There are times when, after hours of sitting in cars or standing at teas or on platforms, every muscle in my body feels like a separate ache.

"The day before, another group of people drove me round for two hours, and I really think I have tasted every experience that New Orleans has to offer. I have had a Jubilee cocktail and an 'ol' hen' cocktail (bright green and pale pink respectively) at Antoine's in the old French quarter, where also I have eaten *oysters Rockefeller* and *oysters Ellis*. . . . I was taken there twice."

I might have added that I had also sampled a number of other famous dishes—*Bisque d'Ecrevisses à la Cardinal, Pompano en Papillote, Pommes Soufflées, Poulet Chanteclair, Crêpes Suzette*, and *Café Brûlot Diabolique*, a potent variety of black coffee burned with cognac and flavoured with spice.

Antoine's, I learnt, was one of the world's illustrious restaurants, and undoubtedly it deserves its reputation. I have known only one other—a restaurant on Margareten Island in the Danube at Budapest, where G. and I were taken during our honeymoon by a Hungarian banker—which has equalled it in aesthetic and gastronomic satisfaction. From the time that Antoine Alciatore opened his eating-house on St. Louis Street in 1840, Antoine's has never descended to orchestras, jazz walls or gilded ceilings. Clean and severe, like a well-scrubbed Paris kitchen, it depends for its reputation upon food alone.

"When you go to Antoine's," announces its souvenir leaflet, "it is to give your palate an undisturbed treat."

In pursuit of this experience, every species of celebrity from Sarah Bernhardt to General Pershing has visited the restaurant. President Roosevelt, I discovered, had lunched there as recently as April 29th, and a photograph of the occasion, cherished by Roy Alciatore, the grandson of Antoine, showed him seated between the Governor of Louisiana, Richard W. Leche, and the dark mayor of New Orleans, Robert S. Maestri.

As the day after my arrival in this Catholic city was All Saints' Day, I was taken from luncheon at Antoine's to see the famous Métairie Cemetery in its annual full dress.

"Yesterday," reported the New Orleans *Tribune* for November 2nd, 1937, "all the saints were thanked en masse on bended knees, with offerings of flowers and love and devotion. All Saints' Day, the day New Orleans keeps her rendezvous with death, and makes a holiday occasion of it, is more than a mere religious rite. It has become an historic pageant that people come from all over the world to see."

In spite of the elaborate above-ground tombs, with their separate spires and cupolas towering amid the green feathers of the lofty palms in assertive memory of the once wealthy dead, this immense burial garden on the edge of the swamps reminded me, as I wrote to G., of the great *Zentralfriedhof* outside Vienna, which Winifred and I had visited on All Saints' Day in 1924. Only the insertion of the word "mere" in the *Tribune's* paragraph emphasized the fact that I was not in Europe, but exploring the United States.

"There was the same atmosphere of subdued festivity and the same masses of expensive flowers—only here the flowers were mostly gigantic chrysanthemums specially trained to grow an incredible size by cutting off the buds, and the cemeteries looked quite different because owing to the swampy ground the dead have to be buried above the earth and literal fortunes are spent upon colossal marble or granite vaults like individual temples. But the Americans don't sell 'hot dogs' at the cemetery gates as the Viennese sell ham sandwiches and frizzling Frankfurters, nor do the

American mourners eat their luncheon parked in groups upon the family tomb."

After the cemetery, I related, I was shown the Shushan Airport, with its small flower-dotted lozenge-shaped lawns, where a large silver Army aeroplane had landed close to the white-painted Lindbergh Hangar. We drove back to the city along a wide road skirting the sandy beaches of Lake Pontchartrain, which joins the Gulf of Mexico at its narrow eastern corner. Little wooden summerhouses stood on piles erected several yards out into the lake itself, and gaily painted boats still danced on the water's edge beyond a long line of bright-hued boat-houses.

My Cook's Tour of New Orleans continued the next day with a run round Audubon Park and the elegant oak-lined St. Charles Avenue, followed by a trip to Chalmette's plantation, where the virile Americans conquered a British force twice their size at the Battle of New Orleans on January 8, 1815, and the British General died beneath the moss-festooned Pakenham Oaks. From the heavy boughs my escort pulled a handful of this blue-grey moss, which clothes the forests of the Louisiana swamps. It hangs from the trees in swinging banners of feathery softness, but in the hand it is strong and dry, like tough grey string.

I found it typical of the United States that my final expedition should take me straight from a tenderly guarded historic battle-ground to the latest and most spectacular feat of New World engineering. The Southern pinnacle of a civilisation quite other than the old placid culture cherished by New Orleans antiquaries, the Huey P. Long Bridge, conceived by the ruthless intelligence of Louisiana's dictator, enshrines his memory in a grand two-mile sweep of soaring steel. This colossal bridge, which spans the wide Gulf-bound Mississippi and its dense surrounding swamps, is visible over many miles of verdant marshy plain. Arching into the sky like the curved skeleton backbone of some prehistoric monster, it typifies for me "the desire of the moth for the star" as truthfully as any flight of the poetic imagination. It is another example of the unlimited aspiration represented by America's skyscrapers, and it explains finally why the new civilisation has absorbed the older and less vigorous cultures of the American continent.

"I was told," ran my letter to G. embodying my final impressions of New Orleans, "that for ages they couldn't bridge the Mississippi in Louisiana because of the quicksands in the river bed, but now they have discovered a method of sinking enormous concrete blocks which descend through the quicksands and rest on the solid bottom beneath. Doesn't it seem ludicrous irony that men should divert their talents to inventing destructive war machines, when they can achieve such feats of construction!

"This country, more than any I have ever been in, makes one realise the conquering triumphant energy of humanity, in spite of its fragile, short-lived vulnerability. They were up against so much more here than the old civilisations of Europe and the Middle East—the distances so much greater, the rivers wider, the climate fiercer, the storms more violent. And what a standard of comfort and cleanliness they have achieved! New Orleans has the lovely mellowness of old European civilisation, its rich vegetation, its soft southern climate, but no smells, no dirt, no noxious ubiquitous insect-life—nothing worse than occasional bites on one's ankles by a mild mosquito. They have even invented a cream which completely eliminates under-arm perspiration, so that you can safely go about without dress-preservers on the hottest day. I suspect that this may ultimately prove as inimical to the normal process of nature as those astringent douches which all the women are so fond of—but what a comfort to go into a crowded store on a hot day without being overpowered by the odours of sweating humanity!"

However unlimited might be the successive achievements of scientific civilisation, the emotional impulses of human curiosity apparently remained unaffected by progress. By the time that I reached New Orleans, America's interest in England's monarchical crisis had risen to a loud crescendo owing to the proposed visit of the Windsors to the United States.

"Now that our ex-sovereign lord and his Duchess are to arrive here in a week's time," I told G., "it is again impossible to be interviewed about anything else; whatever one says, that is the item that gets reported! I was pursued up to my bedroom by reporters and photographers at all hours of the day."

Numerous pictures of the ex-King and his bride invariably showed Edward VIII with a worried, distraught expression, but the Duchess calm and beautiful. Side by side on its front page, a New Orleans "tabloid" published the smuggest atrocity of a photograph that I have ever had taken above the caption "Takes Up for Eddie", and an affable portrait of the British Ambassador and his wife labelled "Vague over Wally". "*POT BOILS AS WALLY NEARS*," ran the screeching headline, more mildly paraphrased on an inner page as "Orleans Pulsates over Windsors' Visit". Charles Bedaux, on his way to the United States, was already provoking the hostile comment which ultimately checked the Windsors' visit, and the Baltimore Federation of Labour scathingly emphasised the former Wallis Warfield's youthful indifference to the problems and poverty of American workers.

"Probably," remarked a leader in the *Atlanta Constitution*, "the least worried folk in Washington over the coming visit of the Duke and Duchess of Windsor are the British Ambassador, Lady Lindsay and the embassy staff. The charming Prince may be a former King-Emperor to you and me, but he is simply a member of the British royal family, no more nor less, to Sir Ronald Lindsay, his majesty's envoy extraordinary and minister plenipotentiary in Washington. To the highly civilised and perfectly correct members of the British diplomatic service, that painful event which occurred 'at long last' simply hasn't occurred."

On November 8th, the *Raleigh News and Observer* from North Carolina summed up the week's events in an article entitled "Those Ex-Quantities":

"The week's news revealed a curious parallel in the plight of the Republican party in the United States and the government of Great Britain. The Republicans have a nosey ex-President on their hands, and Great Britain has a foot-loose ex-king to worry about. Both solved problems of considerable embarrassment during the week by identical method. Britain, more or less tactfully, stalled the Duke of Windsor's anticipated visit to the United States, while the Republican National Committee crimped the Hoover proposal for a mid-term convention of the party."

Wherever I travelled, I instantly became a vicarious target for all this excitement. The mere chance that I happen to be small, slight and dark, and to part my hair in the middle, was sufficient to make several listeners describe me as "the spit and image of Wally". One or two quite irrelevant lectures owed their success solely to this illusory resemblance. When the newspapers throughout America alternately asserted and denied that Edward's trip had been cancelled, reporters vied with one another in demanding my wholly uninformed but topically British opinions. It was a relief to escape into the leisurely day-train which carried me from New Orleans to my next lecture at the University of Alabama.

"Thank Heaven," I wrote home, "I am on a peaceful, deliberate eight-hour journey to Tuscaloosa, and alone, alone! These journeys can hardly be too long; they represent the only time that I get to myself. . . . This really is a grim travel schedule, giving me only four to six hours' sleep for three successive nights, and then three nights running in the train. I have four successive lectures on four nights in four different states—Louisiana, Alabama, Georgia and Tennessee. . . .

"We have just left the Louisiana swamps behind—thick rich undergrowth interspersed with clumps of cypresses, brown grass spangled with a tallish yellow marsh flower like a super-buttercup. The swamps are full of little miracles—birds, flowers and butterflies. Everywhere hangs the grey moss . . . it appears at its most exquisite when the autumn leaves have turned scarlet against its grey.

"Here in Mississippi the swamps have disappeared and the pine-trees grow more thickly from rough brown grass with patches of green. Little velvety cows with leaf-brown coats browse here and there beneath the branches. Except for the fields of dry sugar-cane and occasional clumps of scarlet sumac, we might be in Hampshire."

At Tuscaloosa I was greeted by Professor Hudson Strode, the dark, energetic head of the English Department at the University of Alabama, and author of *South by Thunderbird;* G. had met him the previous summer while staying with Rebecca West. Apart from the station and a brief glimpse of the Campus, I never learnt the appearance of Tuscaloosa at all, for Professor Strode drove me straight to the house of the Dean of Women. Before I left it to dine with him, the swift eclipsing darkness of the Deep South had shrouded the little town with its velvet blackness.

Deans of women, as I now realised, were purely American phenomena; the career was one for which England, with her mere 35,000 undergraduates of both sexes, as yet offered no opportunity. In a country where the girl students alone amount to hundreds of thousands, women of a selected type are trained from youth to fulfil this rôle, which combines the functions of parent, university teacher and hospital matron. Nearly all the deans of women whom I have met have had dominant, gracious personalities and a powerful physique. The Dean at Alabama, true to her calling, presented me with benign Southern courtesy to a score of attractive young women—members of the University "Mortar Board" who were sponsoring my lecture.

Later, at Hudson Strode's house, I met Harriet Hassell, his former student and literary "discovery" whose first novel, *Rachel's Children,* had just been accepted by Harper's in New York and Peter Davies in London. Her book, he believed, justified a comment quoted by Lewis Follett in a recent number of the *Birmingham News:*

"The literary barrenness of the South has been overstated . . . both as to quantity and quality. A new day has come, and with it a new literature marked by new energy, new freedom and self-analysis and descriptive power."

I read *Rachel's Children* in England some weeks later, and shared Professor Strode's opinion of the author. In the spring of 1938, the New York Press reinforced us both: "Compassion, Tenderness and Brutality," ran the heading of Rose C. Feld's review in the *Herald Tribune*. "If *Rachel's Children* were a first novel written by a person of deep maturity in years and experience", she added, "it could be called a work of profundity and excellence. Coming from the pen of a young woman . . . it demands evaluation insistent upon the use of the word 'genius'."

When I met this girl from an Alabama farm, whose youth, in her own words, had been spent "looking at the green hills in my father's pasture", she was just twenty-six, slim and quiet, and simply but very skilfully dressed in a plain black velvet dinner gown which emphasised the radiant fairness of her skin and hair. Over her serious young face her emotions, controlled to the point of intensity, moved as delicately perceptible as the wind which ruffles the surface of a pool.

After the lecture I was driven through sixty miles of dark uninhabited woodland country to Birmingham, the capital of Alabama. A sudden night frost made the journey bitterly cold; I was wearing only a silk lecturing frock beneath a thin coat, and felt numbed and stiff by the time we reached Birmingham. Here I had to pick up an early-morning train and snatch, in the interval, what sleep I could—a chronic drawback of lecture itineraries over Southern railroads in a country where the main-line trains, reflecting the bitter divisions of the Civil War, run with lavish magnificence from east to west but with niggardly reluctance from north to south.

I saw even less of Birmingham than of Tuscaloosa, but I know no American city to which I have taken so keen a dislike in so short a time. It was hardly, perhaps, to be expected that the management of the large hotel where I spent the comfortless remnant of the night would display conspicuous interest in a guest who arrived after midnight and left again before 7.30 a.m., but I never encountered an American hotel which made its indifference so clear. I was told, though I did not see it, that opposite the Southern railway station in Birmingham, a massive signboard proclaimed "The Magic City". This description, I felt, must represent the pious but unfulfilled hopes of its founders, for in the grey unflattering light of early morning no habitation could have appeared less glamorous than the dingy sprawl of artisan dwellings surrounding the desolate railroad track.

Later I learnt that this dilapidated city of a quarter-million inhabitants—once known as the "Murder Capital of the World" owing to its high homicide rate—symbolised both the defeat of the agrarian by the industrial ideal in the "New South" of the Reconstruction era, and the subsequent demoralisation of Southern industry by "loan sharks", absentee landlords, local upheavals and industrial depression. The dismal evidences of Birmingham's poverty, like that of the small townships through which I passed on the weary journey to Macon over the Central of Georgia Railroad, illustrated an article by Professor Henry Steele Commager of New York University that I read some months afterwards:

"The New South differed from the old in many respects, but it did not differ from it in class arrangements. The planter class was no longer in the ascendancy, but the industrialists were just as cavalier towards the underprivileged farmers and workers and Negroes as the planters had been. The old plantation feudalism disappeared, but in its place came a new feudalism, the feudalism of tenant-farms and textile-mill villages."

From the grubby day-coach jogging through Alabama into Georgia, I sent G. a long unheroic grumble which may nevertheless serve to warn innocent English lecturers who propose to visit America of the train schedules that they may expect in the South.

"I had to get up at 6.0 to make this train at 7.40. Nominally five hours' sleep—actually about three, as I was too tired to rest even with aspirin. Now I am on one of those terrible little day coaches for another eight hours, equipped with a chicken sandwich and two bananas, as it has no buffet, and periodically boils up to volcano point. It is now 11.0; we don't get to Macon till 3.10, and already I feel as if I'd been on it all day. We are passing through lovely country—the lower slopes of the Appalachians; beautiful low peaks about the height of the Apennines covered with orange and scarlet woods—but it is an effort of will even to look at them. When I get to Macon I have to be driven fifty miles to Milledgeville; the lecture isn't till 8.30, and then I have to be driven back. It will be at least midnight before I reach the hotel at Macon again, and tomorrow I have to catch a train at 5.30 a.m. to get to Nashville via Chattanooga for another evening lecture. This means getting up at 4.0 a.m.—another four hours' sleep at the very most. My back is now so painful from the incessant sitting and standing and getting no exercise, that I can only relieve it by taking three or four hot baths a day when I am in a hotel."

Outside a small station near Macon, I saw for the first time a gang of negro convicts in their striped zebra-like uniforms, working with pickaxes on a dusty road. Whatever their crimes, their dark, patient countenances, shiny with sweat, showed the same resigned, good-tempered endurance as those of "the gang" in Margaret Bourke-White's photographs which illustrate the moving, superb study, *You Have Seen Their Faces*, made by herself and Erskine Caldwell of the pitiful victims of share-cropping in the South.

When we reached Macon I tumbled dizzily from the dirty, stuffy train, sick with dread lest I should meet some strenuous organiser who would expect sociability, bright conversation, and hours of hand-shaking at a tea-party. But for once God tempered the wind to the shorn lamb. A friendly and considerate Englishwoman from the Music Department of the Georgia State College for Women, where I was lecturing, stepped forward to greet me. Her name, she said, was Beatrice Horsbrugh, her second cousin Florence Horsbrugh, the Member of Parliament for Dundee. Though she had lived in America since the age of eleven, she retained an intuitive knowledge of British habits and British limitations.

"I'm going to give you a cup of tea at the Dempsey Hotel," she said, "and then we'll drive you to Milledgeville. You shall have a bath and lie down till supper-time, and we won't ask anyone in."

This unusual programme—which was carried out to the letter—so cheered me that during the pleasant run to Milledgeville I conquered the faintness which had threatened at Macon, and was able once more to appreciate the ripe unspoiled beauty of the Southern autumn land.

"What a lovely State Georgia is!" I wrote afterwards to G. "So rich and warm-looking with its rust-red earth, red-brown grass, and rose-red and copper trees. It is like a study in all the softest and warmest colours in the world; even the little pine-trees which are being grown everywhere all over the South to supply the growing Southern paper industry which makes paper from pine-wood, are of a special mellow green. And the rolling wood-clad hills look so beautiful after the flatness of Texas and the Middle West."

When the lecture was over the eager audience of women students applauded till I reappeared on the platform; they had received with joyous appreciation my description, in a talk on "The Changing Scene", of the pre-war chaperonage system at Oxford, which ended only a few years before I went up in 1914. Their mirth, however, was not provoked—as in the East and Middle West—by the peculiarities of a long-dead respectability, but by the fact that the young womanhood of the South suffers even today from the same protective vigilance. Rested, encouraged and cosily wrapped in a thick coat and rug lent by the generous Miss Horsbrugh, I was driven back to the Dempsey Hotel at Macon. My night there was even shorter than the night at Birmingham, but the sympathetic interest shown by the management in my arduous programme was typical of Southern courtesy at its best.

Travelling next day from dawn onwards to Nashville, Tennessee, I learned that the long-distance train from

Jacksonville, Florida, into which I had to change at Chattanooga, had been delayed by a Georgia train-smash.

"Porter tells me," I scribbled in my notebook, "that
train wreck occurred near Americus, Ga., yesterday, to a
passenger train on the Central of Georgia line. If it was
anything like the hick train I travelled on, I wonder they're
not all wrecked every day. I seem fated to be delayed on
these tours by the very few train-wrecks that occur in this
country."

At Chattanooga, committed to an indefinite delay which
only resolved itself into a certain four hours when it was too
late to use them, I wandered about the city until a sudden
soaking shower drove me back to the station. In shabby
contrast to the modern Walnut Street Bridge and imposing
white marble Post Office like a memorial sarcophagus, a
jumble of faded houses and factories straggled along either
side of the river, filling the Tennessee Valley with their
smoke. But for the sweeping dimensions of the great river
basin, I might have been in some industrial dale of the
West Riding. When I walked next day in the sharp November air round the garden of the Hermitage, Andrew Jackson's historic home outside Nashville, I noticed that the
atmosphere of Tennessee is misty from the soft coal burnt
there, and the hills, like English hills, have gentle, elusive
outlines.

Only seven miles from Chattanooga, the Chickamauga
Dam was in process of construction by the Tennessee
Valley Authority, but overwork and a crowded schedule had
limited the direction of my intelligence, and I did not
realise how close I was to the steel and concrete monuments
of regional economic planning which the New Deal has
erected to its permanent glory. Ignorantly in search of
relevant information, I walked out of the saturating rain
to the usual station stall where a local vendor sold cigarettes,
candies, postcards and guide-books.

"What's the name of the river that goes through this
city?" I inquired.

"Couldn't tell you," he responded amiably.

"But," I protested, picturing the primeval flood of water bisecting the main business centre and visible for miles down the wide smoke-dimmed valley, "I mean *this* river—the river the city's built on."

"Sure," he agreed, "but I dunno its name." A bright idea struck him. "Tell you what, let's look it up on one of these maps."

He picked up a local guide book and examined the attached map with newly awakened interest.

"Why," he exclaimed, "it's the Tennessee River!"

In return for this surprising item of intelligence, I purchased a copy of the *Chattanooga News* and sat down to read it over a late luncheon in a restaurant opposite the station. At once I perceived a rhymed paragraph which faithfully reflected the current direction of American emotions on the universal topic.

"Wherever Dave and Wally go they're stepping on somebody's toe; it's labour now, in Baltimore, that's trying hard to shut the door. Poor Windsor bears a heavy load, he's got to tread a rocky road; old England's nose is in the air—Well, Chattanooga'll take the pair."

Late in the afternoon, when the "Dixie Flyer" finally appeared, it proved—like most American "flyers" which are not of the new streamlined variety—to be one of those unhurried, dignified trains which stop at every small station to deposit mails and loads of freight. The darky waiters were all contentedly asleep in the restaurant coach when I appeared at 4.30 to order tea and cinnamon toast; as usual, they looked at me as if I were completely demented to want a meal at that hour, particularly tea. At 5.0, I knew, various passengers would come in and begin to order "dinner", consisting of lamb chops, roast pork or chipped beef hash, with numerous accessories such as crackers, biscuits, vegetables and salad. I have never understood why the average American eats his meals so early though he goes to bed so late.

Whenever I could forget to wonder whether we should reach Nashville in time for my eight o'clock lecture, the

Us

ponderous locomotive gave me adequate opportunity to admire the beautiful Tennessee mountains through which we were passing. With the imperturbable deliberation of a massive tortoise, the train was now ascending the steep incline of the Cumberland Plateau, until I could see, beyond the embankment, tier upon tier of bronze forest-clothed peaks. The unrolling landscape appeared as a vast tapestry in rich shades of brown, ranging from pale tawny tan to glowing burnt-sienna, until the sudden flame of a brilliant sunset turned the steel structures of the Cumberland Cement Company into golden palaces, and the red-brown mountain ranges faded to violet-blue shadows.

The endless day resembled one of those nightmare dreams which never come to an end. It had gone on so long that I had already eaten two breakfasts, a luncheon and a dilatory tea. Out of the previous forty-eight hours I had slept only seven, but thinking of the lecture still to be given, I fought desperately against drowsiness when dusk enveloped the forests, and pin-points of stars appeared like miniature lanterns above the fading vermilion afterglow which threw into startling relief the black summits of the distant hills.

Arriving at Nashville with only half an hour to spare, I flung on an evening dress and rushed to my lecture. When I returned to the hotel at 11 p.m., the mail clerk handed me twenty-five letters; they had accumulated because I could not be reached during the hurried trips through Alabama and Georgia. Like all lecture-tour correspondence, which often demands urgent telegrams, they had to be read then and there. By the time that I flopped into bed at one o'clock after being on the move since 4 a.m., my head swam and my legs felt as weak as though I were convalescing after a severe attack of influenza.

I had just fallen into the sound sleep of complete exhaustion, when I was violently awakened by a bright light flashing into my eyes and a uniformed figure standing beside my bed. A surly voice irately inquired: "Wha' d'yer mean by going t' bed with y'r door unlocked?"

Apologetically I tried to explain that I had hardly been

in a condition to observe the key, let alone turn it, but my English expostulations were as Greek or Hebrew to the Tennessee night-porter.

"Don' get you," he cut in summarily. "Jus' lock y'r door."

I obeyed humbly, and spent the remainder of the night alternately chasing fitful snatches of restless sleep, and listening to the unidentifiable early-morning noises in the imposing square outside the Hermitage Hotel.

At the end of my lecture a young man had made himself known to me; he was Norman Berg, the manager of my publisher's Atlanta office. With typical courtesy he had taken an eight-hour journey to hear my address and look after me at Nashville.

Next morning at breakfast I welcomed the quiet support of his presence through a discussion with a fundamentalist interviewer, who did her persistent best to make me allege that I believed in a divine plan for the universe. The lecture-going section of the city, I gathered, was rent with controversy over my address on "Youth Morals"; the young had liked it, but their elders disapproved. Later I joined an assembly of Nashville youth at Vanderbilt University, where another Dean of Women had taken me to inspect a dress show organised by the students to raise funds for a college scholarship.

As a succession of skilfully rouged and painted young women paraded before me in scarlet tweeds and jade-green velvets, I tried to imagine Somerville or Girton collecting scholarship money by a mannequin parade. But how good for them, I thought, if only they could! Dowdiness, after all, is a form of lethargy too often confused with high-minded concentration; no college authority need despise the energy required to achieve and maintain an attractive appearance.

That night I travelled with Norman Berg to Atlanta, where I had arranged to spend Sunday on the way to an engagement at Richmond, Virginia. I wanted to visit the Macmillan office in that spreading garden of a city so pleasantly laid out amongst copper-brown oaks and golden maples; I also hoped for a few moments' conversation with the author of *Gone with the Wind*. This hope was shared by our mutual publishers, who had written to Margaret Mitchell to announce my coming.

But when I arrived, I found that the fugitive, over-pursued young woman had apparently vanished from the confines of Georgia for the entire week-end; not even for an English author whom the ocean would shortly remove a safe three thousand miles from Atlanta was she to be recaptured. The only traces left of her in the city were her father's handsome white mansion on Peachtree Street, the deliciously named chief avenue, and the old-fashioned yellow brick apartment house where she herself still lives. Royalties amounting to half a million dollars had apparently caused their owner to cling with the greater tenacity to a modest apartment quietly overlooking an unpretentious side street.

Such momentary disappointment as I suffered was more than compensated at Richmond by the gracious vivacity of Ellen Glasgow, the author of *Vein of Iron* and a dozen equally distinguished novels. A note of introduction from Hudson Strode brought her back early from an afternoon conference, to give me sherry in a typical Victorian drawing-room which could hardly have been changed since her childhood. Her deafness did not hamper our discussion of the Abdication and other controversial topics, upon which, like a true Virginian, she challenged good-humouredly every view that I expressed; with unembarrassed verve she handed me her private ear telephone so that we could argue freely.

A great woman, with the profile of Ellen Terry, she embodied for me the staunch, courteous conservatism of an indomitable tradition which has survived defeat, disintegration and decay.

V

THE 14TH OF November, 1937, was as fresh and sparkling a Sunday as I had ever known in New York. It followed an Armistice week in which grief for Dick Sheppard and memories—now nineteen years old—of the War's mournful ending had been incongruously mingled with a trip to Providence, the *New York Times* Book Fair and two Victory Balls.

As I wrote, in the train to Providence, Rhode Island, a letter to Canon Stuart Morris who was to take Dick Sheppard's place as Chairman of the Peace Pledge Union, I looked out of the window and thought I had never seen that rocky, indented coast shine with so pellucid a radiance. The New England landscape wore the vivid, poignant beauty which the earth seems to put on when a friend who loved life has left it, as though the unshed tears of a survivor's sorrow create a mirror in which the significant details of a half-familiar scene are magnified and enhanced with peculiar clarity.

The trees were bare now except for the golden maples, which still shimmered like celestial shrubs in the bright sunshine of a belated Indian summer. In the dense thickets, though an occasional tangle of green leaves and scarlet berries recalled the gentler march of England's seasons through woodland undergrowth, the little thin silver birches gleamed stark and leafless; already their fragile boughs were snapped by early visitations of the frost which causes New England's winter woods to resemble a shell-torn battlefield. The earth and vegetation of these Eastern states had turned to the uniform sombre brown of a dead leaf, in contrast to the rust-red soil of Georgia and Tennessee. Tiny islands of sepia rock, tufted with bare, dry bushes, dotted the sapphire blue of irregular inlets where the white vanishing fringes of the shining waves caught flashes of gold from the afternoon sun.

Every twenty minutes or so we passed through small towns, their little green-gabled houses painted white or yellow. Against the pale azure sky stood the white puritan spires of New England's barnlike churches, sometimes varied by the tall rounded chimneys of a red-brick factory. At Westerly I noticed a ridiculous toy of a cannon—perhaps some relic of the Civil War—dominating with Lilliputian dignity an empty public square close to the station. What a cosy, compact land this was, compared with the titanic bareness of the Southwest, and the slow, difficult communications of the South! I marvelled, as always, at the adventurous curiosity which had driven so many of its original settlers to leave these clustering small cities and their warm, gregarious humanity for the menacing, inhuman silences of the great states stretching between the imperial ramparts of the Rockies and the perilous swamps bordering the Gulf of Mexico.

On Armistice morning, a member of the Macmillan Company took me to the outdoor municipal ceremony before the Eternal Light in Madison Square. Though General Pershing was present and Mayor La Guardia of New York gave a vehement address, the celebration lacked the moving quality which had raised the dead to an hour of resurrection three years before. The listening assembly would have appeared sparse and indifferent but for the reinforcing presence of the American Legion, its sharp-eyed, stern-lipped members so strangely unlike the mild and much-enduring British ex-soldier. It seemed to me that the eager, scrambling crowd which came that afternoon to Radio City to hear Ralph Thompson, McKinlay Cantor, Stephen Vincent Benét and myself speak at the Book Fair, recaptured more faithfully the spirit present in St. Thomas's Church.

When I told Stephen Benét that Winifred Holtby and I had admired together his poem "1936", which describes the marching skeleton dead of the next Great War, he read it aloud while the great audience listened in tense, acutely comprehending silence:

"All night they marched, the infantrymen under pack . . ."

The grave, gentle voice and sinister warning words seemed all too appropriate to the war-clouded Armistice Day of 1937.

Now, on a Sunday morning of sunshine dancing upon pavements washed clean by a night of furious wind and driving rain, grief and fear and fatigue were temporarily banished by a return of that invigorating exhilaration with which, through the mere fact of being, the living perpetually cheat the dead. Though accumulated work had again prevented me from leaving the city for the week-end, I seized an hour of freedom to wander through the sunlit streets and avenues round Washington Square.

Up and down Fifth Avenue, sprucely clothed men and elegant women crowded into their respective churches, the decorous guardians of sabbatarianism in a predominantly pagan country. Their sober manners and discreetly chosen finery might have belonged to an English congregation, but the success-slogans and calls to efficiency, which took the place of biblical texts on the framed placards outside the churches themselves, were typically American in their direct application of religion to the business of living.

YOU CAN FEAR YOURSELF TO FAILURE
OR FIRE YOURSELF TO SUCCESS,

announced the arresting silver letters on one black-painted poster. Later in the year, I was to find this challenge to resolution rivalled by another:

REMEMBER HOW STEEP THAT ROAD AHEAD ONCE LOOKED? THEN WE WENT STRAIGHT FOR THE TOP OF IT—AND LO! IT FLATTENED OUT.

Even in the sermons arranged and announced, America's admiration for invincibility took precedence of the gentler scriptural virtues:

DR. NORMAN V. PEALE
WILL PREACH

11 A.M.
"THE ART OF SELF-MASTERY"

8 P.M.
"MANHATTAN SINNERS"
ALL WELCOME

The churches, as usual, were not alone in their efforts to commandeer the attention of Manhattan sinners. Near Madison Square, a small shop showing a colourful collection of rubber-plaited doormats used the same silver-lettered blackboards as the clerical advertisers for its own modest proclamation: "Now is the time to be mat-minded." In Broadway a well-patronised Automat Cafeteria announced the following attractive "Breakfast Specials" for only twenty cents (tenpence) apiece:

1. Fresh fruit juice, one fried egg, one strip bacon, fried potatoes, toast, roll or muffins with butter.
2. Fresh fruit juice or hot cooked cereal with cream, two fresh eggs (fried, poached, boiled or scrambled), toast, rolls or muffin with butter.
3. Fresh fruit juice or hot cooked cereal with cream, two griddle cakes, syrup and butter, fresh country sausage.

Even fifteen cents (sevenpence halfpenny), I discovered, would buy a poached egg on buttered toast, with two strips of bacon.

Over and over again, in England, I have recalled with rueful envy the rational food values embodied in these well-planned, inexpensive meals. Only recently, at a large commercial hotel in Cheshire, I caused a small commotion by asking for an orange with which to conclude a five-and-six-penny dinner solidly composed of proteins and starches. After prolonged search, the startled waiter produced the only fresh fruit to be found in the hotel—one small hard pear, and a weary-looking little bunch of yellowish grapes. No wonder the figures of American girls are naturally slim, their eyes bright, their complexions clear! The beauty parlours of the United States achieve so marked a success because they begin with such excellent material. England has still to learn the lesson that beauty experts cannot work miracles upon the lifeless hair, unhealthy skins and unwieldy figures produced by conservative cooking and an ill-balanced diet.

From Broadway I crossed the impressive terminus of Fifth Avenue into Washington Square. The leaves, now fallen from the naked city trees, drifted sere and dry over the small enclosed plots of scrubby grass, but the mellow, gentle air still held the lingering mildness of late September. A fragrant smell, almost English, rose from the damp autumn earth, and a little notice-board on the edge of a grassplot made a wistful appeal:

> Let no one say, and say it to your shame,
> That all was beauty here until you came.

In the railed-in lozenge of the well-used sandpit, a baby playing with a blue and scarlet engine flung handfuls of sand over his navy coat and white-edged navy cap. Small neatly dressed children swung down the asphalt paths on roller skates; slim leash-held dogs of various breeds nosed one another suspiciously. The seats fringing the paths were filled with men and women of a dozen races eagerly discoursing in as many languages. Some would remain there until the sinking sun turned the upper windows of the sky-scrapers into shields of flame, and the white ghost of a three-quarter moon floated like a puff of cotton wool in the pallid eastern sky.

I walked back to my hotel past the flower-shops of West Eighth Street, multi-coloured with their royal treasure of

rich November blossom. Massed in the doorways stood vases
filled with single dahlias of a clear, bright orange, sweet
olives with white velvet petals now opened wide against
their shining golden-green leaves, tawny and yellow chrysanthemums smaller but no less vivid than the monster mops
of New Orleans. Pottery bowls ranged inside the windows
held proud purple orchids, orange marigolds, sulphur-hued
antirrhinums, a bunch of forget-me-nots, and the miniature
ruby-tipped buds of mignon roses. Their scent and colour
came back to me two days afterwards, when I heard Dr.
Hu Shih, Professor of Philosophy at the University of Pekin
and once a student at Cornell University, describe the ruin
by high-powered Japanese bombs of Chinese gardens
cultivated at Soochow since the twelfth century.

The week which followed that peaceful Sunday gave me
a programme of nine lectures in seven days. From a confused
recollection of small towns and lecture halls in Connecticut,
Scarsdale and New Jersey, the memory of the P.E.N.
Club dinner in New York at which Dr. Hu Shih spoke,
alone remains clear.

I had gone to the Algonquin Hotel not knowing the
names of my fellow-speakers, and wondering whether the
extra fatigue of this additional engagement was really worth
while. These doubts disappeared when I found my co-guests
to be Susan Ertz, Dr. Hu Shih and Eugene Lyons, the young
ex-Communist debunker of Soviet idolatry who had just
published the story of his newspaper life in Moscow. Thanks
to an enthusiastic criticism by Dorothy Thompson, the
powerful prima donna of American journalists whose word
now made and destroyed reputations, this brilliant study,
Assignment in Utopia, was already a best-seller. The author's
speech proved as witty as his book; it also released that
hard-headed, sophisticated New York gathering from the
unexpected mood of religious solemnity into which it had
been plunged by Dr. Hu Shih.

Without vehemence or bitterness, this Dante of modern
China spoke of the Japanese invasion. His dignified words

reflected in their mournful beauty the noble magnanimity of a race which was to pray in its temples for its enemies during the spring of 1938, and to send its airmen to Japanese islands carrying, not bombs, but messages urging the people of Japan to throw off their military ruling caste and make friends with the people of China. He began by describing a night which he had spent as a patient in a Chinese hospital, where a number of wounded had been brought in from a recent battle. At midnight a Japanese air-raid burst from the sky, producing a panic such as I myself remembered twenty years earlier in France, when German aeroplanes dropped their bombs near the wards of shell-shocked patients in the Army hospitals.

"After it was all over," he said sadly, "I stood beside my window and looked at the beautiful moonlight flooding the city. Once again the night was peaceful, and I mourned over the evil in humanity which could use for such a purpose this lovely moonlight so well suited to poetry and romance."

Later, in a letter sent home from Boston, I recalled the rest of his grave, unforgettable story.

"He then related his own efforts to establish the use of the flexible Chinese vernacular, in which the old novels were written, as the literary language of China (just as the vernacular of Tuscany became the literary language of Italy) instead of the old inflexible form. He told how, inspired by the example of the President of Chicago University, who toured the country to get vigorous, distinguished scholars to hold the various chairs, he got the Government of China to finance twenty-two new chairs in the University of Pekin, and how the new University had opened just three days before the first Japanese invasion of Manchuria in 1931. He described how these progressive educational movements which were transforming the old into the new China were completely held up by the War, and said sorrowfully that China expected no help from the civilised world, that she knew that neither England nor Russia nor the United States would help her to defend herself, and was relying only upon her enormous territory, her almost inexhaustible man-power, and her ability to go on manufacturing small arms, which despite modern inventions were the chief mainstay of a Chinese army in a war of this type.

"He ended by describing, without any bitter comment, the falling of Japanese bombs upon the exquisite gardens in Soochow. . . . It was one of the saddest and most impressive little addresses that I have heard in my life. The dinner meeting sat as immovable as a church congregation during a fine sermon. . . . My own speech, on the war generation of English writers, was taken up by Hu Shih in his remark that the war generation in China had hardly known anything but war throughout their lives—and that yet another war generation there was now involved."

That night, in my room close to Washington Square, the gentle exhortation which I had read two days previously rang through my mind like a plaintive bell:

> Let no one say, and say it to your shame,
> That all was beauty here until you came.

How much more appropriately it might have been addressed to the imperialist despoilers of peaceful territories, from whom, all too efficiently, Japan had learnt her lesson!

At Saratoga Springs, where I lectured at Skidmore College on the way to Montreal, I found myself in the real Buxton of America, complete with parks, spouting wells, summer horse-racing, medicinal waters, a sunny, bracing climate, and several large hotels now closed for the winter. Placid, beautiful and artificial, with a population of only 13,000, it was the smallest American city in which I had spoken.

The sudden, palpable quiet after the noisy racket of New York made me keenly conscious of its sharp cold and my own anxious, half-buried sadness. As I walked up and down the frozen paths of the little city park before going to the College, I found myself suddenly seized with an inexplicable

feeling of illness, and had the hardest fight of my experience
to finish the lecture without breaking down. Now that the
clamour of the previous week had receded, memories of
Dick Sheppard filled my conscious mind, and I never suspected that a telepathic explanation might exist for this
strange physical discomfort until letters and cables from
home ten days afterwards told me that, just at this time,
my little daughter had become seriously ill with influenza
which threatened, for a brief interval, to develop into
pneumonia. Shivering and dejected, I returned to the hotel
to write to G.:

"I have been thinking about Dick's funeral—those crowds,
the pathos of the tugmen, the downs and outs on the Embankment. Surely nothing like it was ever known except for
the funeral of a sovereign, with all the preliminary pomp
and publicity—and this was spontaneous. . . . I don't
think pacifism was his simple idea so much as the *consequence*
of his simple idea. He once told me, coming back from a
meeting, that his only motive was to follow Christ. To
him the Christian doctrine meant love, and love involved
pacifism. The tribute paid to him in his life and after his
death seems to show that, in the long run, that simple
idea was more powerful, even to the representatives of
tradition in the shape of the Bishop of London and the
Archbishop of Canterbury, than the entrenched interests
of the State, the Church, hypocritical convention, self-
regarding materialism and so forth. When the spirit of man,
at its noblest and best, does shine through, unimpeded by
worldly interests, compromises and all the artifices by which
men deceive themselves, it appears to have a more compelling influence upon other men than anything else in the
world."

In Montreal that week-end, the Canadian newspapers
and their readers were discussing the proposed London-
Washington and Ottawa-Washington trade pacts. Conservative opinion, strong in French Canada, regarded the proposed commercial treaty between Great Britain and the
United States as a menace to interests based upon Imperial

preference, but the more progressive groups saw the triangular economic union of three great democratic communities as a strong check to the growth of Fascism.

The previous June a keen American observer, Leland Stowe, had attended a conference at Kingston, Ontario, on Canadian-American relations, and afterwards contributed to the *Montreal Star* an article which described the conflicting emotions of the Canadian people. Canada's dilemma lay, he said, in the clash between her geographical position and her inherited loyalties. Should she be British first and North American second, or should her environment dominate the inherited bond of blood and the traditional symbol of the British Crown? If another Great War were to break out in Europe, Canada would have to choose, and she was no more ready to choose than the United States had been in 1914.

Because of this dilemma, I found the three organisations to which I spoke—the Women's Canadian Club, the Canadian Institute for International Affairs, and the People's Forum of Montreal—equally anxious to discuss the threatened equilibrium of Europe. The Women's Canadian Club had asked me to speak on "Literature and World Peace"; the Canadian Institute—which excluded women from its membership and had departed from its normal practice in inviting a woman speaker—listened to my account of the English pacifist movement with more interest and no greater scepticism than I had anticipated.

The secretary of the People's Forum—an organisation of quite another type—told me that G. had addressed them on one of his visits to Canada during my long absence from the New World. Virile, progressive, argumentative, with a membership open to both sexes, the Forum seemed an astonishing source of thriving democracy in the Catholic conservative centre of a province where women were still prohibited from voting. I could only suppose that its vitality had developed as a consequence of reaction against reaction. When the secretary took me, at my request, round the East End of Montreal on the Sunday morning, I saw the destitute

homes, with their twisting outdoor iron staircases, of a
devitalised population which spent its substance on the upkeep of costly churches and shrines. Yet the atmosphere
of the Victoria Hall in Westmount, where the Forum was
held, was that of the Kingsway Hall in London before
a Fabian lecture by S. K. Ratcliffe or Mrs. Sidney
Webb.

Remembering that in 1925 a thunderstorm had prevented
me from seeing the city, I snatched the first available
moment to climb halfway up the steep ascent of Mount
Royal above the main business section. Turning at the foot
of the bleak brown woods, I looked down upon the province
of Quebec unrolled like a map from the silver coil of the St.
Lawrence to the austere hills of Vermont on the distant
horizon. I did not linger, for the air was even colder than
at Saratoga Springs, and sudden gusts of wind whirled
flurries of snow against the high windows of the Mount
Royal Hotel.

Taking possession of my room there, I had the strange
sense of a wheel having turned full circle—an impression
strengthened by an eager greeting from the Macmillan
Company of Canada in the person of its sales manager,
Mr. E. H. Morrow. In the absence of my friend Hugh
Eayrs, who was now recovering from sudden illness in a
New York hospital, he had come to the Mount Royal Hotel
to organise the Montreal Book Fair. With this exacting task
he nobly combined the self-imposed duty of protecting from
invasion such little leisure as my week-end in Canada
allowed me.

"I thought," ran a letter to G. that Sunday, "you might
like a line of greeting from this city, and this hotel which
represented my first habitation upon the continent that
I entered with you twelve years ago. I never dreamed then
how much of America I was ultimately to see, nor the
welcome that this side of the Atlantic would give to my work
after its initial rejection. As though to illustrate the extraordinary change that twelve years have brought, I have
just come from a luncheon given for me by Mr. Morrow of

the Canadian Macmillan Company, at which, in the capacity of a Macmillan author, I acted also as hostess. . . .

"The People's Forum, for which I am speaking tonight, still remember with pleasure the talk on the Prayer Book that you gave them some years ago. Mr. Fraser, their secretary, spoke of it this morning to me with great appreciation. He also said that in your speech you made constant references to your wife and what she thought—and it impressed him because he had never heard of her, and wondered what on earth there was about her which made you speak of her with so much respect!"

At Rouses Point on the way to Boston, I found the Canadian-American frontier guarded by no more aggressive an international barrier than three American flags on white poles outside the station.

Soon after we passed the border the train began to cross Lake Champlain, running along a raised embankment constructed through the water from island to island with the nonchalant directness of American engineering. Along the eastern shore of the lake stretched the state of Vermont, cold, flat and homely, a country of isolated wooden houses and small hamlets dominated by their simple churches. Bare trees, grey sky, neutral-shaded grass and steel-coloured water gave a uniform impression of cold austerity. Towards the centre of the lake the country changed to an enlarged likeness of Scotland; chains of fir-clad islands receded towards distant blue mountains with snow lying lightly upon their topmost peaks.

From a fellow traveller—later identified by my Boston friends as the Professor of Geology at Harvard—I learnt that the railway track through Lake Champlain was laid along a "fill" of marble, provided by imperfect blocks from the Rutland quarries, and built upon a subterranean ridge. The level of the lake, he said, created an international problem of an unusual kind. It was maintained by the existence of rocks in the rapids at St. John, but the French Canadian fishermen of that coast constantly removed them

in order to create pools for trapping eels, which they sold
to Germany as an ingredient in the manufacture of a cure
for rheumatism.

"How quickly is the level being lowered?" I inquired,
and was told that it had fallen two feet in the past hundred
years.

"But geologically speaking," my companion added,
"the land in the whole of this area is 'tilting', which raises
the water three inches in a century. So the total reduction
is one and three-quarter feet."

The problem, he concluded, reminded him of a student
who rushed up excitedly to a famous geologist at the conclusion of his lecture on the coal-fields of America.

"Did you really say that American coal resources are going
to be exhausted in a thousand years?"

"Why, no!" replied the lecturer. "It was ten thousand
years that I said."

"Thank God!" exclaimed the student, mopping his
brow.

Two days of overwork and persistent unaccountable
malaise followed the long journey through New England
from Montreal. They concluded with a lecture at Waterville, Maine, a pleasant little town on the Kennebec River,
where a red sun was setting peacefully over the lightly
powdered snow which now covered the brown earth of
New England like icing on a plum cake.

At Boston the next morning, a wintry sea-wind whistling
round the docks and warehouses made me contemplate with
thankfulness the five days' respite from travel and fatigue
which now lay before me. I climbed gratefully into the
Springfield train to spend Thanksgiving in Massachusetts,
with Mary Ellen Chase.

VI

MARY ELLEN CHASE, Professor of English Literature at Smith College and the author of several distinguished novels, was the first of three outstanding American women whom I came to know during the last weeks of 1937.

Of the second, Dorothy Thompson, it has become strictly incorrect to say—in the glib fashion habitually used where a female reputation is under discussion—that she is the chief *woman* journalist and lecturer in the United States, for in the field of political journalism and speaking no man overshadows her. Her syndicated articles on current topics in the *New York Herald Tribune* are read all over America by men and women alike, and the prestige which her lecturing and broadcasting have won for her may be measured both by the demand for her services and by the astronomical fees which these command. *Time* recently stated that the eight lectures which she gave during the winter of 1937-38 for an undisclosed figure were selected from over seven hundred invitations at fees ranging up to $1,000 a lecture. During the same period her husband, Sinclair Lewis, gave twenty-three lectures for a total fee of $23,000.

The third woman was Mrs. Franklin D. Roosevelt herself. The English title of her recent autobiography, *The Lady of the White House*, describes her unfairly, for long before Mr. Roosevelt became President, his wife had acquired a personal reputation as social reformer, lecturer and journalist which will remain hers after his term of office has ceased. At Mary Ellen Chase's home I received a friendly letter signed "Eleanor Roosevelt", inviting me to luncheon at the White House, which proved that the surprising suggestion made to me in Texas was more readily capable of fulfilment than I had supposed.

I had met Mary Ellen Chase in London at an authors'
luncheon given by Harold Latham at Brown's Hotel. When
I saw her again, very briefly, in his New York office, she
invited me, with typical American generosity, to spend the
five free days of Thanksgiving at her house in Northampton,
Massachusetts.

Only those who realise the number of letters and telephone calls which beset a travelling author-lecturer can
estimate the degree of hospitality contained in an invitation
from someone who is herself afflicted with a similar
avalanche of daily business. I had not passed twenty-four
hours at the house on Smith College Campus which she
shared with her English friend Eleanor Duckett, Professor
of Latin Language and Literature and author of *The Gateway
to the Middle Ages*, before I recognised in Mary Ellen Chase
a first-class hostess and a born *raconteuse*. What a joy she
must be to her lecture audiences, I thought, observing her
stimulating vivacity, her keen wit salted with an occasional
touch of the don's critical asperity, her clothes-conscious
sophistication which achieved a gracious elegance all too
seldom characteristic of academic women in Great Britain.

My five days of peace included breakfast in bed and
several walks round the Campus, of which my visit to the
Institute for the Coordination of Women's Interests in
1926 had left not a shred of memory. At the pleasant
sociable meals arranged by my hostesses, I met guests
representing all sections of the College, from Principal
William Allan Neilson himself to a picked group of English
Literature students. Another visitor was Marian Dodd, the
owner of the Hampshire Bookshop, one of the finest college-
town bookstores in America. A rousing tea-party, packed
by students, which she gave for me there, tempted me
back the next morning to buy Christmas presents for G.
and the children. Before I left, she presented me with a copy
of Guy Chapman's *Vain Glory*, a war anthology just over
from England which I had longed for weeks to possess.

I knew already that England was as familiar to Mary
Ellen Chase as America had become to me; she had lived

for two years in a Grantchester cottage, writing her novels in the intervals of research within the haughty and austere precincts of Cambridge University. In her book *In England— Now*, she has described the cottage with buoyant enthusiasm, the haughtiness and austerity with humorous restraint. Uncomfortably recalling Oxford's arrogant habit of putting foreign scholars and students into the place mentally reserved for them, I pressed her for further details of Cambridge. Only after persistent questioning did she admit good-temperedly that never once, during her two years' residence, had she been invited to address a learned society, a literary society, or even a gathering of would-be literary students. On the contrary, it appeared that Cambridge lecturers, complacently disregarding the emotions of Rhodes scholars and American graduates in their audiences, were accustomed to relegate New World scholarship to a comprehensive category of comfortable insignificance.

"There's a crude type of humour in this book," Miss Chase and her compatriots would be assured. "It will probably appeal more to our trans-Atlantic friends than to us." Or, with even more direct if heavily unconscious insolence: "This is a product of trans-Atlantic scholarship, so you must not expect profundity or thoroughness."

Almost inevitably, these examples of the sterilising contempt periodically meted out by our older Universities to scholars from abroad, led to a story of A. E. Housman, whom Miss Chase had met. He was lecturing, ran the Cambridge legend, to a mixed audience of students, when his topic required him to describe the matrimonial problems of a primitive community in the South Sea Islands.

"It's difficult," he said, "for the men to make satisfactory domestic arrangements because the women are so few. Even the ladies from Newnham and Girton would have a good chance of marriage if they went there."

One or two women students, deeply offended, got up to leave the lecture as a protest, but Housman forestalled them. Coming down from the platform, he opened the door for them, adding politely: "There's no hurry, ladies, no hurry whatever! The next boat doesn't leave until Friday afternoon."

As always, I wondered what process of inward emotional combustion turned that acid scholar into a poet. Perhaps, I suggested, Miss Chase's contacts with English literature outside Cambridge had proved a more genial experience?

Oh, yes, she assured me appreciatively; everybody had been perfectly delightful. But again the details, when acquired with difficulty, hardly supported this charitable judgment. In spite of direct requests to English acquaintances, she had been unsuccessful, it seemed, in meeting R. C. Sherriff, whose simplicity of style and honest personality greatly attracted her. But one animated writer whom she did meet had repaid a week-end of hospitality by three pages of sarcastic comment on "learned ladies" in her next book of memoirs.

With the amused detachment characteristic of both women, Eleanor Duckett read aloud to me one evening these lively, malicious pages. I listened ruefully, wishing that any but an English writer had perpetrated this tasteless jest on her American hostesses, and wondering why their gracious, orderly existence had appeared a suitable subject for facetious banter. I have known English university women whose cloistered academic seclusion acted as an intellectual antiseptic upon their normal emotions, but this circumscribed bleakness has nothing whatever in common with the rich life and exquisite environment which Mary Ellen Chase has created for herself and others.

Seldom indeed had I lived in an atmosphere of such peace and beauty. Externally the house appeared neat and compact; but its many connecting rooms were designed with the elegant spaciousness of America's well-planned homes. The front windows faced a quiet road running across the Campus, but the back looked over a beautiful sloping beechwood, now leafless, to the silver surface of a flooded creek appropriately known as Paradise Pond.

In my bedroom—which I suspected was Miss Chase's own —I lay beneath a pale gold eiderdown and crochet coverlet of fine creamy lace on a high, comfortable bed, from which I could look upon grey walls and emerald lawns through casement windows enclosed by delicately tinted curtains of mauve, jade and deep rose. Throughout the house, cream walls and pale fawn carpets made a perfect background for elegant china, coloured glass, and the framed pages of richly illustrated Latin parchments. Above the practical desk in Miss Chase's study hung a picture of the old Maine sailing ship, *Don Justo*. Here the linen curtains, specially woven in England, combined fresh, vivid shades of crimson, orange, primrose and green. In the living room, where vases of talisman roses and a bowl of narcissus stood on little polished tables, the darker, bolder stripes mingled purple, magenta and blue.

"Everything," I reported to G., "was spotless and the best of its kind . . . and nothing was ever out of order. The cooking was irreproachable, the service efficient and immaculate. In the bathroom were the usual amazing selection of tinted and embroidered towels of all kinds (how *do* people afford it, with laundry so costly here, and so cheap in England where we offer visitors the soiled family towel more often than not?) and a collection of Elizabeth Arden soaps and bath-salts. . . . It was almost like the specimen apartments which house-agents show people in luxury flats, except that here were all the latest books and a lavish selection of the newest intellectual magazines—*Atlantic, Saturday Review, Literary Digest*."

It was inevitable that the perfect working conditions provided by this little oasis of beauty and quiet should fill me with fleeting but acute regret for the crowded pandemonium of my own existence.

Should I ever have time for the thought and study which give to the writings of Mary Ellen Chase their serenity and wisdom? I could not help comparing the orderly elegance of her home and its enchanting treasures of books, pictures and china, with my large, noisy, ramshackle Chelsea household, where in every room except my own little fifth-floor study overlooking the Thames, my husband strews his documents as irrepressibly as the children scatter their toys, and small family problems are brought to me for solution however deeply involved I may be in a piece of work.

By nature I am a tidy individual to whom complete concentration comes easily the moment that disturbances cease, but fate has seldom bestowed upon me either the order I enjoy, or the freedom from interruption that I covet with a passion to which the thirst of the hart for the water brooks is a mere vagrant fancy. As long as I can remember, I have craved for the privilege—accepted as a matter of course by the masculine world—of a life organised to fit the needs of my work, instead of one constantly requisitioned by miscellaneous external claims to which my work has perforce to adapt itself. Even the escape from adverse conditions which might have destroyed it altogether— such as the frustrations of small-town existence in both England and America—has meant only an incomplete victory over time and conflict.

For all the political feminist triumphs of the past two decades, men alone remain able to satisfy their biological impulses without partially ruining their intellectual accomplishments. This sex monopoly of balanced human development will probably continue until a generation arises with sufficient courage, generosity and sense of justice to repudiate the prevailing assumptions upon which most marriages are based. At present the sentimental emphasis placed by average middle-class society upon the possession of a husband and children overshadows the importance, for a woman scholar or artist, of that ideal working environment for which I envied Mary Ellen Chase.

Nevertheless, the lovely, devastating responsibilities of wifehood and parenthood, once acquired, cannot be lightly regarded. By the time that I left Northampton to continue my tour, a cable from G. had told me of our daughter's illness, though he assured me that she was now recovering. I faced the last fortnight in the Middle West with an overburdened heart, wondering—as so many mothers must have wondered before me—why a child that remains in perfect health for two or three years on end, invariably elects to become seriously ill the moment that one or both of its parents are temporarily absent. A lecture tour cannot be impulsively cancelled, since only a real emergency justifies the infliction of heavy financial loss upon manager and organisers, and nothing is more difficult than to judge, from cables and letters in which the whole truth may be suppressed from the kindest motives, whether or when that emergency exists.

Torn by conflicting claims and indescribable anxiety, I took the train at Springfield, Massachusetts, for a twenty-four hours' journey to Rockford, Illinois, which would carry me yet another thousand miles from home.

Too troubled to read or write letters, I looked from the window at the Berkshire Hills through which we were passing between Springfield and Albany.

In the fine, clear autumn air their steep slopes, covered with spruce and silver birch, appeared as gigantic brushes with stiff bristles against the pale afternoon sky. Below the railway embankment ran swift shallow streams spanned by little stone bridges, occasionally forming crystal pools which mirrored their grey fringe of withered ragwort. Across the tawny-green earth glowing golden in the slanting sunlight, thin shadows of pine-trunks stretched like long spectral arms from thicket to thicket. Occasionally tiny villages of white or red-painted houses appeared within the mountain hollows. Outside Albany, the silver streak of the Hudson divided an open stretch of blue-grey landscape, pink-tinged beneath the sunset. Along the horizon the familiar outline of the Catskills, a dim blue shadow, recalled an allegorical storybook of my own seven-year-old childhood, *The Distant Hills*.

It was not until I reached Buffalo on December 5th for a return engagement with the First Presbyterian Church, that a cable saying "All well—Poppy normal", brought my fears to an end. The message caught me just as I was leaving the city at 7 a.m.; I learnt afterwards that my publisher, to whose assiduous care these vital cables from England had been entrusted, had sent it off at midnight with a series of emphatic instructions. That week's lectures, at Rockford, Milwaukee, Toledo, Buffalo and Elkhart, had carried me up and down the monotonous stretch of railway-line between Buffalo and Chicago, but now a less familiar journey took me once more to St. Paul and thirty-six hours of Ruth Gage Colby's society.

I had dreaded this trip in the "Burlington Zephyr", the grey blunt-nosed steel dragon drawn by an 1800-horsepower Diesel-electric engine, which covered in six and a half hours the four hundred and ten miles between Chicago and St. Paul. Mark Twain had required a week to travel over this empty expanse of pristine wilderness beside the young Mississippi, and my experience of a "stream-lined" rush from Boston to Waterville, Maine, had left me with the impression that the leisurely transit methods of his America were infinitely preferable to the competitive scrambles of mine. The Pullman car of the little New England "flyer" had boiled up to the temperature of an enclosed steel oven; it must have been nearer ninety degrees than eighty, and I felt roasted alive, though none of my heat-hardened fellow travellers seemed conscious of discomfort.

But the journey to St. Paul modified, though it did not remove, my rational objections to high-speed travel. It was true that I could not write at all, nor eat nor walk without wary ingenuity, but so long as I "stayed put", the aeroplane-like interior of the armour-plated monster was comfortable enough. Behind the high-powered Diesel-electric car, the grey-cushioned, chromium-furnished cocktail lounge, dining car, parlour cars and grey-carpeted coaches carrying a hundred and twenty passengers, followed with a remarkable freedom from jerks and bumps. Outside the windows, the landscape seemed to fly past with the effect of a double-speed kaleidoscope. To the left of the line from Savanna onwards stretched the frozen Mississippi, broken at intervals

into channels encircling numerous islands, and widening
beyond the Zumbrota and Chippewa rivers to form the
crescent-shaped Lake Pepin. Fed by eight large tributaries
and many smaller streams, and sometimes hardly distin-
guishable from its snowy banks, the Mississippi flowing
through this uninhabited country seemed wider and more
impressive than at St. Louis or New Orleans.

At every bend of the river, the train passed beneath harsh
bluffs and grotesque rock formations, or swept above wooded
valleys backed by rolling hills. From Rock Island, I learnt,
to the mouth of the Chippewa River, three hundred
thousand acres of forests, rivers, marshes and islands had
been preserved as a wild-life refuge, and much of the land
remained as it was known to the tribes of native Indian
hunters—the Algonquins, Sioux, Chippewas, Winnebagos,
Sacs and Foxes. In summer and autumn this river region—
which in 1934 I had passed through at night—was alive
and clamorous with red-winged blackbirds, wild ducks,
black bass, beavers and muskrats, but now, except for an
occasional automobile crossing the solidly frozen river, there
was nothing to be seen but miles beyond calculation of grey
ice and snow-covered marsh. Except for the pale azure
sky, the scene was colourless until sunset incarnadined
the flawless surface of the snow. Mark Twain, I was
told, had named the country of the Upper Mississippi
"Sunset Land" because of its splendour of sanguine
skies.

Occasionally I noticed formidable-looking structures half
concealed by snowdrifts along the river; these, I gathered,
represented eleven out of the twenty-six dams built along
the Mississippi as part of the Government's project for flood-
control and the development of navigation. From time to
time we stopped at small cities originally settled by various
nationalities—German, French, Italian and Indian—as
tiny trading posts. Many of these settlements were still no
more than villages, with populations of less than one
thousand. The largest city, La Crosse, had given its name
to the national game of Canada; it was once the ancient

meeting place of Indians, who had played this game during
their tribal congregations.

At St. Paul I was interviewed for the *St. Paul Dispatch*
by James Gray, Minnesota journalist and word-writer
whose books appeared on my American publishers' list.

In his article he wrote—not, I conjecture, without a
shrewd awareness that feminine dogmatism, however impressive, is only seldom an attractive quality—that I talked
with an air of authority obviously derived from frequent
appearances on public platforms. Actually, I had never felt
less authoritative in my life; the previous night had been
rendered almost sleepless by a 1 a.m. arrival in Chicago
from Elkhart, and the breathless journey to St. Paul had
left me with no conscious emotion but a neuralgic longing
for a cup of tea.

I had read, too, several reviews by this tall, clever young
man which at first sight appeared as deceptively innocent
as himself, but on a second reading had left a subtly un-
favourable impression, couched in most generous and sympathetic phrases, of the book or author reviewed. As he
catechised me earnestly on the distinction between "collective security" and the principles of pacifism, I suspected
uncomfortably that he was trying to make fun of me—or
rather, to manœuvre me into a position where I should
inadvertently make fun of myself. Even when the coveted
cup of tea had been hospitably provided, my philosophy of
life was not easily defined after a wakeful night and six
hours of precipitate travel. Nor was the luxurious sociable
drawing-room of a successful newspaper-editor the most
appropriate place in which to make confession of a principle
only completely accepted after months of mental conflict.

This time my visit to St. Paul was brief; the lecture to a
dinner meeting of the College Club kept me there only one
night. I returned to Chicago on the morning Zephyr in
the company of Ruth Gage Colby. We found the city
scourged by relentless bitter gales blowing inland from
Lake Michigan, and twelve hours later, when I reached

Springfield, Ohio, the Middle West was firmly in the iron grip of premature "zero weather".

"Temperature at Springfield this morning was five above zero," I wrote to G. "Brilliant sun, clear blue sky, pavements bone-dry, a powdering of white snow over the fields, but attractive as it looked, it was impossible to stay out for more than about twenty minutes, because of the icy wind which cut one's face and froze one's hands."

Travelling eastward again on December 11th, my night train was held up for over an hour by a snowstorm outside Buffalo. I arrived late in New York for my final ten days, which included a stimulating week-end of walking and skating at the Bretts' Easton farm, and a speech for the National Woman's Party at the Carlton Hotel in Washington.

VII

IT WAS DURING these final days in New York that I met Dorothy Thompson.

Her invitation to luncheon was brought to me by a mutual friend, Betty Gram Swing, wife of Raymond Gram Swing, the international radio commentator and editor. Through Betty, a zealous and able feminist known to me for some years on both sides of the Atlantic, my dinner address to the National Woman's Party had been arranged.

Generously anxious for her American and English friends to meet, Betty took me up to the beautiful apartment, with its Epstein head above the fireplace, and its wide tall windows looking over Central Park, in which Dorothy Thompson and Sinclair Lewis live with their small son. Sinclair Lewis himself was not present; the Irish-American artist, Georgia O'Keeffe, made the fourth member of our luncheon party. Dark, dreamy, and brown-skinned as an Irish colleen, Mrs. O'Keeffe brought richness and warmth into the challenging political atmosphere. When luncheon was over, Betty and I went with her across New York to her top-floor studio above the East River, where her rare, symbolic paintings of flowers and shells and Mexican deserts recalled me from the tumultuous world of partisan controversies to another in which the only sound is that of a still, small voice.

It would hardly, I felt, have been possible to find throughout America a woman who contrasted more sharply than Dorothy Thompson with both Georgia O'Keeffe and Mary Ellen Chase. Here was no detached philosopher who sought, from the stronghold of a serenity both material and spiritual, to express the eternal values through the lovely cadences of the English language or the vivid colours of an artist's palette. Here was a woman who plunged grimly, with the gloves off, into every political fight, asserting her positive convictions with nervous dogmatic intensity, writing, speaking, broadcasting, without rest for herself or respite for her opponents, in order that her conception of the truth might prevail.

As one who desperately endeavours, in the time left over from external claims, to lead each type of life in turn, I am hardly a judge of which is the more essential to the complex pattern of modern society, but my own experience leaves me in no doubt whatever as to which is the more exhausting. Dorothy Thompson looked, I thought, more tired than any individual in normal health should be, but her very appearance of fatigue added to the effectiveness of her passionate power. Even on topics about which she admitted that she could not make up her mind, her indecision was stated so decisively that it wore the aspect of a clearly defined creed.

It was only natural that my conversation with this brilliant woman who had been expelled from Germany for her fearless criticism of Nazi intolerance and persecution, should centre upon Fascism and the alternative attitudes of those who claimed to be lovers of peace. In her syndicated *Herald Tribune* column, "On the Record", for December 22nd, 1937, she endeavoured, with the generosity characteristic of all great men and women, to do justice to a point of view which she thought incompatible with her own vehement beliefs.

"We, and every other person and nation in the world, who believe in peace, have a choice of two attitudes," she wrote under the heading of "Resistant Pacifism". "We can either believe in non-resistance, in which case we ought to be prepared to carry that attitude to its ultimate conclusion, or we can believe that peace is a positive—not a negative— thing . . . and that it is our duty as passionate peace-lovers to defend that condition of affairs . . . by positive resistance to encroachments upon it.

"I have the deepest respect for the first attitude when it is whole-hearted. I have, for instance, the deepest respect for Mr. Gerald Heard, the British pacifist, and for Miss Vera Brittain, the English novelist, with whom I had the pleasure of a conversation this week. Miss Brittain went through the last war . . . and has come to a final conclusion, as far as she herself is concerned. That conclusion is: War is evil. Any kind of peace is better than any kind of war. Better a Nazi invasion of Great Britain and its occupation for several generations, than to try to overcome war with war. Endure anything, rather than resist with force. For resistance with force turns you, yourself, your country and your nation, into the pattern of behaviour of the aggressor. You cannot defend civilization, I think she would argue, except with the instruments of civilization. Resort to the instruments of barbarism, and you, yourself, become a barbarian. . . .

"If you believe that life is a struggle between good and evil—if you have a dualist philosophy—this will not be your viewpoint. You will conceive of peace as the positive demonstration in life and behaviour of certain positive principles. It is not very difficult to define what those principles are. They are, that individuals as well as nations must live with the most sensitive respect for each other and conduct their affairs inside the spirit and letter of law.

"It is quite impossible, in the long run, for either individuals, or groups, or nations, or classes inside nations, to live together in peace without the implicit and sincere acceptance of certain standards, and codes of behaviour. The resistant pacifist will cherish these standards as the first condition of peace, and will resist their violation at every single point. For his thesis will be, that the accumulation of failures to resist encroachment upon these standards, will progressively contribute to abolish the standards altogether, and eventually land us in a world where there is no code, no law, no principle, and no standards. And such a world is the barbaric domain of naked force. Such a world means chaos, which is the opposite of the ordered relations between men, which is peace."

There is, I think, less difference of outlook between

Dorothy Thompson and myself than she imagined from our conversation—in which I was suffering from one of the periodic fits of tongue-tiedness that so often afflict me in social intercourse, though not (as yet) on the platform. A person of a highly intellectual and sophisticated type always appears to relegate me, for the moment, to the narrow, unintellectual provincial society in which I was brought up, and I am filled with a pervading inferiority complex. The more passionately his or her convictions are put into words, the more deeply I tend to be temporarily impressed. It is only afterwards, when I have had time to think, that I remember that truth is more likely to be expressed through the still small voice than by the most ardent controversialists, however indubitable their burning sincerity.

If I had been able, with the added foreknowledge of her article, to answer Dorothy Thompson at all, my reply—though thanks to the diffidence with which that imperious personality imbued me, I could never actually have made it—would have run something like this:

"I agree with you entirely that peace is not negative, but the positive demonstration in life and behaviour of certain positive principles, and I am not a believer in passive non-resistance to the forces of evil which threaten those principles. I do not even believe that any kind of peace has always been better than any kind of war; it is the wholesale massacres involved in modern warfare, and its penalisation of those who are most helpless and least responsible, which causes me to regard war as the greatest calamity that can afflict a nation today. With Aldous Huxley and Gerald Heard, I believe in any method of resistance which does not involve the destruction of human life and the debasement of civilisation, with all its treasures, to a wild, hideous chaos where those positive principles, according to which we both believe that life should be lived, would have no chance of survival.

"It is chiefly because of the incalculable, insensate and indiscriminate destructiveness of the modern war machine, that I deny that the principles, codes and standards of civilised living can be inculcated or maintained by force. There are other ways of resisting 'encroachment upon those standards' without resort to the arms which are in themselves the most fatal attack upon them, and which destroy them in the very process of nominally defending them. Have you ever considered how far the methods of non-violent resistance can be carried in restraining an aggressor? 'Is there', you ask, 'a possibility of living dangerously, in behalf of the things that the very word Peace implies?' But living dangerously is the actual method that the pacifist employs; the difference between him and the war-monger is that he himself will he the first to endure whatever suffering may result from his methods. He alone is prepared to undergo, for peace, the risks that the war-maker is ready, with suicidal blindness, to impose upon others.

"I say that the blindness of men today is suicidal because to fight Fascism by arms is merely to abandon ourselves to the supreme ineptitude of imitating its methods. To attempt, yet again, to 'defend democracy' by war requires, if that war is to be effective, the acceptance of military regimentation and the abandonment of every democratic principle. It means exterminating *en masse*, on the battlefield or in raided cities, not the dictators themselves but the common people, the raw material of democracy. These ordinary men and women have no quarrel with one another; they have acquiesced, in several countries, in the uncongenial rule of dictators because alternative methods brought them nothing but poverty and humiliation.

"In your article you say: 'Christian gentlemen, in this era, have sat down at dinner with murderers, in more countries than one, and discussed politics with men whose ideas of behaviour are exactly those of the New York underworld.' But do we get any nearer to the millennium by murdering the murderer—even supposing it is he whom we can reach —instead of trying to discover and remove the motive for his murders?

Ys

"Slowly, in our national codes, the civilised world has come to accept the idea that 'making the punishment fit the crime' is unscientific as well as inhumane; that murders are not diminished by hanging the murderer, nor robbery with violence prevented by flogging the robber. It is the gradual civilising of a community which eradicates these crimes, and vengeful punishments, however well deserved by the individual, brutalise instead of civilising society, and thus defeat the very ends that they are intended to serve.

"I cannot believe that the successful conduct of international relations depends upon a precisely opposite principle. The acid test of our willingness to negotiate comes when our adversary is aggressive, intolerant and unattractive; when he displays those qualities which arouse humanity's primitive desire to fight. Anybody can make terms with an antagonist who sees with his own eyes, accepts the same standard of values, meets his point of view half-way. The peace movement has no integrity unless its willingness to negotiate is maintained when the angry passions of its members are aroused by those who retaliate with injustice for the injustices suffered over fifteen years. Today, when our dictatorial opponents are nasty, brutish, provocative and unscrupulous, will prove whether the advocates of peace have meant anything at all by their twenty years of protestation; or whether they prefer to be captured by those intoxicating animosities through which it is always so much easier to stimulate the applause of the unthinking crowd, than by any exhortation to sanity, charity and historic realism.

"If we look to the past we shall see that the greatest peaceful diplomatic triumphs of history—such as the Rush-Bagot Convention of 1818 and the Cobden Treaty of 1860 —were made when the negotiators had the courage and foresight to seek a ground of common interest with those whom they hated and feared. Germany, today, is the France of the nineteenth century, but with one fundamental difference. The French are at heart a liberty-loving people; the Germans are not, and never have been since

Frederick the Great wrote the principles of authoritarianism into his *Testament Politique*. They love regimentation, autocracy, control; they do not understand the American passion for freedom nor the British admiration for compromise. Hitlerism in 1937 is only another variant of 'Prussianism' in 1870 and 'Kaiserism' in 1914. It is improbable that a people with this mentality will ever for long support a form of government which appeals to the British, French and American temperaments, with their natural preference for democratic institutions, or rouses the sympathy of the Soviet Union, which has so strangely enthroned democracy in a dictator's chair.

"A philosophy of life cannot be suppressed by arms; like an indestructible phoenix it rises from the ashes of defeat, adopting a new name with each reincarnation. Are we then to visualise, in each generation, a repetition of ideological conflicts between Germany and her democratic neighbours, until civilisation itself perishes in the process? Surely even the most ardent advocate of 'Resistant Pacifism' will cry 'God forbid'!, and will recognise that the true pacifist, in seeking for some plan by which people with incompatible ideals can live at peace until the slow advancement of mankind allows the more civilised ideal to dominate, is merely recognising the primary condition of human survival."

One week before I sailed, I took an early-morning train to Washington in order to lunch with Mrs. Roosevelt at the White House before my evening engagement with the National Woman's Party. Her autobiography, *This Is My Story*, had been published in America just before I reached Northampton, and I bought a copy to read on the final tedious journeys through the Middle West.

Much of it, she told me afterwards, had been dictated on trains to secretaries while she accompanied the President on his speaking campaigns—a fact which accounted for a conversational informality of style. The book related, with unmitigated honesty and a disarming freedom from compunction for herself, the story of an energetic, courageous woman,—capable, as only a few are capable, of learning from life the lessons that it has to teach,—who developed idealistic standards and a social conscience out of a highly privileged background. Although America has no official aristocracy, Mrs. Roosevelt was born an aristocrat as certainly as any English Duchess. It was, in fact, of an English Duchess that she most reminded me.

The luncheon was a small intimate party in an upstairs room, half library, half boudoir. Apart from two members of the household, the only guest besides myself was a Washington newspaper woman, Mrs. Eleanor Patterson. While we waited for Mrs. Roosevelt, I observed that the room was furnished with a striking chintz, of a strawberry pattern on a white ground, like the clear transfers on Sèvres china. A low bowl filled with little pink roses of a similar shade stood in the middle of the luncheon table. Vases of deep magenta-pink carnations were distributed round the pleaant, informal room, with its numerous small bookcases and its window overlooking a white stone arch which framed a green vista of garden.

From the moment that Mrs. Roosevelt came in, I was too much preoccupied with our conversation, and the endeavour to appear less *gauche* than I felt, to observe what we were eating, but I remember that we ended the meal with tall glasses of pink jelly, covered in cream and delicately flavoured with wine. I noticed them because they matched the carnations. At the time I felt as dumbfounded as a schoolgirl; I thought that as usual I had listened instead of trying to talk, but according to Mrs. Roosevelt's account of the luncheon in her syndicated column "My Day", I seem to have said more than I imagined.

Apparently we even discussed war and peace, but her attitude to the subject resembled Dorothy Thompson's only in so far as conspicuousness breeds a commanding authority of manner in all who attain it. For Eleanor Roosevelt, peace, I felt, was not a political battle to be waged, but a humanitarian ideal to be achieved. Later, in April, 1938, a paragraph published by the London *News Chronicle* left the same impression:

> Mrs. Eleanor Roosevelt, wife of the President, went to see the newsreels of the Barcelona bombings.
>
> Next day she wrote in her diary (syndicated in 62 newspapers of the U.S.A., with over 4,000,000 circulation):
>
> "I felt positively disgusted with human beings. How can we be such fools as to go on senselessly taking life this way?
>
> "Why the women in every nation do not rise and refuse to bring children into this kind of world is beyond my understanding."
>
> Reporters asked: Was she really advocating a motherhood strike?
>
> Mrs. Roosevelt flared up.
>
> "Well, isn't it perfectly stupid for women to go on having babies just to see them killed?"

Benevolent and hospitable as she was, I found her more impressive than I had expected, and a little alarming. Her demeanour conveyed the whole story of her upbringing and background—its dignity and self-assurance, its privilege and security, together with the tradition of *noblesse oblige* developed by the last two or three generations. Most photographers, in their endeavour to create a suave and pleasing portrait, fail to do justice to her resolute, penetrating, blue-grey eyes beneath their strongly marked brows. Looking at those eyes, I forgot every other feature as she spoke emphatically of American women and their failure to qualify themselves sufficiently before taking public posts.

How often I too had heard in England the senseless parrot phrase, "We must have a woman on this committee" (as though being a woman were in itself a qualification for anything whatever). I could endorse her words with reciprocal vehemence when she stated that the woman who accepted a position which required expert knowledge without possessing it was letting down her sex as a whole.

"Our women in authority don't know enough of their own country," she said. "They'll travel for days on conventional journeys and spend the fall in New York and the winter in Florida, but they don't take the trouble to go about and discover how ordinary people live."

I had not expected to see Mr. Roosevelt at all, for the *Panay* had been sunk a day or two before, and I knew that he was considering the American Note to Japan. But to my surprise, the brief after-luncheon talk abruptly terminated with an announcement from a butler: "The President is ready." The butler took me down to the ground floor, and I followed him through a series of dark corridors to the closed door of a secluded study.

This unexpected courtesy and the wait outside the door made my heart thump a little when I was finally shown in, but at the first sight of the smiling seated figure in a large chair pushed back a little from the big imposing desk, my nervousness vanished. A day or two afterwards, when I saw on a New York stage the satiric drama, *I'd Rather Be Right*, to which the theatre-going community was crowding, I thought how different was the portly, pink-faced, complacent President of that vivacious skit from the pale and purposeful reality. But his pallor and the lines of strain which hollowed his cheeks seemed only to intensify the invincible charm of his manner and the genial informality of his greeting.

Like all great men, he sought, not to instruct me, but to acquire whatever small contribution I could make to his own knowledge.

"You've been lecturing in the Middle West, I understand? Have you noticed whether there is less sectionalism in that part of the country than you found last time you were there?"

"Yes," I replied, remembering the farmer at Cedar Rapids in 1934. "Three years ago I was hardly asked any questions about the European situation; in fact some people seemed to dislike hearing about it. But this time they all wanted to know."

"I quite agree," he assented. "I've noticed exactly the same thing on my own campaigns."

Realising that the *Panay* dispatch must be in process of composition, I rose to leave without further delay.

"It was specially good of you to see me today, sir. It's an anxious moment for both our countries."

"It certainly is," he responded, but the reassuring smile with which he dismissed me suggested that if anyone could find a way out, it was Franklin D. Roosevelt.

With a pleasant sense of going home to congenial colleagues, I spent the afternoon at the Headquarters of the National Woman's Party. Only recently, I had been taken by Eleanor Flexner, the young daughter of Dr. Abraham Flexner, to see Clare Booth's vehemently discussed play, *The Women*, and the Woman's Party was a welcome guarantee that American life would never be dominated by the emotion-ridden parasites so ruthlessly portrayed.

The audience which the Woman's Party gathered that evening at the Carlton Hotel was probably the most distinguished that I had addressed in America. Composed as it was of Senators, Congressmen and other political personalities with their wives or husbands, it certainly ought to have alarmed me; but somehow it did not. Feelings of friendly expectation seemed to animate the men and women who had come to hear Senator Edward R. Burke of Nebraska, Raymond Gram Swing and myself give a blessing to the Equal Rights Amendment to the Constitution of the United States.

The friends of the Woman's Party—led by Senator Burke, who acted as sponsor of the Equal Rights Amendment in the Senate—seemed infinitely more numerous and powerful than they had been at the time of my first visit to National Headquarters nearly twelve years before. When dinner was over, Senator Burke talked of the Equal Rights Amendment, and Raymond Gram Swing spoke on the relation of the woman's movement to the business recession. In his speech the Senator quoted a letter written by Abigail

Adams to her husband, John Adams, the second President of the United States, while he was serving as a member of the Continental Congress:

"I long to hear that you have declared an independency, and, by the way, in the new code of laws, which I suppose it will be necessary for you to make, I desire you would remember the ladies and be more generous and favourable to them than were your ancestors. Do not put such unlimited power into the hands of husbands. Remember all men would be tyrants if they could."

"Women," added the Senator, "have progressed a long way since those words were penned. In the face of the most stringent opposition they have demanded and received some degree of recognition of their right to be educated, to participate in government, to enter the professions, to work—in a word, to live their lives in their own way as free human beings. There remains only the adoption of this simple amendment to the Constitution and women will stand upon an equal footing with men. You ask no special privileges. You crave no favours because you are women. You are willing to match your strength and your intelligence with your brothers. Write into the Constitution this amendment, and women will be free to make their fullest possible contribution to the building of a better America."

My own speech followed. In that autumn during which conflicting philosophies of life were leading to ever more sinister wars and rumours of war, it seemed not inappropriate that I should conclude with an appeal to the women of America to defend and strengthen their liberties by the constructive methods of peace:

"The future position of women depends today upon the conflict between the reactionary ideas of Fascism, and the democratic theories in accordance with which so large a measure of emancipation has already been achieved. It hardly seems possible that the great western democracies, such as your country and mine, will endorse any policy involving complete retrogression. It is our job today, as never before, to be on the lookout for reactionary tendencies, and to support any step which seems likely not only to stem the menacing tide of Fascism, but to carry still further forward the victories already achieved. For this reason England has been watching with great interest the stand made by the National Woman's Party on behalf of an Equal Rights Amendment to the Constitution of the United States. We feel that, particularly on this question of the freedom of half humanity, England and America should work in co-operation.

"The woman's movement found success in the past through two methods—the freeing of women from the old restrictions and the liberation of thought and speech from the old repressions. Are we to move forward to a higher order of human relationships in which war is no more, the exploitation of man by man unknown, and the subjection of women a cruelty of the past? Or are we to solve our problem negatively, by the method of death, as the problems of ancient Rome were solved? Are we to descend into a second 'Dark Age', in which all that civilisation has achieved by centuries of struggle and pain will be lost? That is the problem which confronts the men and women of the western democracies today.

"Surely the solution lies, not in war against those with whom we disagree, but in the preservation, strengthening and development of those principles and institutions which make for freedom and progress."

As I travelled back to New York by the night train after this final engagement, I calculated that my two tours of 1934 and 1937 had involved a programme of seventy-seven lectures, raised by broadcasts and various shorter speeches to a total of at least a hundred "appearances". In addition there had been innumerable Press interviews and social functions, not one of which I had cancelled or postponed; I had not even been late for an engagement except on the two occasions when railway accidents had retarded my trains.

"It must be something of a record," I had already written

proudly to G., "considering that the two tours together have involved nearly 50,000 miles of travel, and this time I haven't even once disgraced myself as I did by fainting at Toronto—no colds, no sickness, and my worst enemy (headaches) not nearly so violent as last time owing to the air-conditioned trains."

Looking back upon the fear of breaking down which had haunted me before the earlier tour, and the care with which I had taken out insurance policies against the cancellation of lectures through illness or injury, I realised that I had never for a moment expected to achieve this unbroken record. Its fulfilment, which had taught me that one could be tired to the utmost limit of endurance and yet go on effectively working, was a salutary shock to my inherited faculty for nervous apprehension.

Between 1919 and 1934 the physical memory of my youthful war years, which carried the same lesson, had faded, and I had come to look upon long journeys as fatiguing, lectures as exhausting, and a minor illness as a good reason for cancelling an engagement. The first little lecture tour that I ever made, round a number of Scottish Border villages in 1923 when I was still a girl, so depleted my energy that I hardly knew how to talk to my hosts and hostesses between the speeches. In 1934, when the publication of *Testament of Youth* had sent me, almost before I realised what was happening, racing up and down England and America addressing strangely assorted collections of insistent audiences, I realised that it was possible to endure an unremitting sequence of journeys and engagements without any serious risk of collapse. By 1937, when I was fourteen years older than I had been at the time of that first Scottish experiment, I had learnt to travel all day, sleep soundly on trains, and give a reasonably interesting lecture after several successive nights each allowing for only three or four hours' sleep.

The last experience is still one that I do not welcome, and I have not modified my view that lecture managers ruthlessly underestimate the amount of sleep which a normal person

—or at any rate a normal English person—requires if a
task is to be efficiently performed. But even this experience,
in its way, was beneficial; it completely changed my per-
spective of daily achievement, and altered my estimate of
my capacity for work. Today the journeys from London to
the North of England or Scotland which once seemed
immense, have dwindled to agreeable little trips that offer
a welcome sequence of uninterrupted hours. I know now
that the after-effects of fatigue can be quickly overcome;
that, however ill or tired I may feel, I can make myself
do a job quite capably if it really has to be done. I have
learnt that endurance breeds the power to endure, and that
courage springs mainly from one's belief in this power.

Appropriately enough, this very realisation had first
been crystallised for me by a passage from Mrs. Roosevelt's
autobiography. In a description of the exhausting official
journeys which, as a young woman, she had made with
her husband when he was appointed Assistant Secretary of
the Navy, she had put down some conclusions that might
usefully be committed to memory by all whose work is
likely to make them conspicuous, or who cherish any ambition
to occupy what Earl Baldwin has called "the high places
of this world."

"I think I knew instinctively," she wrote, "that these
trips were just one of the tests that life put in your way as
a preparation for the future. They were feats of endurance,
and, in the doing, they built up strength. I learned that I
could be tired, and that it did me no harm. Some time or
other I had to catch up on sleep, but I learned that if I
kept myself well, when I had an exhausting strain to endure,
it could be borne.

"I could never say in the morning: 'I have a headache
and cannot do thus and so.' Headache or no headache, thus
and so had to be done, and no time could be wasted. . .

"I knew that I did not actually have to go, but I was
interested in seeing my own country, and there was a sense
of pride and obligation which made me feel that I must
not add to the difficulties of the trip. At the time I was not

conscious of this, but as I look back upon it now I realise that the very strenuousness of some of these experiences built up a confidence in my ability to stand things which has stood me in good stead throughout the rest of my life."

How much I wished, as I recalled these courageous paragraphs, that I had acquired the same measure of permanent wisdom at so early an age! After all, my sense of pride in my own unblemished programme was a very recently justified emotion. More constructive than personal complacency would be some useful conclusions on the functions fulfilled by this vast and profitable industry of American lecturing, and the extent to which strangers from Great Britain could contribute to its value. Had six months of travelling and speaking in thirty states, added to my earlier experience of life in America, taught me anything of value which I could pass on to other visitors from England who hoped to play a similar part?

VIII

IN ONE DELIGHTFUL chapter of *In England—Now*, Mary Ellen Chase pays a generous tribute to British courtesy. She does not add, as she might well have done, that when English lecturers cross the Atlantic, this engaging attribute often tends to be left at home with the furniture. Long experience of that type of behaviour which the British call "snootiness" and the Americans, even more expressively, describe as "high-hatting", has made graciousness and good manners about the last qualities now expected from English performers on American platforms.

One reason for many misunderstandings is the appalling ignorance of the United States typical of most Europeans. It is not, let me add, a reciprocal ignorance. Americans are accustomed to visit Europe as frequently and in as large numbers as time and funds will allow. They publish and read as many books by English as by American writers; they listen to lecturers from every European country. Their newspapers contain long columns of information on English politics and the complex problems of Europe, whereas the British Press—apart from occasional informed articles in such dignified publications as *The Times*, *The Observer*, *The Spectator* and *The New Statesman*—leaves America severely alone except when some violent manifestation of her dramatic climate provides "news" for its acutely weather-conscious readers.

This habitual ignorance is the source of vulgar and tact-less generalisations which not only exasperate the Americans, but invest those Europeans who do venture into the New World with an advance battery of senseless and unfounded prejudices. One favourite generalisation is the statement that the Americans are a naïve, superficial people, whose lecture-going propensities merit exactly the same type of patronising indulgence as certain adults extend to a child's passion for dolls or engines. This assumption, like so many others, is both insulting and inaccurate. The *blasé* amusement with which we of more ancient, less vital countries dismiss America's enthusiasm for lectures gives us no reason for pride.

After two years of American living and two experiences of American lecturing, I seriously believe that as much damage is done to Anglo-American relations by those Europeans who contentedly pocket the huge fees paid for lectures by American organisations but secretly cherish a supercilious Old World contempt for the whole lecture business, as by any other single factor. It is hardly to be expected that a sensitive, ambitious and progressive people will be inspired with respect for European "celebrities" who bargain with American lecture managers for fees and publicity, accept in full measure the lavish and generous hospitality of American households, and then go home to talk slightingly of "thirsters", pour ridicule on lecturing as an occupation, and deprecatingly explain that only the low level of their bank balances obliged them to descend to this shoddy method of money-making.

There is nothing shoddy or ridiculous in America's fondness for public lectures and open discussion. Her eagerness for knowledge is not only a symptom of national vitality; it is also one of the best assurances for the survival and development of democracy. In no other country where I have lectured—not in England, Scotland, Ireland, Holland or Canada—have I found audiences so free from the cramping liability to be shocked or offended, so ready to give complete freedom to a lecturer with whose opinions they do not agree. By this widespread ventilation of controversial questions, the United States is creating that awareness of political tendencies and social movements which is mankind's best defence against a drift into war. The great lecturing industry of America, which we in England so foolishly and ignorantly deride, is in itself a guarantee that liberty of conscience, speech, publication and assembly will survive the destructive inroads of Fascism.

"We are fighting insidious and deadly bacteria which breed with miraculous rapidity in the stagnant pools of ignorance, greed and apathy," stated George V. Denny in his Harvard lecture. "The sword will be of no avail in this fight. Only by constant and continuous use of that life-giving serum we call education can we hope to triumph over the virulent forces of authoritarianism."

To Mr. Denny's reply to the question asked by every foreign visitor, "Why do Americans go to lectures?" Dr. Alvin Johnson of the New School for Social Research has added another:

"We Americans go to lectures because they give us the straight truth at the least cost of time. As we become a wiser, a more enlightened and cultivated people, more of us will attend lectures, and more persistently."

In her study, *Why Forums?* Mary L. Ely shows that the immense network of American lecture organisations has developed throughout the country a critical attitude, an interest in current events, and a desire for liberation from the narcotic influence of political shibboleths. The facts given by innumerable foreign lecturers at the public "forums" have gradually substituted accurate knowledge for the "stereotypes" so largely responsible for international ill-will—such as the assumption that all the French are immoral, all the Germans cowardly bullies, all the British complacent patriots, and all the Americans swaggering dollar-chasers. "There are few institutions operating in America," President William Allan Neilson has written, "that do as much for individual thinking about public problems; and in some respects the effect of the forum is greater than that of the church and the press."

I have often noticed the stimulus given to family conversation in America by this habit of open public discussion. If the conversations at the great majority of British meal-tables were compared with similar conversations in the

United States, I fear that we should appear dull and limited in
our thinking and talking. No doubt the large and miscellaneous programmes in which many American lecture-goers
indulge do produce a good deal of superficial knowledge,
but it is better to have superficial knowledge of world
events than no knowledge at all and, still worse, no interest.
Their discussion, even at home, leads those who take part to
discover first what they think, and then to say exactly what
they mean. Both these processes are invigorating mental
exercises, sedulously avoided by the great majority of the
British public. If the large apathetic community of British
middle-class matrons were to substitute attendance at
lectures for their universal preoccupation with knitting
jumpers, finding new recipes, and playing Bridge, our tiny
thinking minority would quadruple itself tomorrow and
bring us nearer to a peaceful, just and equal society.

An industry so enormous as American lecturing has, of
course, other defects besides the tendency of the listener's
knowledge to be superficial. A type of audience exists, and
is widely distributed, which estimates a lecturer's external
assets much higher than his intelligence.

"One kind of organisation," I once wrote bitterly to G.,
"will pay \$250 to look at a gold frock and a blue sash . . .
far more readily than another will pay \$100 to hear a
scholarly lecture. Even the grand reputation of X. Y. Z."
(a well-known English novelist) "will not persuade a
second-rate organisation in N. to pay \$75 to hear him.
Gold sleeves and a new finger-wave matter more than
brains."

To this criticism—which applies only to one variety of
lecture amongst very many—it should be added that most
British lecture-goers and lecture-givers would probably be
horrified by the unashamed and relentless commercialisation
which much American lecturing has undergone. We are a
sanctimonious people who like to pretend that all our work is
done from ideal motives which take no account of the
large profits incidentally acquired—a fiction that extends
from armament manufacturers downwards. For my own

part, I prefer America's frank recognition of the principle that the labourer is worthy of his hire—and that if he isn't, he won't be hired again. It has at least been responsible for the high standard which the American lecture platform has maintained.

British ignorance of the standard required has created the blithe illusion that American audiences are prepared to pay vast sums for the doubtful privilege of hearing an Oxford accent, though our lack of respect for American lecturing, and our failure to understand and sympathise with its aims, remains the chief reason why many established British lecturers have been unsuccessful in America. There are, however, other causes, less easily remediable by the growth of good-will. The immense difference between the conduct and organisation of English and American lecturing is the most obvious, and is closely related to the lack of importance which we attach to the occupation.

Lecturing in England is a simple, amiable and amateurish proposition, which need deceive no English speaker into imagining that success upon the platforms of his own country in itself qualifies him to appear before the exacting, critical and experienced audiences of the United States. Since the English lecturer is regarded by his own countrymen as a mere semi-professional whose work is incidental to other jobs, he is lucky if he receives a fee which even partially compensates for the time and trouble involved. Apart from a limited group of organisations, such as women's luncheon clubs and the wealthier nonconformist chapels, the line between professional and amateur speaking is almost indecipherable. As soon as anyone becomes known as a lecturer, constant pressure is put upon him by political and social organisations to make him feel a moral obligation to speak for them, usually for his expenses only, but sometimes without the offer even of these.

When my English agent arranges commercial lectures for me in provincial towns, voluntary societies from the same cities besiege me with invitations to extend my visit in order

Zs

to address them *gratis*. This is not because I am in any way a remarkable speaker, but because the prospect of getting something at the expense of another organisation is irresistible to minority groups with limited resources. The free lectures demanded include talks to schools, colleges, religious brotherhoods, welfare centres, and political bodies.

A year or two ago, at a large seaport town, I found myself involved in the arrangements for a midnight supper which was to follow an exacting lecture to a big chapel audience. No mention of a speech was made in the original invitation, which came from a group unconnected with the organisers of the lecture, but at the last moment, with an early train to catch in the morning and a further series of engagements to follow, I was abruptly notified that a half-hour speech was expected of me after two other speeches at the close of the meal. If the tired worm turns—as this worm did on that occasion—he risks unpopularity, the hostility of the local press and the loss of subsequent professional engagements. Nowhere in America have I encountered the same naïve impression that an overworked lecturer is honoured by an invitation to address an obscure group for nothing.

Curiously enough, the sponsoring organisations—unlike their American counterparts, whose commercial exclusiveness is usually a welcome protection—seldom raise any objection to this method of exploiting both themselves and their speakers. At the end of the year the English lecturer—unless he teaches himself to disregard criticism and grows impervious to the national dislike of giving offence—usually finds that his voluntary lectures have vastly outnumbered the paid variety, and that his platform eloquence, far from being a financial asset, is a source of constant interruption and considerable expense.

No doubt it is because we regard lecturing as a free amateur entertainment rather than a serious economic proposition, that English audiences are seldom either intimidating or critical. Most members of the British lecture-going public—which in comparison with American listeners is an extremely small proportion of the whole population—

are themselves accustomed to getting up and "saying a few words" at informal dinners, "old school" gatherings, athletic clubs, women's institutes or local government committees. They prefer to feel that they and the lecturer are informally discussing a subject together, rather than that a "celebrity" or an "expert" is telling them what they ought to know.

With some English audiences it is almost a solecism for the lecturer to be too efficient. In the older universities, those traditional homes of sweetness and light, the members of the Senior Common Rooms are moved by really eloquent lecturing to an antagonism which approaches contempt. The ringing voice, the dramatic gesture, savour to them of an exhibitionism incompatible with pure scholarship— as though the quest for truth somehow acquired greater integrity by being presented without charm or skill. The English academic world seldom awards its highest prizes to its most successful lecturers. Their lecture-halls may remain full while the audiences of the mumbling scholars melt rapidly away, but the appreciation of students does not count in England to the extent that it counts in America. Sometimes, when I was an undergraduate myself, it seemed to me that the inability of a university lecturer to hold his audience appeared to his eminent contemporaries as a matter for congratulation. Had the enthusiasm of his listeners been greater, his colleagues' faith in his scholarship would certainly have been less.

It is difficult for an English lecturer, accustomed to the tradition of good-humoured, semi-skilled amateurishness so congenial to the English spirit—which expects something, but not a great deal, for nothing—to realise the hard, exacting and rigidly commercial standards to which he will be expected to conform when he crosses the Atlantic. Much of the failure of English lecturers in America is due to the happy belief that American audiences are delighted to pay the immense fees only merited by an outstanding professional performance, for the same inept, unskilled exhibitions of public speaking which are offered *gratis* to English listeners.

The sooner it is realised that this comfortable notion is ripe for discard, the better it will be for Anglo-American relations. Should some nightmare future ever produce a war between the United States and the British Empire, the historians—if any—who record the subsequent Dark Ages will certainly have to include amongst the causes of conflict the long tale of inordinately remunerated "high-hattings," unprepared improvisations, social chit-chats and political gossipings meted out to American audiences as slovenly substitutes for the carefully reasoned addresses to which they justly believe that their high fees entitle them.

So habitual has this letting-down process become, that American organisers are apt to show pathetic gratitude for any signs of industry on the part of English lecturers. I was told during my first tour that Winston Churchill won high approval in America by recognising the responsibility involved in his large guarantee and preparing a series of lectures worthy of the sum offered. I learnt on my second that Phyllis Bentley had pleased many audiences by the obvious perseverance and skill with which she had collected and arranged her material. No remark of mine on American platforms has been better received than the statement that a particular lecture took nearly a month to prepare.

American lecture agents would do well to explain more carefully to their prospective clients the standards of intelligence, eloquence and (in the case of women lecturers) external decoration which the average American audience expects. If I have been fortunate enough in my own tours to avoid some of the more egregious blunders characteristic of my race, I owe my good luck partly to my previous knowledge of America, and partly to the vigorous and uncompromising realism with which my American publisher expounded the technique of the lecture business.

"Lecturing," he warned me before I sailed from England, "is a game which must be played by definite rules, for it is more affected by rules of thumb than most anything one could do."

These rules, and the infinite possibilities of breaking them inadvertently, present his first problem to an English speaker, who has never conducted a lecture campaign with the same formality, never been hedged about with so many regulations as those stipulated in his contract (itself an alarming document with which no British lecture agent would trouble his clients), and finally, and most formidably, has never been the object of so many conflicting interests.

The first essential for a lecturer—especially if he or she is an author—who desires a successful tour is not a fascinating personality, nor a resonant voice, nor a syllabus of arresting lecture-titles, nor even the "name" which originally attracted the interest of both agent and audiences; it is a training in diplomacy. Somehow or other the visiting author-lecturer, if he is not to return home a lugubrious failure, has to please his manager, his publisher, the organisers of the individual lectures, the audiences which gather to hear them, the Press which reports them, and the principal bookstores in the city where the lecture is held. It would be a hard enough task to satisfy all these individuals if their interests were the same; but they seldom are. The manager is concerned with pleasing his organisers, and the organisers are preoccupied with contenting their audiences; the Press wants a "story" which may be anything but the right type of publicity for the lecturer or his listeners; the publisher—whose support is extremely valuable to the lecturing author—is interested in selling his books to the bookstores, and the bookstores are anxious to persuade the public to buy them.

Occasionally an agreeable co-operation does exist between the representatives of all these interests—in which happy and unusual event the lecturer heaves a sigh of relief, thanks God that hard work is so much less exhausting than diplomacy, and gives himself up to an orgy of hand-shaking, question-answering, book-autographing and interviewing. When this co-operation is not forthcoming, his sense of being a bone between several competing dogs quickens until it fills him with dismay. In those disturbing situations in which the lecture-organiser regards the book-autographing demands of the local bookstore as an unwarranted encroachment upon the time of the lecturer-author for which organiser and audience have paid, the bewildered source of conflict is at his wit's end to know how to do justice to both his agent and his publisher.

It is seldom possible to foresee which of these alternative situations will develop, since organisers vary enormously in their demands upon the lecturer. Some regard the lecture itself as fulfilling his financial obligation to those who have promoted it, and are exceedingly generous in their estimate of the amount of time (which cannot possibly be exaggerated) that he requires for correspondence, bookstore visits, meals, packing and telephone conversations. Others apparently consider themselves entitled to purchase the lecturer, body, mind and spirit, from the time that he enters a city until the moment that he leaves it—usually by a midnight train after lecturing for one hour, answering questions for a second and autographing his books for a third.

I am, of course, aware that diplomacy of this type is a quality required by American as well as by English lecturers —though to a lesser degree because errors of judgment are always more conspicuous in a stranger. The English lecturer has, in addition, certain difficulties which arise from the mere fact of being English, and hence unfamiliar not only with the rules of the game, but with the varying psychology of audiences in different parts of the United States. In some regions, and especially, as I have discovered, in parts of the Middle West, many listeners have an anti-English bias which they conceal with infinite care and cordiality, but which subsequently betrays itself in the expressions of relief and gratitude which are forthcoming if the English lecturer avoids offending them in the way that they expect.

Once or twice, in spite of gracious words and welcoming
faces, I have felt waves of hostility coming towards me
from an audience before I have even begun to speak, and
have discovered these to be due, not to a narrow Monroe
Doctrinism nor to a stubborn Main Street psychology, but
to errors of tact (to give them no harder a name) on the
part of previous English lecturers.

It is, no doubt, possible that some temporary economic
aberration may have overcome the charming speaker who
had her hair shampooed in the beauty parlour of a middle
western women's club, and then charged the fee to the
account of her entertainers who had extended to her the
courtesy of their premises. But no such charitable explanation seems to fit the political lecturer who announced his
anxiety to acquaint himself with the amenities of American
home life, only to treat his locally distinguished hostess
and his fellow guests with such condescending discourtesy
that in at least one American city no private household
will ever again run the formidable risk of offering hospitality
to English lecturers.

How many other unhappy "incidents" are due less to
British gaucherie than to unexpected areas of American
oversensitiveness, it is difficult for a stranger to estimate; I
only know from my own experience that even after long
acquaintance the possibility of saying or doing the wrong
thing still remains terrifying. I had some bad moments at
the end of my first tour, when I left America without
receiving a farewell letter or message from my lecture
manager. This silence, I felt, was undoubtedly sinister.
Which of the customary blunders had I unintentionally
made? Was I guilty of the suggestion that some treasured
piece of architecture, old in the eyes of a young country,
was new according to the standards of our ancient
and shabby little island? Had I made some tactless
reference to inter-Allied debts, or been too insistent on
the subject of the League of Nations? It was a real relief
when my manager's letter—forwarded from my publisher's
office the day after I sailed—followed me to England with

indications that I had apparently avoided those particular solecisms.

Perhaps, even by my fellow speakers, I may be forgiven for offering one or two suggestions which might prevent that loss of normally good manners which seems so inexplicably to befall English lecturers who cross the Atlantic. A first lecture tour might be preceded, for instance, by a visit to Washington, with its austere monuments to the great, and its long record of the illustrious dead in Arlington Cemetery. No one who has stood in the precincts of the White House, or has read, even in the rain, the extracts from Lincoln's speeches on the marble walls of his Memorial, could continue to regard America as a land of barbarians with no history worthy of the name.

A trial course of lecturing in England might also indicate at least some of the pitfalls of public speaking to those who have never lectured anywhere, yet who imagine that a fortune can be made in America by some trivial anecdotes or a few shallow witticisms if coupled with an Oxford voice, an ancient name, a military title or a political ancestry. Sometimes I marvel at the patience and tolerance of American listeners who continue to invite English speakers to address them after the sorry treatment that they have often received at our hands, but I shall never cease to fear them for their critical judgment, their exacting standards, and the formality which regulates the whole process of American lecturing.

Its very terminology suggests how formidable it is. In England a lecturer just turns up, but in America he is always "presented", while the informal questions put by an English audience at the close of an address are elevated, by American listeners, to the dignity of a "forum". As for the organisers, they would never be satisfied with merely arranging lectures, inviting guests and selling tickets; they become programme secretaries, hospitality chairmen and finance committees. The more imposing the title, the more impressed will be the audience and the better pleased the recipient.

No aspects of this American lecture business are more intimidating to unaccustomed English visitors than the size of both auditoriums and audiences, and the enormous distances which must be covered by speakers who have hitherto regarded the four-hour run from London to Manchester as a long and tiring journey.

The immensity of American auditoriums seems to me yet another example of that national *Sehnsucht* for grandeur and enlargement which puts up a building of fifty stories in the midst of a hundred square miles of undeveloped prairie, and gives such a name as "Grand Rapids" to an insignificant stream with a very small dam over which used to float the logs required for the local furniture-making industry. Recently, in New York, someone suggested to me that if we knew what lay behind the desire to build skyscrapers, we should understand the fundamental fact of American psychology. It is, I suppose, this "devotion to something afar" which makes America appear, to those Europeans who appreciate her zest for self-improvement, a Renaissance country alive with the experimental audacity of fifteenth-century Italy. Whenever I approach New York from the sea I recall Leonardo da Vinci's prophetic words, and I am physically in love with its challenging towers, its azure skies undimmed by the smoke clouds of apathetic industrial England, its palpable and almost tangible vitality, its monuments to those pagan deities of speed and human efficiency which have dethroned the conventional gods of the older religions.

I believe that I understand why little Saratoga Springs describes the pleasant enclosed garden which divides its peaceful streets as "the city park", and I sympathise with the dusty Georgian villages which attach the word "city" to their insignificant names. I am also able, for all my alarm, to feel a sense of admiration when I find in some small midwestern town a Masonic temple, capable of accommodating a regiment, which looks forward to the day when that embryo municipality will be a large and flourishing metropolis. The fact remains that strange English eyes, accustomed to the dimly lit soberness of provincial town halls and suburban Wesleyan chapels, are liable to be dazzled by the brilliance of American auditoriums, and unpractised English voices to be defeated by the effort of making the last row of listeners hear even the substance of the lecture.

The farther the English lecturer penetrates into the resistant heart of the Middle West, the greater this problem of intonation and vocabulary becomes. Speakers who never receive complaints of inaudibility at home may well be forewarned of the disappointment that they will suffer when from some huge middle western audience, which has apparently received a lecture with vociferous enthusiasm, the criticism eventually comes that the lecturer could not be heard. Usually this does not mean that his voice was inaudible, but that his unfamiliar pronunciation and choice of words were not understood. I realised how this could happen when I heard ex-Governor Whitman give his Armistice Day address. Nothing could have been clearer than that deep, insistent voice, yet some quality in it defeated my English ears and I had continually to ask G. for enlightenment.

However pure one's English, it is useless to be vain about it amongst the listeners of the Middle West. No standard of purity avails when the language itself is becoming an alien tongue, and will one day, perhaps, sound as strange in American ears as the Anglo-Saxon from which our own speech is descended has become to modern England.

The intimidating distances to be covered throughout the whole vast territory between New York and San Francisco, and the conditions of living which so much travelling entails, also explain a good deal of the disappointment felt by American listeners in English lecturers. Nearly all English speakers who are unfamiliar with the United States appear on American platforms at their worst instead of their best. Accustomed as they have been to short journeys, small halls, slow, benevolent audiences, and above all to frequent returns home to repack suitcases and answer correspondence, the perpetual driving activity of an American tour brings many of them before their hearers impaired by travel, fatigued by social functions, and nerve-racked after sleepless nights on long-distance trains.

The exploits of many American lecturers, who appear to thrive under these conditions, must leave American lecture agents with a poor opinion of British powers of endurance. I doubt if the most impervious Englishman could rival the stalwart American philosopher who, according to his gratified manager, gave eleven lectures a week for five months and made forty thousand dollars. These figures as I write them still seem to me incredible, but I believe that I recall them correctly.

In retrospect the inexhaustible hospitality that I have received in America—the interrogative luncheons, the crowded teas, the dinners, drives, visits and conversations, the long reception-lines before lectures and the frequent political questionings which succeeded them and often extended far into the night—comes back to me as a triumphant kaleidoscope gay with spectacular colours, not one of which I would now wish to forgo. But my correspondence to friends at home during my first tour reveals a constant apprehension lest I should fail to deliver an adequate lecture after the expenditure of so much vitality upon other activities, and though I acquired confidence from the second, I suspect that this rôle of quasi-cinema-star can only be effectively maintained after a long period of intensive training. Genuine cinema stars, unlike most authors, can afford to travel with secretaries who will dispose of the enormous correspondence which even on a short tour perpetually threatens to overwhelm the foreign lecturer who has no opportunity to return at intervals to his base.

Only second to the demands of "fan-mail" is the constant unpacking and repacking of suitcases, especially for a woman lecturer who is endeavouring to modify in her listeners the excusable American belief that all Englishwomen are homely and dowdy, addicted to heavy tweeds, large brogues and thick woollen stockings.

Since we are not always as drab as we are painted it is worth while to dispel this allusion, even though the consequent visits to beauty parlours add several hours a week to the obligations of a tour. But the endeavour always to present an attractive appearance lays on the travelling Englishwoman a burden heavier than that of a man lecturer, and one seldom allowed for by listeners or organisers. As I wrote Winifred Holtby from St. Louis in 1934, she has to be not only the star performer, but her own maid, laundress and secretary as well. I cannot recall how often on both my tours I longed, almost with tears, for a travelling companion who would unpack the garments which had usually to be unearthed from my suitcases and pulled on—after a hasty steaming in the bathroom to eliminate the worst creases made by packing—immediately on arrival in each new city. Theoretically the task of cleaning and pressing is carried out by the hotel valet service. In practice one requires the dress in twenty minutes, and is told that one can have it in two hours.

At the risk of being numbered with other transgressors from my country, I therefore venture to doubt whether the amount of hospitality which normally accompanies lecture tours is the best policy when the lecturer is English. It is valuable, perhaps, in so far as it makes upon him that impression of gaiety, kindness and exuberant vitality which causes England to seem, by comparison, as flat as the plains of Illinois and not half so amusing. Personal contacts may be, in themselves, better worth while and more conducive to Anglo-American friendship than the most successful lectures, but they do not always produce the best results from the address as such.

I still remember the strange amnesia that once seized me in 1934, when I arrived at a university college after a sleepless night to find myself booked up for a series of interviews, a luncheon, a motor-drive, a tea during which I stood, tealess, in a reception-line for one and a half hours, a dinner, the lecture itself, and a Press interrogation afterwards. The lecture passed off without mishap, but during the forum which followed I was asked a simple question about the Saar Valley and the probable outcome of the plebiscite. On this occasion the word "Saar" awakened no responsive chord in my mind, although I had often heard the problem discussed at Geneva and had once spent several days in Saarbrücken, where I interviewed the Governing Commission and was taken all over the Valley in one of their cars. I was obliged to reply to my questioner, lamely and inaccurately, that the Saar was not a subject I had studied.

Never since the Viva Voce which followed my Finals at Oxford had I fallen victim to such a strange lapse of memory. The moral appears to be that most British lecturers are vulnerable creatures, the products of an old, slow civilisation, for whose fragile equilibrium the vitality of American listeners at times proves overwhelming.

A contributor to the *Atlantic Monthly* once suggested, as a solution of this lecture problem, the limitation of America's annual quota of English "celebrities." I would certainly endorse the wisdom of such an expedient, which could easily be accomplished by automatically eliminating after their first visits the inept, the cantankerous, the "high-hatters", the gold-digging orators without professional qualifications and the qualified specialists without platform technique. But I would go still farther, and limit also the extraneous demands made upon English lecturers by American listeners.

Some of us, after all, really do want to deliver the goods. We object to taking American money on false pretences; we prefer to give our lectures with zest and vitality, to marshal our prepared facts with intelligence, and to speak in voices audible to the back row of the gallery in the mammoth auditoriums of the Middle West. But vitality and intelligence and audibility are qualities which demand a reasonable measure of physical fitness from the speaker, and physical fitness is difficult to maintain when the alien traveller's nerves are on edge from curtailed sleep, and his unfamiliar voice is hoarse from incessant conversation.

For reasons which I have suggested here, I suspect that complete success in America is impossible for any English lecturer, but we should get nearer to giving our money's worth if our listeners had more mercy on our national limitations and remembered that we are but British.

IX

IN NEW YORK now, Christmas was everywhere.

On December 21st, my son's birthday, I sat late in the Macmillan Board Room finishing an article for the *Saturday Review of Literature*. Suddenly I stopped writing, for a band playing in the street recalled to me the carol singers outside the nursing home on the evening of his birth ten years before.

> "Nowell, Nowell! Now-ell, Now-*e ll*!
> Born is the King of I - Is - ra - el."

The previous Sunday, as I walked back towards the Bretts' house after lunching with Julia and Oswald Garrison Villard in East Seventy-ninth Street, the chimes of St. Thomas's Church had played "Hark, the herald angels sing" and "O come, all ye faithful." In Fifth Avenue, the shops were jubilant with gold tinsel and red berries and silver bells; in many windows, scarlet ribbons and wreaths of holly surrounded little tableaux of the Babe in the Manger. Up and down the wide pavements moved the Christmas crowds, laughing, talking, gazing at the treasury of Yuletide gifts which each store displayed, as light-heartedly as though no "business recession" had ever existed.

Here, if anywhere, I reflected—quite unable as I watched them to distinguish which families belonged to the eager middle class and which to the self-respecting masses of American labour—the ingredients of true democracy exist. In this land, as nowhere else in the world, different social and economic groups mingle without rigidity of distinction; the interchange of ideas is not confined to one status or one occupation. But, because the machinery of co-operation between man and society is still incomplete, the theoretical

equality upon which America's civilisation was founded,
and which shows itself perpetually in the habits and values
of her people, has too often been betrayed by the ruthless
operations of unimpeded individualism. What an additional
lead America could give to the struggling threatened
democracies of the tired Old World, if the vision, enterprise
and courageous vitality of these men and women could be
harnessed to the welfare of the whole nation, instead of to
the property interests of the few!

Although, I thought, waiting for the lights to change at
Fifth-seventh Street, there is, as Walter Lippmann said, less
willingness to be just to antagonists than at any time in
the life of his generation, I nevertheless believe the United
States to possess more capacity for tolerance and a greater
potential sense of justice, than any other part of the world
today. Without the ability to accept alien habits and respect
unfamiliar opinions, she would never have welded her
incompatible races and temperaments into the American
people. Toleration has been of the essence of her experiment,
social justice a basic need in the development of her democracy.

Here, less than anywhere, is there a final risk that
authority will centre itself in a small group under the leader-
ship of a demagogue; the very bitterness of anti-Roosevelt
propaganda shows how quickly and jealously America
defends her privileges against even an imaginary threat.
Those freedoms which she cherishes and which her lecture
platforms help her to guard—freedom of thought, of speech,
of assembly, of the radio, of the Press—are, after all, the
only real liberties remaining in an interdependent world
where an individual's economic status and political policy
are largely regulated by great international forces beyond
his control. Because these liberties remain inviolate, America's
respect for justice will ultimately transcend the fanatical
desire to discredit opponents, and the pursuit of honest
opinions through knowledge will reverse the post-war
flight from truth which even the New World has not wholly
escaped.

The day before I left America, Isabel Brett took me to a matinée of *Father Malachy's Miracle*, in which the leading character persistently reminded me of Dick Sheppard.

When the play was over, I saw her off at the Grand Central Station. Her two sons were already at Easton; her husband would follow on Christmas Eve. Regretfully I watched the train disappear, envying them the gay Christmas party which they would celebrate while I was pitching on the Atlantic. How gladly, instead, would I have joined them again in skating on the polished ice which left clearly visible the little water turtles at the bottom of the pool, or in stirring the steaming cauldron of soup on the huge log fire in the wooden shelter!

Sounding through the vast echoing cavern of Grand Central Station as I left the crowded platform, came the familiar words to which I had listened outside St. Thomas's Church:

"O come, all ye faithful,
Joyful and triumphant,
O come ye, O come ye to Bethlehem! . . .
O come, let us adore Him,
O come, let us adore Him,
O come, let us adore Him, Christ, the Lord!"

They poured triumphantly from loud speakers erected high above the excited multitudes, broadcasting Christmas hymns which made this super-achievement of American commercial architecture appear more than ever like some great twentieth-century Cathedral, strangely combining the quintessence of ancient and modern religions. When posterity comes to put up statues to the New World pioneers of the present age, the features commemorated in marble or bronze should surely not be those of Coolidge, or Hoover, or even of Franklin D. Roosevelt, but of the architect of the Empire State Building, of the designer of the Huey P. Long Bridge at New Orleans, of the engineer whose bold imagination was responsible for the Wilson Dam at Muscle Shoals.

AAs

Sooner or later, I mused, making my way through the hurrying throng into Forty-second Street, this country will have to evolve a political theory to match its architectural vision of the future, and a political machine worthy to interpret that theory. The rest of the world, which can now only begin to understand the United States by coming here and looking at them, will then learn where America is going. But where is she going? It was the old question that I had asked myself repeatedly between 1925 and 1927, and had again recently put to G. I knew the answer a little better now, I felt, though probably no European would ever find words sufficiently elastic to convey the essence of America's complex spirit, or sufficiently expressive to embody the philosophy which inspired her audacious valiance.

Because, that autumn, I had visited the South and Southwest as well as the East, the Middle West, New England and the North, the extreme, bewildering contrasts which make up modern America had become clearer to me than on any previous visit. I had seen her great wealth and her excruciating poverty, her high urban sophistication and her vast territorial rawness; I had discovered her capacity for tolerance and assimilation at the same time as her violent political and racial prejudices; I had witnessed both her limitless generosity to friends and her ruthless cruelty to opponents. And arising from these contrasts I had observed—particularly, as I told President Roosevelt, in the Middle West—a sympathy with the problems of other peoples even greater than the anxious, newly awakened interest which I had noticed in the last year of the depression.

America, it seemed, had learnt from the chaotic years since 1929 that the life of a generation and its wealth or poverty, peace or conflict, security or peril, is mainly determined, even in so vast and self-sufficient a country as the United States, by events in other lands—their wars, revolutions, financial collapses, political alignments and scientific inventions. In the words which M. van Zeeland, the emissary of Great Britain and France, was even then drafting into his Report, "no country can avoid being influenced by general movements of the international economy, whether for good or for evil".

Realising that the wealthiest and most powerful nations could no longer, either politically or economically, live or die to themselves, America had shown a willingness that autumn to approach Great Britain, and discuss an Anglo-American agreement, which even the "business recession" had not diminished. To many commentators the mood of the United States, in spite of her enormous rearmament programme, seemed more favourable to Anglo-American co-operation in the interests of genuine peace than it had been for two decades. At the beginning of January, 1938, a leading article in a London newspaper was to conclude with these words:

"The tide of Anglo-American co-operation is running more strongly than at any time since the end of the War. That it may continue to do so, fostered by the contributions which must be made by either party, will be the earnest prayer of far-sighted men and women who see in it the surest safeguard of peace on this earth."

Because both nations were democracies, and the dignity of free, judgment-exercising citizenship ran in the blood of their peoples, the achievement of this co-operation depended, as I now knew, upon mutual friendly understanding between individuals in a way that it could depend in no other two countries. Such understanding demanded, in its turn, the abandonment of precisely that critical outlook and those obstinate national prejudices which I—an Englishwoman whose war experience should have given her more wisdom—had carried with me the first time that I crossed the Atlantic. Twelve years of intermittent contact with the United States had taught me, and this time for always, that no one can hope to interpret the spirit and aspirations of a country which is new to him, without sympathy for its problems and an open-minded readiness to learn the meaning of the unfamiliar.

As I drove back through the brightly lit streets to my

publisher's house I noticed—as in a smaller city those twelve years ago—that tall illuminated Christmas trees cast their glowing nimbus of light over every dark square. At a street corner facing the Macmillan offices stood one of the largest, its gaily coloured electric bulbs shining like myriad stars of Bethlehem through the frosty darkness. Later that night I found the entrance hall of the Plaza Hotel, where George Brett had taken me for a farewell dance, decorated with grey-green fir trees illumined by lamps of a soft celestial blue.

For one week of the year, New York had forgotten her anxieties in the cheerful business of transforming herself into a fairy city of bright lights, ringing bells and gay, brilliant colours. How strange it seemed that this virile, pagan country should make so much more of Christmas than England with her traditional lip-service to historic faiths! Even as we danced to jazz music almost obliterated by the animated conversations at the crowded Plaza tables, an inspired editorial writer in the offices of the *New York Times* was preparing his Christmas message that love endures, that hatred and fear cannot dominate the world for ever, that the upward impulse of mankind survives in spite of human cruelty and anguish.

"It is a struggle at best," he wrote. "So it has been throughout the ages. Socrates knew it, and Buddha, and Christ. The heart of man is darkness shot with light. He is an animal who rises at times to kinship with divinity, a god who sinks despairingly through bleak and terrible abysses. But the light strives upward, and will not die. It is not put out when the bomb slips earthward, when the artillerymen stand to the guns hurling shells into the defenceless city, when the machine guns silence forever the diggers, the builders, the inventors, and the singers of songs. It cannot be quenched by edicts, nor blotted out by censorships. Not by hate nor cruelty, nor selfishness— though these things remain—can it be forever extinguished. Always the hope returns, always the dream straining outward and upward. . . .

"Fear and sorrow, and the hate that is born of them,
bestride the earth. They hold their lines, advance their
armies, destroy cities, trample down growing crops, parade
in bitter triumph with the thumping of hobbed boots and the
flash of bayonets. But we know on Christmas morning that
their strategy is doomed to fail. The human spirit will not
endure for a long time the degradation of their presence.
God will not be mocked forever—nor will man. Ever the
truth will force its way through the dust of battle. We are
of one body and one flesh—the black, the yellow, the white,
whose prayers go up to one God under different names. It
is our own flesh that is torn when the shell explodes, that is
pierced by the thrusting bayonet. Our hate recoils upon us
and destroys us. It is only our love that survives and is
immortal."

The *Aquitania* sailed from New York at noon on
December 23rd, 1937.

Ten minutes earlier, Harold Latham, who came with
me to the boat, had said goodbye at the landing stage as
the loud gong sounded for the departure of friends. By
12.30, the gigantic promenade deck was deserted. Perhaps
the handful of Christmas passengers were preparing for
luncheon; perhaps the bitter December wind, blowing
stronger as we passed from the Hudson into the open sea,
had driven them indoors.

I seemed to be alone in the stern of the great steamer,
but I did not want yet to go down to my cabin, even
though it was richer than ever before in the gifts and
messages of which I had once written to G.: "One should
remember to cable one's friends when they are sailing
anywhere. It *does* make a difference—takes away the feeling
of isolation one gets when a train slips round a curve, or the
quay at last vanishes out of sight and one can't see people
waving any more."

There were flowers, I knew, from George and Isabel
Brett, and from kindly Edith Jarvis of the English Speaking
Union who had taken me to see *I'd Rather Be Right ;* books

from Harold Latham and Mary Ellen Chase; "comics" and a book for my children from the English Speaking Union secretary, Edith Briggs; an exquisite *crêpe-de-chine* bed-jacket from Ruth Gage Colby; cables from the Villards, Betty Gram Swing, and the National Woman's Party; letters and Christmas cards from Izetta Winter Robb and many members of the Macmillan office staff. But this time even these lovely heart-warming evidences that America remembered me could not quite combat the feeling of desolation with which I had taken leave of my friends in the New World.

My love for America had now become a passion, almost a creed. The courage, vitality and generosity of her people were qualities that I could worship; her hopes and desires for herself were essentially civilised aspirations with which I would gladly identify my own. If human society could count on a future, America would be called upon to supply an indispensable part of its design for living. No other country today had the same matchless advantages of a virile people, material resources, abundance of technical and scientific inventions, and the incomparable experience of co-operation, assimilation and nation-building, with which to counter political lunacy and economic insecurity.

It seemed incredible that a time had ever existed when I left America with relief, for now I did not want to leave her at all. I wished that my family could come over to me, instead of my crossing the ocean to go back to them; I faced with reluctant sadness this return to England and the European squabbles, dangers, passions, prejudices and traditions from which America was so triumphantly setting herself free.

A few of her people, as I had discovered in Texas, were still hampered by the old inferiority complex, the needless intimidation before the arrogant complacency of ancient cultures, but even they, together with every valiant and vital community throughout the country, were engaged in breaking each restraining tradition which bound it to the Old World past. Some lines came into my head that I

had seen a week or two earlier over the name of E. Leslie
Spaulding in the *Chicago Tribune :*

> Only the rooted souls demand things constant,
> Weather and women change, come cold or heat;
> It matters not how much you be remonstrant
> So long as you do not admit defeat!

In their doughtiest moods, this experimental people
wanted to rid themselves even of our art, our philosophy
and our creeds, for where, after all, had our centuries-old
habit of sitting down in couples and solemnly discussing
the state of the world brought us but to the edge of the abyss?
It may be, I thought, remembering how haughtily I had
once condemned the co-operative gregariousness which
America so obviously preferred to the isolated introspections
of the unsociable British, that mankind will not eliminate
war and poverty and injustice by cautious and sententious
philosophising. Perhaps, in the end, we shall overcome
evil only by boldly doing, constructing, improving, by
soaring on wings like the wings of a mighty swan to unimagined regions of human experience, without troubling
ourselves overmuch about the obstacles we may encounter
or the risk that we may fall on our flight. America, at any
rate, has begun that experiment, and we of the Old World
have not made such a conspicuous success of man's residence
on this planet as to claim that her method is inferior to
ours. Let us at least have the humility to watch and wait.

A few following sea-birds, last messengers from New
York, wheeled crying in plaintive semicircles against the
stormy sky. How passionately I wished that I could remain
with them in the New World until I understood completely the secret of that future which it was magnificently
evolving! Some day, perhaps, this destiny would be possible
for my children, but it was not, and probably never would
be, possible for me. Even now, when I desired most ardently
to stay, I knew that I had to go back. Acutely I realised
that only a coward would run away and leave others
striving, in their tiny minorities, to mitigate the doom

that threatened, to urge charity and sanity upon men and women before it was too late.

Whether I liked it or not, I was the product of an old country and an ancient civilisation; I had inherited its follies and its perils with its history, its culture and its beauty, and so long as the breath remained in me, my heritage impelled me to join with those who were struggling to save it from annihilation. America might be in process of building a new society, but for us Europeans the old one still lived, and while the slenderest hope of victory remained in the strife against ignorance, prejudice and hatred, we could not abandon that which created us to the fate of dead cities where jackals howl in the moonlight and bats wheel blindly above the silent dust.

In the wake of the speeding ship, fading rapidly now into a grey-green phantom, the Statue of Liberty held its torch aloft in perpetual salute or valediction. Across the Bay, the skyscrapers of lower New York, still dominated by the Empire State Building from whose record height I had once surveyed Manhattan and its encircling rivers, vanished fast into the distance until they appeared like the geometrical doll's-house towers of medieval Italian painters.

But never, now, could I cry farewell to this city as dear to me as my own London, and far more compelling in its forward-looking, unbounded faith in that which was to be. Let me come again, I silently implored the future, and learn some more of this ever-changing land.

POSTSCRIPT, 1938

All night they marched, the infantrymen under pack,
But the hands gripping the rifles were naked bone
And the hollow pits of the eyes stared, vacant and black,
   Where the moonlight shone.

The gas mask lay like a blot on the empty chest,
The slanting helmets were spattered with rust and mould,
But they burrowed the hill for the machine-gun nest
   As they had of old.

And the guns rolled, and the tanks, but there was no sound,
Never the gasp or rustle of living men
Where the skeletons strung their wire on disputed ground . . .
   I knew them, then.

"It is seventeen years," I cried. "You must come no more.
We know your names. We know that you are the dead.
Must you march forever from France and the last, blind War?"
   "Fool! From the next!" they said.

STEPHEN VINCENT BENÉT,
   "1936"[1]

SINCE I RETURNED to England from America the international stage has darkened, as again, all over Europe, the lamps have been put out one by one.

Already, this year, we have had an Austrian crisis, a Polish crisis and a Czech crisis. Before this book is published, more Czech crises will certainly have threatened, and it may well be that even larger catastrophes—a Danubian crisis, an Italian crisis, a French crisis—are also in store for a generation wearied to death of bitter dawns and horizons without light.

During the Toronto broadcast in which I took part at the end of October, 1934, my interviewer referred to a

[1] From *Burning City*. Copyright, 1933, 1935, 1936, by Stephen Vincent Benét. Published by Farrar & Rinehart.

remark made by a German student which I had quoted in *Testament of Youth*: "Oh, you in England don't know what Europe is. How can you? You're so *safe*."

Today we in England are safe no more. With our small area, our many industrial centres, our teeming London population so accessible to every adjacent country's air-force, we are probably less safe than the wide agricultural areas across the Channel or even the potential fighting line of the future. In the narrow, crowded streets of London's East End, the released death-dealing waves of poison gas would linger for days longer than they ever survived in the open spaces of No Man's Land and the wind-blown air above the trenches. Even assuming that "bomb-proof shelters" offer any measure of reliable protection, their construction is as Utopian as Paradise in districts where families occupy one room apiece.

Does anyone in America realise the tension under which we have been living throughout this spring and summer, watching experiments with searchlights, listening to air-raid warnings being tested even in the early hours, reading perpetually about conscription, air-raid precautions, and plans for "evacuation"? There have been days in which I could not continue the writing of this book; days when I could only read the newspapers, listen to the radio, and wander restlessly up and down Chelsea Embankment while the air-raid warning siren on the great power-station across the river practised its horrid shriek, like a titanic banshee rising and falling upon the wind. These last few months have often recalled to me Iris Tree's sad little poem, the lament of a girlhood robbed of its birthright by the War:

> The days come up as beggars in the street
> With empty hands, as summers without sun
> That bring no gold of corn. With weary feet
> We tread our ways not caring where they run.

Again and again I have wondered whether the Jugger-naut wheel which crushed my youth has turned full circle so soon, and have felt remorsefully that my son and daughter should never have been born. We, the women whose lovers and brothers were cut off in the lovely flowering of their earliest manhood, see our children threatened before we have even grown old enough for the acute edge of memory to be blunted by time. How dare any of us, in such an hour, live as artists alone? How can we escape the responsibility of saving that young generation from another Day of Wrath?

Whatever the immediate future may be, we who strive for a peaceful society know that we cannot suffer ultimate defeat. If war comes tomorrow, we may be mocked and reviled, thrown into prison, confined in concentration camps; but we shall not be conquered. At long last the guerdon will be ours, since we care nothing for the temporary expedients, successively entitled Balance of Power, Concert of Europe, and Collective Security, by which those who claim a monopoly of righteousness endeavour to get the big battalions on their side. We work neither for enthroned pomp nor for embattled power, but for the triumph of an eternal principle, the substitution of love for hate. I have often heard this vision of a world released from the apprehensions of power-politics described as "pathetic". It is not we who merit such pity. The term applies rather to those who allow themselves to be seduced by the arrogant hatreds of the hour.

"Obviously," wrote Kingsley Martin in the *New Statesman and Nation* for June 4th, 1938, "a threat may keep the peace at a particular moment, but equally obviously it brings no hope for the world in the future . . . If war comes people may call it war for democracy, Socialism or Christianity (they actually said that in the last war!), but . . . it is in fact unlikely to produce anything except the general disintegration of our civilisation. It is ideas and systems of thought that we have to combat, and war has become a monstrously inefficient instrument for that purpose. If the last war was fought against Prussianism and produced Nazism, what incredible horror are we likely to get out of a war against Hitler? All sane men agree about this. The job —the only one worth attempting in the world and becoming daily more difficult to accomplish—is to defeat Fascism without war; if it comes to war the battle is lost."

I know that the genuine will to peace—as distinct from the pseudo-will which finds "peace" a convenient excuse for warlike preparations—is a plant of slow growth, but I have no doubt whatsoever that one day it will cover the earth. I am even still hopeful that it may flower in my lifetime, since the last stage of history's progressive impulses tends to be short. In 1908, when I was a child at school, the possibility that universal suffrage would be granted in England during the lifetime of their generation was ridiculed by the suffrage leaders themselves. Yet only twenty years later, the incredible occurred.

But peace is not yet. Once again, Europe and Asia echo from west to east with the tramp of marching armies; in many countries the bugle summons the youth born in one period of slaughter to destroy itself in another. Driven by the suicidal "principle of death" which appears to lie at the root of their being, the hate-besotted nations of this crazy Old World may bring upon mankind one more period of wild anguish, in which the destroyers will trample underfoot the tattered banner of peace together with those who struggle to hold it aloft.

"It might be wise," Izetta Winter Robb wrote me recently, "for us to go to some South Sea Island. But a bullet is probably preferable to boredom. Dearly as we have loved each other, we have led lives in the thick of events, and I fear we could not stand the strain of quietness."

If fate demands that I remain in Europe to perish with the remnant of my generation which has already died in one major war, it may be that America, distant, vast and inviolate, will receive my children who are too young to kill but old enough to suffer, give them a home and offer them a future. There are no friends to whom I would more

readily commit them, no schools and universities where I
would rather see them educated, no civilisation of which I
would prefer that they became a part.

Thirteen years ago, America appeared to me in the guise
of an antagonist. Nine years later she became my friend;
today she represents the beloved refuge to which I would
gladly entrust the lives that I hold most dear. From the
forward direction of her aspiring, invincible spirit, freed
from the impulse of death that leads ancient cultures to
compass their own destruction, arises one sure and certain
hope that for those whom she shelters, the dawn of tomorrow
will break. Beyond the turmoil of her past and the unresolved
conflicts of her present lies a future in which, like the Catskill
Mountains of my waking vision, the sunlit slopes of a wiser
age will climb above the shadow of our night to new ranges
of eternal experience.